The Public Prosecutor of the Terror, Antoine Quentin Fouquier-Tinville;

THE
PUBLIC
PROSECUTOR
OF
THE
TERROR

Antoine Quentin Fouquier-Tinville
From a mezzotint after Duplessi-Bertaux.

THE
PUBLIC PROSECUTOR
:: OF THE TERROR ::

ANTOINE QUENTIN FOUQUIER-TINVILLE
TRANSLATED FROM THE FRENCH OF
ALPHONSE DUNOYER BY A. W. EVANS
WITH A PHOTOGRAVURE FRONTISPIECE
AND NUMEROUS OTHER ILLUSTRATIONS

HERBERT JENKINS LIMITED
ARUNDEL PLACE HAYMARKET
LONDON S.W. :: :: MCMXIV

THE
PUBLIC PROSECUTOR
:: OF THE TERROR ::

ANTOINE QUENTIN FOUQUIER-TINVILLE
TRANSLATED FROM THE FRENCH OF
ALPHONSE DUNOYER BY A. W. EVANS
WITH A PHOTOGRAVURE FRONTISPIECE
AND FOURTEEN OTHER ILLUSTRATIONS

HERBERT JENKINS LIMITED
ARUNDEL PLACE, HAYMARKET
LONDON, S.W. ⊕ ⊕ MCMXIV

LONDON AND NORWICH PRESS, LIMITED, LONDON AND NORWICH

INTRODUCTION

IN the famous oval room of the Soubise Palace, where, amid the gilded garlands of foliage and flowers, the eighteenth-century painter, Charles Natoire, grouped the supple and youthful figures which he had borrowed from the legend of Cupid and Psyche, there is a melancholy glass case which to-day contains the will of Louis XVI and the last letter of Marie Antoinette.

A note it is, rather than a letter. Two yellow, rumpled, ink-stained sheets on which the Queen of France, condemned to death, expressed her last thoughts and addressed her final recommendations to her sister-in-law, Madame Elisabeth.

The note was written at the conclusion of that terrible final appearance before the Revolutionary Tribunal. It is dated, "This 16th of October, at half-past four in the morning." Seven and a half hours before the execution!

"It is to you, my sister, that I am writing for the last time. I have just been condemned, not to a shameful death, that is only for criminals, but to join your brother. Innocent as he, I hope to show the same firmness in these last moments. I am as calm as one whose conscience has no reproach; I feel profound regret at leaving my poor children, you know that I only existed for them and for you, my good and tender sister. In what a position do I leave you who in your affection have sacrificed everything to be with us! I have learned from the speech for the defence in the trial that my daughter has been separated from you. Alas! poor child, I dare not write to her, she would not receive my letter; I do not even know if this will reach you. Receive for them both this my blessing; I hope that one day, when they are bigger, they will be re-united with you, and enjoy to the full your tender care; let them both think of what I have not ceased to inspire in them, that the principles and exact execution of one's duties are the fundamental basis of life, that their friendship and mutual confidence will cause its happiness Let my daughter feel that at her age she ought always to help her brother by the counsels that her greater experience and affection inspire her with ; let my son, on his side, render to his sister every care, every service that affection can inspire , lastly, let both feel that in whatever position they may find themselves, they will be truly happy only by their union , let them take example from us How much consolation has our friendship brought us in our misfortunes ! Happiness is doubly enjoyed when one can share it with a friend , and where is a more tender or devoted friend to be found than in one's own family ? Let my son never forget his father's last words which I repeat to him expressly , let him never seek to avenge our death.

" I have to speak to you of something very painful to me I know how much trouble this child must have caused you. Forgive him, dear sister , think of his age and of how easy it is to make a child say what one likes, and even what he does not understand A day will come, I hope, when he will better realise the value of your goodness and tenderness towards both It remains for me to confide my last thoughts to you I should have liked to write them to you from the beginning of my trial, but, besides the fact that I was not allowed to write, its course has been so rapid that I really should not have had the time

" I die in the Catholic, Apostolic, and Roman religion, in that of my fathers, in that in which I have been brought up and always professed ; having no spiritual consolations to expect, not knowing if there are priests of that religion here ; and if there were, the position in which I am would expose them too much if once they entered here I sincerely ask God's pardon for all the faults I may have committed since I came into being , I hope that in His goodness He will hear my last prayers as well as those that I have long made that He will receive my soul in His mercy and goodness I ask pardon from all whom I know, and especially from you, my sister, for all the trouble that, without wishing it, I may have caused them I pardon all my enemies for the evil they have done me. I here say adieu to my aunts and to

all my brothers and sisters I once had friends the idea
of being separated from them and their sufferings for ever is
one of the greatest regrets that I take with me in dying ,
let them know at least that to my last moment I have
thought of them

"Adieu, my good and tender sister , may this letter
reach you ! Think always of me I embrace you with all
my heart as well as those poor dear children Oh ! God !
how heart-rending it is to leave them for ever ! Adieu !
Adieu ! I am going to occupy myself with nothing more
except my spiritual duties As I am not free in my actions,
perhaps they will bring me a priest[1] , but I here protest
that I shall not say a word and shall treat him as an absolute
stranger "

The Queen has not signed this note, which is entirely
written in her own hand. But the last page bears the five
following signatures —A. Q. Fouquier, Lecointre, Legot,
Guffroy, and Massieu

How is this to be explained ?

The first is the signature of Antoine Quentin Fouquier-
Tinville, Public Prosecutor of the Revolutionary Tribunal
of Paris ; the other four are those of the members of the
National Convention, charged with the verification of the
ex-Public Prosecutor's papers when, after Robespierre's
fall, that magistrate was ordered to be indicted and placed
on trial in his turn.

The gaoler of the Conciergerie had taken possession of
the Queen's last letter , he had handed it over to Fouquier-
Tinville Marie Antoinette's presentiment did not deceive
her when she wrote " Alas ! poor child, I dare not write
to her, she would not receive my letter , I do not even know
if this will reach you " " May this letter reach you ! " she
also wrote Those pages never reached their address The
Public Prosecutor kept among his papers this moving
expression of the last prayers of a dead woman Without
any regard for the final wishes of a mother whom his Tribunal
sent to the scaffold, he arranged among his portfolios the note

[1] A priest who had taken the oath to the Civil Constitution of
the Clergy —Tr

in which Marie Antoinette breathed forth all the pride of her character and all the ardent and simple tenderness of her heart

That is why to-day, after a hundred and seventeen years have passed, those who visit the Princesse de Soubise's drawing-room pause, filled with emotion, before the mystery of this touching letter, countersigned in the clumsy and uncouth handwriting of the famous Public Prosecutor. They ask questions. They want to know. And when they are given the above explanation, many of them remain there, motionless, and ask in low tones and with a sort of shiver in their voice. "What was Fouquier-Tinville then? A brute? A monster?"

Fouquier-Tinville does not seem to have had the appearance of a monster, if we refer to these terms in a note which was sent to him by Thérèse Françoise de Stainville, Princesse de Grimaldi-Monaco, guillotined on the 9th of Thermidor in the year II., the very day of Robespierre's fall —

"Citizen, I ask you, in the name of humanity, to have this packet sent to my children; you seemed to me to have a humane look, and when I saw you I regretted that you were not my judge; perhaps I should not be charging you with a last wish if you had been. Heed the request of an unhappy mother, who perishes at the age of happiness and who leaves children deprived of their only resource; let them at least receive this last evidence of my tenderness, and I shall ever owe you gratitude."[1]

The Princesse de Monaco had declared herself pregnant, but soon afterwards she had written to Fouquier :—

"I warn you, citizen, that I am not with child. I wanted to tell you so; no longer hoping that you will come, I send you word. I have not stained my mouth with this lie through fear of death, or to avoid it, but to give myself a day longer in order to cut off my hair myself and not to yield it to be cut by the hand of the executioner. It is the only legacy I can leave to my children; at least it must be unstained. Choiseul Stainville Josephe Grimaldi-Monaco,

---

[1] Archives Nationales, W. 121, 1st dossier, pièce 100.

a foreign princess dying by the injustice of French judges." [1]

The princess's hair was enclosed in a paper containing two notes, one addressed to her two daughters, the other to their governess.

" My children, this is my hair. I have put off my death for a day not out of fear, but because I wished to be able to cut off this sad spoil myself in order to give it to you ; I did not want it done by the executioner's hand, and I had only this means ; I have passed a day more in this agony, but I do not complain of it ; I ask that my hair be kept in a phial covered with black crape, and locked up throughout the year, and that only three or four times in a year you have in your room before your eyes what remains of your unhappy mother who died loving you, and who regrets life only because she cannot be useful to you I recommend you to your grandfather ; if you see him, tell him that I am filled with the thought of him, and let him keep you in place of everything, and you, my children, take care of his old age and make him forget his misfortunes "

To the governess she wrote —

" I have already written to you one word and now I write another to recommend my children to you ; when you receive this I shall be no more, but may my memory cause you to take pity on my unfortunate children, for that is the only feeling they can then inspire The ring in which my children's names were written, and which you ought to have received, is a keepsake that I offer you It is the only thing of which I can dispose ; let Louise know the reason why I have postponed my death ; let her not suspect me of weakness "[2]

In spite of " the humane look " that the Princesse de Monaco found in him, Fouquier-Tinville did not forward these affecting notes to the orphans for whom they had been written The Public Prosecutor arranged them among the papers of his daily correspondence, where they are preserved in the portfolios of the National Archives

[1] Archives Nationales, W 431, dossier 968, pièce 7
[2] Archives Nationales, W 121, 1st dossier, pp 100 *bis* and 100 *ter*

A sombre and enigmatical figure is Fouquier-Tinville. For a long time his name was in men's memory the symbol of the whole past of the Terror, and for a long time to come this tragic name will remain the symbol of the 'judicial assassinations'[1] committed by the Tribunal established on March 10 1793

Yet in the scales of impartial history the Public Prosecutor's responsibility is a little less heavy than that of President Dumas, President Herman, Judge Coffinhal, Lescot-Fleuriot, the Public Prosecutor's deputy, and the jurors

Paradoxical as the assertion may appear, Fouquier-Tinville displayed sentiments of humanity on rare occasions. The others never did They questioned the accused, and their questions were propounded with such a refinement of perfidy, with such a hypocritical though seeming regard for legality, that the accused felt condemned in advance It is only necessary to read Herman's cross-examination of Marie Antoinette and his summing-up in the Queen's trial to form an opinion of the worth of that civil-spoken and inexorable personage President at the trial of the Girondins, at those of the Duc d'Orléans, of Barnave, of Danton and the Dantonists, this official saw his zeal rewarded by an excellent place which, indeed, was no sinecure and involved risks Three days after Danton's execution, Herman succeeded Paré, he was appointed Minister of Justice, being replaced in the Presidency of the Tribunal by Dumas

Dumas distinguished himself by his brutality He is said to have been an habitual drunkard He was continually in rivalry with Fouquier-Tinville, who at the time of his own trial said, He was my mortal enemy" He was always armed with two pistols which, when in court, he placed on the table before him He interrupted the accused During the adjournment, he would slip among the jury and hold conversations with them[2] He was ferocious, aggressive and ill-tempered His usual procedure, when an

[1] The phrase is that of Boissy d'Anglas in the *Moniteur*, March 23, 1795, p 747, col 3

[2] Arch les Nationales W 500, 3rd dossier, p 63

accused person spoke, was to cut him short, and definitely refuse him the right to speak Fouquier opposed him, and caused witnesses to be heard in spite of the President.

After the law of the 22nd of Prairial, we shall see that Dumas and Coffinhal contented themselves with asking the accused their names and positions, and briefly reminding them of the heads of the indictment brought against them. When the accused answered, Dumas would exclaim " We were expecting what you are saying. You are priests and nobles. That is enough Let us go on to the next "[1]

When he cross-examined Madame Roland, the sculptor Lescot-Fleuriot, Fouquier-Tinville's deputy, propounded to the accused long, embarrassing questions He demanded clear, short answers. Then he interrupted the examination, burst into a rage, and said " With such a chatterbox we shall never finish Besides, we are not at the Ministry of the Interior[2] to indulge in wit "

When Pache, the Mayor of Paris, being compromised in the case of Hébert and the Hébertists, was imprisoned, Lescot-Fleuriot took his place and became one of Robespierre's firmest supporters until the decisive night between the 9th and 10th of Thermidor.

When sitting as President at the trial of the elder Loizerolles, the old man who was arraigned before the Tribunal when it was his son who had been summoned to appear, Coffinhal, on the 8th of Thermidor, calmly allowed the one to be condemned for the other He washed his hands of the matter Some months later, Fouquier-Tinville could justly say " That omission and that crime, if they really exist, are personal to Coffinhal and to the registrar's clerk who had charge of the case." It was Coffinhal who, revising and correcting the list of accused in the " batch "[3] among which the poets Roucher and André Chénier appeared on the 7th of Thermidor, added these words in the margin facing the

[1] Archives Nationales, W 500, 3rd dossier, p 63
[2] Roland had been Minister of the Interior —TR.
[3] *Fournée*, the term generally applied to a number of prisoners tried and executed together —TR.

name of Louis Sers, " captain of infantry in command at Chambarnagot." Chambarnagot for Chandernagor "[1] Some important depositions at Fouquier-Tinville's trial seem to attribute to Coffinhal, " that brutality which was natural to him," the execution of women who were with child.[2]

As for the motley troop of jurors, each of them had his proper share, his terrible share, in the hecatombs of Prairial and of Messidor What about their consciences? Fouquier-Tinville liked to style some of them, " *my solid men* " These solid men had not, on the whole, been more criminal than the others. They liked to utter big words which, for the most part, they did not understand—liberty, equality, fraternity, unity, indivisibility, or death They were proud and happy to speak and write these words, to see them printed on fine engraved paper They were playing an overwhelming part, and thought it agreeable and right to be paid eighteen livres a day for playing that part. Several among them were both members of the Popular Commissions and jurors of the Tribunal of the Terror.

But they themselves experienced the terror they inspired. Veritable tyrants, each in his own Section, in his own Commission, in his own street, at the Tribunal they feared being denounced by men more tyrannous than themselves, and this is why they became ferocious and implacable. They played the part of informers from fear of being accused in that same part. For some of them, it was enough to see the prisoners in order to decide on their verdicts. The mere inspection of a face determined them to vote for death. One of them said " Were I the Public Prosecutor, I would have the condemned bled before their execution so as to weaken their courageous bearing " Another publicly boasted of " never having voted except for death when it was a case of trying priests or nobles, for they were all food for the guillotine."[3] Another having asked permission to address the

[1] Archives Nationales, W 431, No 969
[2] Buchez and Roux, XXXV, p 3
[3] Aubry, the tailor Archives Nationales, W 500, 3rd dossier, p 58

court, said "Is it not enough to show you are an aristocrat, that you have served a noble ² " ¹ This man said to his colleagues, just after they rose from a sitting ' We have only taken two hours and a half this time, because we had only to refer to the letter that was beside the name " Another stated that " when there was no crime, it was necessary to imagine one " Some of them could neither read nor write Others, on the contrary, men of letters or of fashion, or artists, voted for death with a sort of bored carelessness, a mocking air—and to put an end to the matter

It ought to be said that nothing is less just than to attribute entire responsibility to Fouquier-Tinville for the judicial crimes committed by the Tribunal established on March 10, 1793, an exceptional, ' provisional " Tribunal, a sort of " military justice applied by civil judges " It was not he who cross-examined, it was not he who voted for death He was neither judge nor juror ²

A servant of the law, he took care to keep within the bounds of the law What he seemed essentially to desire, " entrusted as he was for eighteen months with the painful duty of seeking out crime and prosecuting it," was to discover the guilty ; and that because his two formidable patrons, the Committee of Public Safety and the Committee of General Security, exacted it The men who composed those Committees made him ' walk " as they wanted He carried out their orders exactly, and in particular the orders of the most violent and most sinister among them, Vadier, Voulland, and Amar ³

At the Committee meetings, to which he went every evening, and where he often remained until an advanced hour of the night, he waited for the lists of persons to be charged, and he handed them over to others He was exact, and fulfilled precisely the intentions and resolutions of the two

---

¹ This juror was Didier Archives Nationales, W 500, 3rd dossier p. 58
² He said so in reply to Cambon at his cross-examination on the 9th of Germinal in the year III (Buchez and Roux XXXIV, p 329)
³ Archives Nationales, W 500, 3rd dossier, p 46 The witness Advenier saw Voulland, Vadier, and Amar go fairly often to Fouquier's room and lock themselves in with him "carefully "

Committees. He remembered this when, torn from his power, imprisoned, and ready, in his turn, to appear before his judges, he wrote, on the 19th of Thermidor "If it is a crime to have given effect to the resolutions of the Committees of Public Safety and of General Security, I confess that I am guilty, I should have been guilty if I did not execute them What then ought I to have done ? " In the same manner, on the 14th of Thermidor, addressing Louis (of the Bas-Rhin) and Moyse Bayle, he wrote · "My defence is limited to a recital of the events that took place between the Committees and myself. . . . Is there a more frightful position than mine, after having spent days and nights in the public service ? " He wrote in one of the memorials for his defence "No appeals of any sort whatever could have stopped me ; the execution of the laws that emanated from the Convention, justice, and humanity—these have been my rule of conduct." He also wrote this to Merlin (of Douai) "It is a slanderous wound which time will heal. I repeat it My crime is that I have been the instrument of too severe laws, and that it was not in my power not to execute them ; hence hatred and resentment."

He is the "executor of the laws." He is the axe and rods, he is the Revolutionary bludgeon. The laws often change A struggle for power, an uninterrupted pitiless struggle, was entered upon by political parties The conqueror slew the conquered, and was himself then conquered and killed It was the business of the Revolutionary Tribunal and its Public Prosecutor to perform this task

It was thus that Fouquier-Tinville drew up in succession indictments against Marie Antoinette, the Girondins, Olympe de Gouges, Madame du Barry, Hébert and the Hébertists, Danton and the Dantonists, the alleged conspiracy in the prisons, etc, etc, until the day when he saw himself obliged to plead in court against his friends, Lescot-Fleuriot and others

The study of the part played by Fouquier-Tinville will be the purpose of the first part of this book. We have entitled it "The Public Prosecutor." The trials have been studied by the historians of the Revolutionary Tribunal, MM. Campardon, Wallon, and Lenôtre, and we do not flatter ourselves that this book contains anything new in this respect But it seemed to us useful and interesting to undertake it for the better understanding of the second part of the book, entitled " The Prisoner." In this latter portion we have applied ourselves to a minute re-examination of Fouquier-Tinville's trial

It is by making this slow and minute re-examination that we best understand the sort of man this tragic Fouquier-Tinville was. In so far as he was Public Prosecutor, he appears to us clearly as a public official, bent on keeping his place and the handsome salary it represented, at the price of every form of servility, even the basest, most criminal, and most dishonourable. Ordered to be placed on trial by the National Convention some moments after having been nominated in the same Assembly as Public Prosecutor for a fresh period, Fouquier-Tinville, a prisoner, fallen, hemmed in, deserted, scoffed at, defended himself with such argumentative vigour, such presence of mind, in a word, such talent , he demonstrated with such skill that he was the scapegoat for others whose exact and untiring agent he had been , he explained so completely the wheels of the blood-stained machine of which he himself had been one of the wheels that moved most easily , he challenged the evidence so audaciously and coolly, especially that of his mortal enemies, the clerks in the registry, that, in spite of his horrible activity, his case became curious and extremely interesting It was that of a former procurator, a former advocate, firmly bound to procedure, a former lawyer whose brain had been misshapen and his reason led astray through the abuse of chicanery, and who, needy and the father of a family, seeking a situation, fell into the midst of the Revolution, was taken seriously, took himself seriously, and into whose hands, companions, as unconscious as he of the responsibility of their acts, placed the machine for judging others The reader will see, in the first part of this study, what effect such a machine can produce, and what

B

in such hands it did produce both before and after the 22nd of Prairial.

And now, let us be pardoned if, in writing the history " of those rigorous times "—to use the words of a contemporary, the poet Vigée—we have not thought it our duty to give details of what befell the family of him who was guillotined in the month of Floréal. His family is not responsible for his judicial crimes. Under what pretext and by what right should we question, in their eternal peace, the piteous and innocent ashes of those whom he loved and who loved him ? As Public Prosecutor of the Terror, Antoine Quentin Fouquier-Tinville is on trial at the bar of History. It is on this ground that he interests us, and on this ground that we mean to study him, not without having always in mind the cynical saying of Carrier, the pro-consul of Nantes, when in his turn brought to trial, he exclaimed " Everything here is guilty, down to the President's bell ! "

A. D.

CONTENTS

PART I

CHAPTER I

FOUQUIER-TINVILLE'S BEGINNINGS

CHAPTER II

" THE DICTATORSHIP OF JUSTICE "

CHAPTER III

FOUQUIER-TINVILLE AND THE CONSPIRACIES IN THE PRISONS

CHAPTER IV

FOUQUIER-TINVILLE AND THE NINTH OF THERMIDOR

CHAPTER V

THE REACTION OF THERMIDOR AND FOUQUIER-TINVILLE'S ARREST

PART II

CHAPTER VI

FOUQUIER-TINVILLE PREPARES HIS DEFENCE

CHAPTER VII

FOUQUIER-TINVILLE'S FIRST TRIAL : THE INQUIRY (VENDEMIAIRE AND BRUMAIRE OF THE YEAR II)

CHAPTER VIII

FOUQUIER-TINVILLE'S FIRST TRIAL : CONTINUATION AND END OF THE INQUIRY. (VENDEMIAIRE AND BRUMAIRE OF THE YEAR III)

CHAPTER IX

FOUQUIER-TINVILLE AFFIRMS HIS INNOCENCE AND HIS HUMANITY. PUBLIC PROSECUTOR LEBLOIS ARGUES AGAINST HIM

CHAPTER X

FOUQUIER-TINVILLE'S SECOND TRIAL · THE INQUIRY BY THE TRIBUNAL ESTABLISHED ON THE EIGHTH OF NIVOSE IN THE YEAR III

CHAPTER XI

CHAPTER XII

CHAPTER XIII

CHAPTER XIV

ILLUSTRATIONS

PART I

THE PUBLIC PROSECUTOR
OF THE TERROR

CHAPTER I

FOUQUIER-TINVILLE'S BEGINNINGS

ON August 14, 1792, four days after the fall of the French Monarchy and the pillage of the Tuileries, a decree of the National Legislative Assembly ordered that the forty-eight Sections of Paris should appoint a *jury d'accusation* and a *jury de jugement*[1] to take cognisance of the crimes committed on August 10 against the people. The Commune did not accept this decision of the Legislative Assembly. It wished to have a Court of Popular Justice.

On the evening of the 15th, it sent a deputation to the Assembly. Maximilien Robespierre spoke on its behalf. He said that public tranquillity and, above all, liberty depended on the punishment of the guilty. The people's vengeance had not yet been satisfied. The men who had hidden themselves under the mask of patriotism, the men who had affected to speak the language of the laws in order to overthrow the laws, " that Lafayette who was not in Paris, but who could be there," were they to escape the national vengeance ? The guilty must be judged, finally and in the last resort, by *commissioners* chosen in each of the forty-eight Sections of the city.[2]

[1] The *jury d'accusation* corresponded in some respects to our grand jury ; but its procedure was not public. It cross-examined prisoners, and prepared the case for trial before the *jury de jugement.* —TR.

[2] *Moniteur* for August 18, 1792.

The Assembly endeavoured to oppose this. The Commune insisted, even threatened. On Friday, the 17th, at ten o'clock in the morning, an orator whom it had sent to the Feuillants proclaimed that a rising would take place at midnight. The tocsin would be sounded, and drums would beat to arms. The people were weary of not being avenged.

The Commune gained the day. The Assembly capitulated. The decree was passed. The extraordinary criminal tribunal was about to set to work. It was to judge the crimes committed on the day of August 10, and " other crimes relative to it " It was to be composed of seven directors of the jury, who were to investigate and arrange its business , of two presidents and six judges ; of two commissioners and two prosecutors , of four registrars and eight registrars' clerks ; of ninety-six members of the *jury d'accusation* and ninety-six members of the *jury de jugement*.

The judges and the members of the jury of this tribunal were appointed during the night between the 17th and the 18th of August Robespierre was at the head of the list,[1] and Coffinhal was one of the judges. On August 25 the electors, in thirty-two sections, chose " Monsieur Fouquier-Tinville " as one of the directors of the *jury d'accusation*.

Antoine Quentin Fouquier was then forty-six years of age. He was born at Hérouel, near Saint-Quentin, on June 10, 1746 " His father," M. Campardon writes, " was a rich agriculturalist[2] of the district, who gave him so good an education that, at the period in his life when his occupations least permitted him to think of Latin, he still liked to remember it , for when he was Public Prosecutor of the Revolutionary Tribunal, he listened with pleasure to quotations from the ancient authors he had studied in his youth. He

---

[1] Robespierre refused this post, as the performance of its duties were incompatible with those of a representative of the Commune of Paris As he explains in a letter, he could not be the judge of those whose opponent he had been (*Moniteur* for August 28, 1792.)

[2] His name was Eloy Fouquier, and he died in 1759, as is mentioned in the *Précis pour le Comte Félix de Pardieu et demoiselle Lelong de Vadancort, son épouse, intimés, contre la dame veuve Fouquier d'Etinville appellante*, preserved in the National Archives.

was destined by his family for the bar ; accordingly, when his studies were completed, he went to Paris and entered a procurator's office ; he then signed himself Fouquier de Tinville, and had himself called by that name. His three brothers acted in the same way, and also added territorial titles to their patronymics , one, Pierre Eloi Fouquier, became Fouquier d'Hérouel , another, Charles François Fouquier, called himself Fouquier de Vauvillé. Both were equerries and agents of the Royal Household. The third, Quentin Fouquier, who was only an advocate in the Parlement, none the less signed himself Fouquier de Forest The future Public Prosecutor of the Revolutionary Tribunal was engaged, up to the end of the year 1773, in obtaining, through the medium of the procurators' offices in the capital, the practical knowledge which was indispensable if he were to perform correctly the duties of the office he desired to purchase. On January 21, 1774, the Chamber of Procurators of the Châtelet of Paris (now the solicitors of the lower court) granted him an *admittatur* " [1] Some days later he received his provisional letters of appointment.

Those letters, dated January 25, gave and conceded to him the office of candidate procurator at the Châtelet of Paris, which had been held and exercised by Jean Louis Cornillier. The customary inquiry had been favourable. He was acknowledged to be " of good life, morals, and conversation, and of the Catholic, Apostolic, and Roman religion." He took the oath, and was put into possession of his offices, Rue du Foin-Saint-Jacques, in the College of Maître Gervais, parish of Saint-Séverin, Sorbonne district. Two years later, he went to live in the Rue Pavée-Saint-Sauveur, " facing the Rue Française." We find him installed there on January 23, 1776 In October, 1778, he was living in the Rue Bourbon-Villeneuve, in a fine house, " by the side of the great balcony, near the corner of the Rue Saint-Philippe."

Maître Fouquier de Tinville's practice was a good one,

[1] Campardon   *Le Tribunal Révolutionnaire de Paris.*   Tome I・ p 13 (Plon 1866)

and included a large number of clients, drawn chiefly from the lower middle-classes—shopkeepers, artisans and traders. Some agriculturalists, farmers and wine-growers from the neighbourhood of Paris, from Charonne, Suresnes, Villiers-le-Bel, and elsewhere, also came to entrust their cases to him ; as did some religious establishments, such as the English Nuns, established in Paris in the Rue des Fossés-Saint-Victor, and the Nuns of Saint-Thomas, of the Order of Saint Dominic, in the Rue Neuve-Saint-Augustin. Fouquier, intelligent and active, was well suited for the management of affairs and for the subtleties of chicanery.

He had married his cousin, Geneviève Dorothée Saugnier, on October 19, 1775, at the parish church of Notre-Dame-du-Mont-Saint-Martin, in the diocese of Cambrai. In the following year a son was born—Pierre Quentin Fouquier. Then he had four daughters—Geneviève Louise Sophie, born on January 2, 1778 ; Émilie Françoise, born on December 7, 1778 , Marie Adélaïde, born on January 19, 1782. Three months later, April 24, 1782, Fouquier's young wife died, at the age of twenty-eight.[1]

Within less than five months, Fouquier married again. His second wife was Henriette Gérard d'Aucourt, the daughter of a colonist who had died at San Domingo. In September, 1783, he sold his practice. For what reasons remains a mystery. It is noteworthy that " for motives of interest " Maître Bligny, his successor, broke off all relations with him for more than ten years, and did not see him again until he had become Public Prosecutor.[2]

At this period he was engaged in doubtful affairs, leading a submerged existence in Paris He no longer lived in the Rue Bourbon-Villeneuve He frequently changed his dwelling In 1785, he was in the Faubourg Saint-Antoine, afterwards in the Rue Vieille-du-Temple ; in 1788, in the Rue

---

[1] All the information given here is taken from the documents preserved among the National Archives. Those documents include many *powers* and *discharges* given by clients to Maître Fouquier de Tinville, procurator at the Châtelet They also include baptismal and death certificates of the children and of Fouquier's first wife

[2] See later p 232.

Saint-Croix de la Bretonnerie, in 1789, in the Rue Barre-du-Bec (which began at the Rue de la Verrerie, and ended at the Rue Saint-Merri and the Rue Saint-Croix de la Bretonnerie); in 1791, in the Rue des Chartres and the Rue des Enfants Rouges; in 1792, at Number 356, Rue Saint-Honoré.

On January 9, 1790, a son was born to his second wife; in 1792, she had twins One of his daughters, Marie Adélaide, having died on May 1, 1786, Fouquier had, at this period, seven children. [1]

Antoine Quentin Fouquier was a robust and strapping Picard, with large and strongly moulded neck and shoulders. His hair was dark and smooth, his forehead high, his face full and pitted with smallpox. He had a Roman nose and extremely arched and elevated eyebrows. His glance was keen, searching, disquieting, and very restless. Contemporaries, who witnessed his trial, said that he was moody, but a good fellow. Many agreed in declaring that he was of a terribly violent and passionate, even brutal, character, a true " despot "

How did this ex-procurator, who had become a vague " man of the law," and fallen into a precarious position, suddenly find a situation in the magistracy and become one of the directors of the *jury d'accusation* established by the law of August 17, 1792 ? The thing has been related by M Campardon with the aid of M. Edouard Fleury's *Camille Desmoulins* and the papers relating to the tribunal of August 17 preserved among the Archives.

Fouquier was a compatriot and even a distant relative of Camille Desmoulins On August 20, 1792, he wrote to him :

" Until the ever memorable day of the tenth of this month, my dear relative, the title of patriot has been not only a cause of exclusion from every office, but even a ground for persecution ; you yourself are an example of this. The time has come at last, we may hope, when true patriotism must conquer. . . . My patriotism is known to you,

[1] See Lenôtre . *Le Tribunal Révolutionnaire* (Paris Perrin, 1908).

C

of affairs. At the beginning of 1793 he was appointed deputy to the Public Prosecutor of the Criminal Tribunal of the Department of Paris, and on February 9 deputy for the Procurator of the Commune of Paris; but he resigned this post in order that he might retain that of deputy to the Public Prosecutor of the Criminal Tribunal as being more suited to his abilities and tastes. Three days later he wrote to the Procurator-Syndic of the Tribunal for the district of Saint-Quentin.

"Paris, this 12th February 1793, year II of the Republic.

'Citizen Procurator-Syndic,

'At the moment when I was elected by my fellow-citizens to the position of judge of the Tribunal for the district of Saint-Quentin, you know that I held the position of director of the two d attached to the provisional Criminal Tribunal established on August 17 last; at least I informed you of this. The duties of this latter position did not allow me to be present at the installation of the Tribunal, and since its suppression I have been busied with the distribution of all the suits in the ten Tribunals. This task has led me further than I expected; and at the moment when I was preparing to take up my duties the electoral body appointed me to be one of the Public Prosecutors of the Criminal Tribunal of the Department of Paris. This position, which I believed it my duty to accept both on account of its importance and as a return for the confidence shown me by this great city, does not permit me to take up the duties of judge of the Tribunal of the district of Saint-Quentin; and by this present letter I place my resignation in your hands. It is not without some regret that I tender my resignation because it would have enabled me to live among my fellow-citizens and my family. But circumstances oblige me to take the present course in spite of the obvious fact that in accepting this post of Prosecutor I impose upon myself the most stringent duty and privation. You will oblige me by conveying to my colleagues my regrets at not being able to join them. Moreover, my successor will not have cause to regret my resignation the more so that as I have not been received and installed he has a right to receive the whole of the emoluments by being himself installed in my place. Even if I had not been appointed to the position of Prosecutor I should still have been obliged to send in my resignation for on Saturday last I was appointed deputy to the Procurator of the Commune of Paris, and I am also about to send in to the Municipality my resignation of that post.

"Signed FOUQUIER-TINVILLE."

On Sunday March 10 1793 the National Convention, which since the preceding day had been occupied with discussing the creation of a Revolutionary Tribunal to try cases without appeal was about to break up exhausted, when Danton burst into the Chamber and cried out "I call upon all good citizens not to leave their places."

It was half past six in the evening. The Convention remained motionless soothed by Danton's voice. It was a critical moment. Liège was held by the enemy, the French army had been compelled to raise the siege of Maestricht, in Paris preparations were being made for a riot.

"Nothing is so difficult," cried Danton, "as to define a political crime. But if a man of the people receives instant punishment for a private crime if it is difficult to overtake a political crime is it not necessary that extraordinary laws taken from outside the social body should terrify the rebels and overtake the guilty?"

"The safety of the people now requires drastic measures. I see no middle course between the ordinary forms and a revolutionary tribunal. History attests this truth, and since some in this assembly have dared to recall those blood-stained days which every good citizen has deplored I will say for my part that if a tribunal had then existed the people who have been reproached so often and so cruelly for those days would not have stained their hands with blood. I will say and shall have the assent of all who witnessed those events, that no human power could check the outbreak of national vengeance.

"Let us profit by the faults of our predecessors. Let us do what the Legislative Assembly failed to do; let us, rather than the people, be terrible; let us organise a tribunal, not a perfect one, for that is impossible, but the best possible, in order that the people may know that the sword of the Law is suspended over the heads of its enemies .... I demand, therefore, that the revolutionary tribunal be organised before the present sitting comes to an end, that the executive power in the new organisation be entrusted with all the necessary powers of action and energy .... Accordingly I sum up what I have said this evening; the organisation of the tribunal, the organisation of the executive power; to-morrow a military advance. By to-morrow let your commissioners have started; let all France arise, rush to arms, march against the enemy! Let Holland be invaded; let Belgium be free; let England's commerce be ruined; let the friends of liberty triumph over that country; let our arms, everywhere victorious, bring deliverance and happiness to the people, and let the world be avenged!'" (Loud applause.)

The sitting was adjourned at seven o'clock in the evening, after Danton's speech, and resumed at nine o'clock. The Convention voted the construction and organisation of an extraordinary Criminal Tribunal. It voted the penalties. At five o'clock in the morning the sitting was adjourned.

This Tribunal, as everybody knows, was to try cases involving every counter-revolutionary enterprise, every attempt against the liberty, equality, unity, and indivisibility of the Republic, against the internal and external security of the State, all plots tending to re-establish royalty or to establish any authority hostile to the liberty, equality, and sovereignty of the people. It was composed of a jury and five judges. The judge who was elected first was to be president. The Tribunal was to have a Public Prosecutor and two deputies, chosen, like the judges and the jurors, by the Convention.

On the 13th the Convention appointed the members of the Tribunal. The President was Jacques-Bernard-Marie Montané, special lieutenant of the Seneschal's Court at Toulouse, born at Grenade in the Haute-Garonne. The Public Prosecutor, chosen by 180 votes, was Faure, his deputies, Fouquier-Tinville (163 votes), Donzé-Verteuil, an ex-monk, and Lescot-Fleuriot, a sculptor (162 votes). Faure resigned. Fouquier-Tinville was appointed in his place by a decree of the Convention dated the 15th, and accepted the post without hesitation. He regarded it "a duty" to do so, as he wrote on March 29, 1793, to the Minister of Justice.[1]

[1] Archives Nationales, BB⁴ *bis* 25.

CHAPTER II

ON April 5, 1793, the Public Prosecutor was invested with the right of causing the arrest, prosecution, and trial of all persons accused of the crime of conspiracy or of "national offences," Deputies and generals excepted. An information lodged by the constituted authorities, or even by private citizens, was sufficient. On his warrant, any individual was at once arrested, prosecuted and tried. The accused was incarcerated in one of the prisons with which Paris abounded from the beginning of the year II.

To analyse the trials, great and small, which occupied the officials and the sessions of the Revolutionary Tribunal from April, 1793, to the end of July, 1794, would be to perform a useless work. They have been examined, and that in a definitive fashion. What took place is known. Moreover, our subject is not the history of the Revolutionary Tribunal, but a study of Fouquier-Tinville's responsibility as Public Prosecutor.

An individual was arrested as a suspect. The official report of his arrest was drawn up at the committee of surveillance of his Section. This document contained the cross-examination he had undergone before the members of that committee. The accused person was then sent, with the documents relating to him, before the Committee of General Security, where he was again questioned. Thence he was despatched to the Revolutionary Tribunal. The documents were sent by the Committee of General Security to the Public Prosecutor, who examined them, made a summary of the facts, arranged the charges, quoted the incriminating

---

[1] Saint-Just's phrase.

words or writings, noted the denials of the accused. In a word he drew up his indictment. He took care to indicate that the accused person acted " wickedly and intentionally " with a view " to provoke the national dissolution and the re-establishment of royalty." In consequence, he demanded that the assembled Tribunal should grant him a writ of indictment, that the person of the accused be seized, and that he be entered on the gaol-book of the house of detention of the Conciergerie, to remain there as in a house of justice.

At the hearing of the case before the Tribunal, Fouquier-Tinville supported the accusation If the declaration of the jury were negative, the accused was set at liberty, at least unless Fouquier demanded his detention in prison as a measure of general security. (We shall see that in this way some accused persons, such as Fréteau, were acquitted by the jury, to be rearrested afterwards by Fouquier, again brought before the Tribunal, and this time condemned.) If the declaration of the jury were affirmative, the Public Prosecutor moved that the law be applied, which meant sending the prisoner to the guillotine.

It would be wearisome to analyse Fouquier-Tinville's writs of indictment, so monotonous is their style, marked as it is throughout with the revolutionary phraseology whose continuous exaggeration and terrible vagueness we can scarcely understand to-day. The only fact that stands out from them is that, during the first period of his magistracy (from April, 1793, to April, 1794), Fouquier drew up his indictments conscientiously enough and in accordance with the cross-examination of the accused persons and the documents that had been transmitted to his office. He showed himself, on the whole, careful in observing the law, and did not go beyond the rights and powers that it conferred upon him. He did not discuss the component parts of the accusation that he had in his hands. He criticised neither their value nor their origin. He did not stop to weigh the for and against. He did not ask whether such and such an affirmation, such and such a denunciation, deserved credit or not. He admitted in its entirety the most questionable evidence.

He accepted everything and gave a summary of all. He expounded and affirmed He was the organ of the law. He adapted himself exactly, with activity, zeal, and application, to the designs and intentions of the legislators His pleadings for the prosecution fell upon the accused like the blows of a club. Moreover, he struck without discrimination all those who were pointed out to him, whatever the social class to which they belonged, and whatever their position, their origin, or their opinions.

But if, in the mass, Fouquier-Tinville's indictments seem to us tiresome to read, we must except some upon which he expended imagination and style. Such, for example, are those of Marie Antoinette and Madame du Barry. "From an examination made of all the documents transmitted by (*sic*) the Public Prosecutor," say the pleadings drawn up by Fouquier against the Queen, "it is clear that, like the Messalinas, Brunehaut, Frédégonde and Médicis, who were formerly described as Queens of France and whose eternally odious names will not be effaced from the annals of history, Marie Antoinette, the widow of Louis Capet, has since her residence in France been the scourge and blood-sucker of the French people ; that she had political relations with the man described as the King of Bohemia and of Hungary even before the happy revolution that has given back their sovereignty to the French people ; that those relations were contrary to the interests of France. . . ."

" Citizens and jurors," said he, when summing up his indictment against Madame du Barry, " you have given your verdict on the plots of the wife of the last tyrant of the French , you have at this moment to give your verdict on the conspiracies of her infamous predecessor You see before you this Lais, famed for the licentiousness of her morals, the publicity and the display of her debauchery, whose wantonness alone made her share the destinies of the despot who sacrificed the blood and treasure of the people to his shameful pleasures."

From the outset of his magistracy, at the beginning of April, 1793, Fouquier was as a rule pitiless towards drunkards[1] and madmen, and on April 10 he asked the Court to inflict the punishment of death on Luttier, an old soldier, who, overcome by drink, asked some workmen at the corner of the Rue de la Huchette "whether they were Republicans and whether they had a soul, affirming to them that he had a soul, that it was for his king who had paid for it;[2] that the king was not dead; but that he still existed and would soon appear, that France was ruined unless there was a king, because France was too large for a Republic . . ." Luttier was guillotined. On April 18, Fouquier appeared against a Paris cook, Catherine Clère, who, on the night of the 7th of March preceding, had been seen to fall down by a municipal officer who was returning home. He picked her up drunk, and she immediately said to him "that she would not allow the son's head to be cut off like his father's," adding that she meant "the little boy who is in the Temple." She was brought to the police station, and called out "Long live the King!" and, say Fouquier's pleadings, indulged in talk which "manifested the disorder of drunkenness." But Fouquier demanded the punishment of death for Catherine Clère, "for having *wickedly and designedly*, in cafés and at the police station, publicly indulged in conversation tending to provoke murder, the dissolution of the national representation, and the re-establishment of royalty in France." Fouquier was not embarrassed by the evident contradiction existing between the disordered ideas and words of the unhappy woman under the influence of drunkenness, and

---

[1] It was not the offence of drunkenness that he proceeded against. He explains his conduct in this matter on the occasion of the impeachment of Menou, an officer of the Carabineers, on the 15th of Messidor in the year II.

" The drunkenness in which it appears that he was plunged at the time of this counter-revolutionary excess cannot serve him as an excuse A drunken republican has never asked for a king; but it is not astonishing that a royalist, masked as a republican, should, in the disorder of drunkenness, allow his secret to escape "—Archives Nationales, W 404, No 933, 2nd part.

[2] He had served in what had been the king's regiment of infantry. Archives Nationales, W. 268, No 4.

the intention of having wickedly, and therefore knowingly, conspired against the Convention. Catherine Clère was guillotined, although her master, M. de Wailly, and other witnesses had come forward to declare they had never known her to be against the Revolution.

We could go on with these quotations, drawing from them sinister or dramatic effects We prefer to expound succinctly but clearly the legislative measures in virtue of which Fouquier's powers become more and more excessive.

This exposition is necessary to give some idea of how the Public Prosecutor, who was only an agent, though a supple, zealous and active agent—one who, moreover, felt himself closely watched by terrible political chiefs—came, quite naturally and by an implacable interpretation of the revolutionary laws, to symbolise Terror and Dismay, at first almost insensibly, then in crescendo to the final butchery We must not forget, that if in thirteen months (from April, 1793, to the 22nd of Prairial in the year II.) 1,259 victims mounted the scaffold ; during the *last forty-nine days of the Terror* (from the 22nd Prairial to the 9th of Thermidor) 1,366 persons were guillotined as conspirators.

On July 19, 1793, Fouquier directed the attention of the Convention to the continuous increase of work that was thrown upon the Tribunal by " circumstances " " The mass of business," he writes, " would require at least eight judges, five of whom would be occupied with the hearings and the other three with the preliminaries. In this way, I venture to assure the Convention that I shall attend to all the business as promptly as circumstances permit."

The external situation of France was most critical. Mayence capitulated on July 23 , Valenciennes on the 28th. After Condé's surrender, General Custines had been recalled to Paris on the 12th. The Convention increased the staff of the Revolutionary Tribunal. On July 24 the number of judges was raised from five to seven. The Public Prosecutor and the President were to have a salary of 8,000 *livres* per annum Then, on July 31, two sections were created The number of judges and jurors was raised to ten ; the number of Fouquier's deputies from two to three; that of the registrar's clerks from three to four[1]; and that of the correspondence clerks from three to four. The number of jurors was raised to thirty.

The following were appointed judges : Coffinhal, an ex-doctor, formerly a national commissioner of the Tribunal of the Second Arrondissement of Paris, Nicolas Grébeauval, formerly Fouquier's secretary; Gabriel Toussaint Scellier, the judge-director of the *jury d'accusation*.

On August 28, Armand Martial Joseph Herman, the President of the Criminal Tribunal of the Pas-de-Calais, a compatriot of Robespierre, was appointed Vice-President of the Tribunal, in Montané's place. Why was Montané replaced ? Fouquier-Tinville had denounced him to the Convention on July 30 for having committed two grave mistakes. First, at Charlotte Corday's trial, Montané had substituted " criminal intentions " for " counter-revolutionary tendencies," a change that might have saved the prisoner's life. Secondly, at the trial of Léonard Bourdon's assailants he had erased from the minute the clause about the confiscation of property.[2] Montané was summoned before the second section of the Tribunal which had just been created, but he did not put in an appearance. He was arrested ; but Fouquier forgot him in his prison, in spite of the entreaties of Montané, who wished to be tried. This touch of humanity on Fouquier's part saved Montané's life. He outlived the 9th of Thermidor, and was acquitted after many months of detention.

On August 25 Marseilles was taken , on the 28th Toulon surrendered to the English. Lyons was in open insurrection.

On September 5 the Sections demanded that Terror should be the order of the day. Merlin (of Douai) told the Convention that the Tribunal was overwhelmed with business ; prisoners were coming in from all parts of France. Still, it was necessary for " prompt justice to be granted to the people." By decrees of September 5 and 14, the Tribunal

---

[1] There was only a single registrar.
[2] Archives Nationales, W. 500, 3rd dossier, p. 91.

was to be composed of four sections and sixteen judges (including the President and the Vice-President), sixty jurors, eight registrar's clerks, and eight correspondence clerks. " The scope of the Tribunal " had to be increased more and more.

In order to make it more effective it was necessary to have the assistance of the Revolutionary Committees. These reorganised Committees were charged with the task of proceeding immediately to the arrest of suspected persons. Full powers were granted them for this purpose. Billaud-Varenne had said . " We must search out our enemies in their dens. Night and day will hardly suffice to arrest them. I demand that we regard as a suspect every noble and every priest who, on the adoption of this decree, is not found residing in his municipality." " There are other suspects," Bazire had added, " there are shopkeepers, wholesale merchants, stock-jobbers, ex-procurators (solicitors), bailiffs, insolent servants, stewards and men of business, men of large independent means, tricksters in essence, profession, and education."

These propositions were carried unanimously.[1]

A decree of September 6 ordered the arrest of all foreigners resident in France   The committees of surveillance [2] were to draw up lists of suspects, and to issue warrants for their arrest.   At the sitting of September 14, Merlin (of Douai) caused the work to be divided among the four sections of the Tribunal.   Every day two sections, alternately, were to try cases , the other two, in the Council Chamber, were to be engaged in the preliminary preparations for other trials.

Fouquier's tasks became very much heavier from day to day.   He took his inspiration from the propositions enunciated by Chaumette on October 10, 1793, at the Council of the Commune.

" Those are suspects who, in the Assemblies of the people, check its energy by astute speeches, turbulent cries, and

---

[1] *Moniteur* for September 7, 1793
[2] Established by the law of March 21

murmurs ; those who, more prudent, speak mysteriously of the ills of the Republic, pity the fate of the people, and are always ready to spread evil tidings with an affectation of grief ; those who have changed their conduct and their language in accordance with events ; those who, silent about the crimes of royalists and federalists, declaim with emphasis against the slight faults of patriots, and, in order to appear republican, affect a studied austerity and severity ; those who contradict themselves when it is a question of a moderate or an aristocrat ; those who pity the farmers and the rapacious merchants against whom the law is obliged to take measures ; those who, having always on their lips such words as liberty, republic and country, associate with the men who were formerly nobles, with counter-revolutionary priests, aristocrats, *feuillants* and moderates, concerning themselves about their fate , those who, having done nothing against liberty, also do nothing for it."[1]

The strength of the revolutionary government lay in " virtue " and " terror."[2] But the people were hungry, were dying of hunger. They were offered the spectacle of the scaffold and the daily execution of conspirators. At the hour of the executions they crowded to the Place de la Révolution. On the 4th of Germinal in the year II., the Chalier Section informed the General Council of the Commune that on that day several unfortunate accidents had been caused by the great crowds of citizens, and the private stands erected on the Place The General Council ordered that in future there should neither be private stands nor carts that could block the way ; that citizens should be forbidden to lift up their canes or their hats at the moment when the sword of the law was about to strike the guilty.[3]

On the 5th of Germinal (March 25, 1794) Fouquier wrote the following letter to Hanriot, the commander-in-chief of the Parisian guard :

[1] *Moniteur* for October 12, 1793
[2] The saying is Robespierre's.
[3] *Moniteur* for the 9th of Germinal, year II.

" Citizen,

" The burial place of the condemned having been transferred to Mousseaux,[1] and the police force of the Tribunal
being insufficient for this daily and continual service of the
Tribunal, would it not be well for you to give orders that
four mounted men should be an escort from the place of
execution to the place where the bodies are deposited ?   In
this manner the police would be able to return promptly
to their post, and the work of the Tribunal would not be
delayed.   I beg you to take this matter into consideration.

" Greeting and fraternity,

" A. Q. FOUQUIER "

The 5th of Germinal was the day following the condemnation of Hébert, Vincent, Ronsin, and their associates (20
accused persons in all)   In spite of virtue, liberty, unity,
indivisibility, equality, in spite of the laws made for them,
the people suffered greatly   They were hungry. They
drank.   The drunkards who were arrested as conspirators
demanded a king " because things cannot go on like this."
They were too wretched.   " As for the crowd of those who
are accustomed to attend the sittings of the Tribunal, indignant as it is," says a police observer, " it sees with uneasiness
the Tribunal pursuing a course contrary to the laws of
humanity and justice "[2]

This phrase of the observer was written at the close of
one of the sittings during Hébert's trial, a trial conducted
rapidly   and   harshly   by   Dumas,   the   Vice-President.
Fouquier did not trouble himself much about investigations or proofs in drawing up his indictment against
the editor of the *Père Duchesne* and his nineteen fellow-
prisoners (one of whom was a woman, Catherine Quétineau,
the widow of the republican colonel who was guillotined on
the 26th of Ventôse in the year II.).   Moral proofs and his
orders were enough for Fouquier.   If he were inspired by
the words spoken by Chaumette at the Council of the Commune on October 10, 1793, he was also mindful of the more

[1] This was the name then given to the village of Monceau
[2] *Situation de Paris du 2 germinal, an II* —Schmidt, II., p 178

recent political speeches of Robespierre and Saint-Just. It was a matter of crushing the " lenient " among the party of the Mountain in the person of Danton, and of suppressing the rising insurrection of the Commune in the person of Hébert. Robespierre branded them as the *moderates* and the *ultras*. At the Convention, on the 8th of Ventôse (February 26, 1794), Saint-Just said —

" What establishes a republic is the total destruction of all that is opposed to it. People complain of revolutionary measures , but we are moderates in comparison with all other governments. . . . A striking sign of treason is the pity shown towards crime in a republic which can be based only on inflexibility. . . . The revolutionary government which had established *the dictatorship of justice* no longer soars as it did . . . Destroy the rebel party ; paint liberty in the colour of bronze."[1] And, when he asked for judicial weapons against the " corrupt and violent " who had sold themselves to the foreigner, those weapons were granted. This is the decree of the 23rd of Ventôse of the year II

" . . . The Revolutionary Tribunal will continue to give information against the authors and accomplices of the conspiracy directed against the French people and their liberty. It will cause prisoners to be promptly arraigned before it and will bring them to trial . . ."

That very night, Hébert, Ronsin, Vincent, and their associates were arrested. " Never," wrote Fouquier-Tinville in his indictment, " has there existed against the sovereignty of the French people and its liberty a conspiracy more atrocious in its object, vaster, more immense in its connections and details , but the active vigilance of the Convention has caused its failure by unmasking it and by handing over to the Tribunal those who appear to have been its principal instruments."[2] Then he summed up the facts in his own way, in conformity with the directions of the two Committees

---

[1] *Moniteur* for the 9th of Ventôse, year II.
[2] Archives Nationales, W 339, dossier 617

Every one knows the piteous attitude of Hébert during his trial. He did not defend himself. He answered with a " yes " or " no." The violent editor of the *Père Duchesne* was in a state of utter collapse On the other hand, Vincent, Momoro, and Ronsin rivalled one another in insolence [1] Three of the accused were acquitted. Laboureau, a medical student, forty-one years of age, was acquitted and received the fraternal embrace He was a police spy. Colonel Quétineau's widow declared herself *enceinte*. She was taken to the Evêché hospital, and was perceived to be four months gone with child The Tribunal ordered a postponement of her execution ; but misfortune followed her. Some days later, she had a miscarriage On May 11, Bayard and Théry, officers of health, handed her a certificate of convalescence. Fouquier-Tinville immediately applied to the Tribunal, and the Tribunal ordered "that within twenty-four hours the judgment of the 4th of Germinal last, which condemned the widow Quétineau to death, should be proceeded with, the whole matter being at the suit of the Public Prosecutor." She was guillotined on the same day.

The Public Prosecutor's diligence was extreme. In order not to lose time in going and coming he lived close to the Palace of Justice, in the Place Thionville (now the Place Dauphine). Rising at dawn, he was in his office before the beginning of the sittings, which generally opened at nine or ten o'clock in the morning, going through the formidable correspondence which reached him from the Departments, preparing the work of the Tribunal, spurring on his secretaries, directing his deputies " Business " flowed in pell-mell How was he to cope with it ? It was necessary to act quickly and to strike hard His political chiefs

---

[1] The day on which Hébert appeared for his trial (1st of Germinal in the year II , March 21, 1794) Legendre, at the Jacobin Club, had energetically expounded what the sentiments of patriots ought to be, he declared that, as soon as the Committee of Public Safety designated those who were factious, all good citizens ought to disregard the bonds of blood and of friendship Legendre himself promised to deliver to the sword of the law those who were dearest to him, if they were designated as traitors. (*Moniteur* of the 5th of Germinal, year II)

D

were there watching him. Would he give it up ? Would he send in his resignation ? He could not even dream of doing so. What would become of him ? What would become of his family ? He must obey. And he obeyed. He was an executive agent.

Hitherto he had contented himself with observing and following the law—that law which changed so often. His indictments were, in reality, only written summaries of the documents that had been handed to him, or of the examinations of the prisoners Fouquier himself was content to execute the law and administer the decrees, and had shown himself a strict and hard observer of that law and of those decrees. Now he was to give proof of initiative, to play a personal part, *to show himself*. He would violate the judicial forms ; he would be partial. He would suggest to his chiefs of the two Committees of General Security and of Public Safety that the powers at his command were too small, that it was possible, by decrees adapted to the circumstances, to go farther, to strike conspirators and suspects more surely.

Hérault de Séchelles had been arrested And Billaud-Varenne had declared it necessary " to kill Danton." Saint-Just had said : " If we do not have him guillotined, we shall be guillotined." On the 10th of Germinal (March 30, 1794), Danton was arrested at six o'clock in the morning. So were Philippeaux, Lacroix, Camille Desmoulins, Fabre and Chabot.

In his indictment Fouquier-Tinville intended to *amalgamate* old charges, recent documents, and quite new denunciations, intentionally confusing political prisoners and those charged with gambling in the funds. The bankers, Frey, Gusman and Deisderichen were to be associated with Danton and his friends on the grounds of complicity in the affair of the East India Company. No proof was adduced to support this audacious affirmation. The Freys, for example, a couple of German Jews who had come to Paris in order, so they said, to breathe " the air of liberty," and who became army contractors in 1792, had doubtless been speculators but not State conspirators. Fouquier describes Deisderichen as " one of the lawyers of the King of Denmark." This is neither a charge nor an argument, but seems to insinuate that he had communications with the foreigner. Just as the foreigners, Proly, Cloots, Pereyra, had, on the 4th of Germinal, been guillotined along with the violent party, the *ultras*, Hébert, Ronsin and Vincent , so Gusman, Frey, and Deisderichen were accused together with the moderates, with Danton and the others This indictment was drawn up from the manuscript of a speech made at the Convention by Amar, a member of the Committee of General Security, on the affair of the East India Company.

General Westermann was also among the accused. " Westermann," writes Dr. Robinet, " was placed in the dock without any of the customary judicial preliminaries. He had not been questioned His indictment, which had not been communicated to him (how then could he prepare his defence ?), had been drawn up by Fouquier on the basis of *documents that he had not even seen, for they were sealed up*, as is proved by the official report made out on that very day at the General's house, 63, Rue Meslé, by members of the Committee of Surveillance of the Gravilliers Section."[1] In fact, the warrant for the General's arrest, the order for his attachment, confirmed by a decree of the Convention, and his writ of indictment are all of the same date, the 13th of Germinal (April 2, 1794).[2] The 14th is the date of the order for his trial by the Tribunal, the verification of the prisoner's identity, his examination and appearance in court. Fouquier drew up his writ of indictment on the 13th, and says in it " that an examination of the report of the questions put to Westermann *to-day* before the Tribunal, as well as of the documents (which the court had not yet at its disposal, and which, on the contrary, it was at that very moment arranging to have seized and placed under seals) shows that Westermann has supported the conspiracy of Dumouriez with all his power."

[1] Robinet : *Le Procès des Dantonistes*, p 440
[2] Archives Nationales, W. 342, dossier 648, 3me partie

But there was more to come, viz. · the part played by the Public Prosecutor at the sitting of the 15th of Germinal (April 4, 1794).

It is not necessary to linger over the charge made by Pâris, the registrar, called Fabricius, against Fouquier-Tinville, at the time of his trial, that he, along with Lescot-Fleuriot, had *selected* the jurors for Danton's trial instead of choosing them by lot. Pâris, the registrar, was a friend of Danton. He was arrested for refusing to sign the document containing Danton's sentence. It is possible that on the day when he had to give evidence against Fouquier, he may, out of ill-will towards him, have imputed everything to him.

In the notes of Topino-Lebrun, who was present at the sitting, it is stated that Fouquier and Herman, the presiding judge, acted together in directing the proceedings. They passed notes to one another of this character ·—

" Herman —In half-an-hour I shall close Danton's defence. . . "

" Fouquier —I have a question to ask Danton relating to Belgium when you have finished your questions."

" Herman.—We must not enter into the Belgian business in regard to anybody except Lacroix and Danton , and when we have reached that point, we must hurry on. . ."

Herman and Fouquier were continually interrupting the prisoners' defence in order to exhaust the three days at the end of which the presiding judge of the Tribunal had a right to ask the jury if they would declare themselves sufficiently informed and ready to close the case.[1]

There is another significant fact—that Lacroix insisted on being allowed to speak, and said that it was impossible for the jury to be sufficiently informed since they had not heard the witnesses. Addressing Fouquier, he asked him if he had summoned the witnesses, a list of whom he had sent him At this question Fouquier was " a little taken aback " He answered that he had lost it Lacroix expressed aston-

---

[1] On the initiative of Fouquier-Tinville this right had been given to the presiding judge by a decree of the 7th of Brumaire in the year II., on the occasion of the trial of the Girondins.

ishment. Fouquier replied that he was within his rights, according to the law, in not giving witnesses to the prisoners. Lacroix and the others pointed out that as they themselves had helped to pass this law, they knew it, and that it did not state what the Public Prosecutor wanted to make it say. Then Fouquier declared that he would write to the Convention in order that "the fact might be cleared up."[1]

During the hearing he wrote, not to the Convention, but to the Committee of Public Safety, the famous letter in which he gave an account of the prisoners' demands.

"Paris, this 15th of Germinal in the Second Year of the Republic one and indivisible."

"Citizens and representatives,

"A horrible storm has been raging from the moment that the session began · the prisoners, like madmen, are demanding the hearing of witnesses for the defence, the citizens and Deputies, Simon, Courtois, Laignelot, Fréron, Panis, Ludot, Callon, Merlin (of Douai), Gossuin, Legendre, Robert Lindet, Robin, Goupilleau (of Montaigu), Lecointre (of Versailles), Brival, and Merlin (of Thionville). They are appealing to the people against the refusal which they say they have received ; in spite of the firmness of the presiding judge and of the entire Tribunal, their repeated demands disturb the sitting, and they openly proclaim that they will not be silent until their witnesses are heard and that without a decree , we request you definitely to lay down a course for us to follow in regard to this demand, the judicial procedure not furnishing us with any means of justifying this refusal.

"A. Q. FOUQUIER, HERMAN, presiding judge."[2]

Saint-Just cynically abstained from reading this letter to the Convention He exclaimed · "The wretches ! They confess their crime *by resisting the law* ! . . . At this

---

[1] Archives Nationales, W 500, 3rd dossier, p 58.
[2] Before composing this letter with Herman, Fouquier had written another, differing considerably from this, which contained the words : " The only method would in our opinion be a decree."

moment conspiracies in their favour are being organised in the prisons ; at this moment the aristocrats are stirring ! " He informed the Convention of the denunciation of Citizen Laflotte, a spy in the Luxembourg prison, showing that a conspiracy with the object of murdering the members of the Convention and of the Tribunal existed among the prisoners and the accused. He proposed a decree depriving them of the right to plead. " Every person accused of conspiracy who shall resist or insult the national justice, shall immediately be deprived of the right to plead." The decree was passed. Amar and Voulland carried it to the Tribunal. Fouquier requested that the decree be read and registered. On the 16th, at the opening of the hearing, he declared to Danton and Lacroix that their witnesses would not be heard. The presiding judge read the decree of the 7th of Brumaire of the year II., authorising the Tribunal to ask the jury if they were sufficiently informed The jury retired. After a fairly long interval they returned. On the same evening, Trinchard, the foreman of the jury, declared that they were sufficiently informed. Fouquier then stated that, owing to the indecency and blasphemy of the accused during the trial, he saw himself obliged to take measures proportionate to the gravity of the circumstances. At his request the Tribunal had ordered that the questions should be put to the jury and sentence passed *in the absence of the accused.* Carts were waiting in the courtyard of the Conciergerie. The Dantonists passed from the audience chamber to the condemned cell. They heard their death sentence whilst they were being prepared for execution. They then set out for the guillotine.

In reality the pleadings had been closed without ever having begun. No document had been read. None of the witnesses who were asked for had been heard. Fouquier had assumed a terrible responsibility. Besides the fact, of which Pâris afterwards accused him, that he and Herman had gone into the jurors' room in order to influence them during their deliberations, he had distorted the character of the protests made by the accused when they insisted on having witnesses, as was their right, and this was a crime. Moreover, when he suggested in his letter to the Committee of Public Safety that it was possible, by a decree, to deprive the accused of speech and liberty of defence, he committed a second crime. He gave Saint-Just a weapon for his judicial *coup d'état*

Later, when he was accused in his turn, he denied that he was responsible for the judgment passed on Danton and for his death.

" I appeal to common sense and to reason. If I had an understanding with the ferocious and sanguinary Robes-pierre and his accomplices[1] to deprive Danton and the other accused of all means of justifying themselves 1st. should I have written the letter of which I have just spoken ? 2nd. should I have informed the Committee that the accused demanded with loud outcries to have a certain number of Deputies heard in their defence ? 3rd should I have stated that the accused appealed to the entire people against the refusal they received ? No, certainly not, unless, indeed, you wish to find evil in the simplest and most correct acts, etc. . . Could I expect that by an act of perfidy as guilty as it was incredible, Saint-Just, who received my letter, *would change its text* and attribute to me the assertion that the accused were in open rebellion, etc. ? "

Why, instead of addressing his letter to the Committee of Public Safety, where he knew Saint-Just and Robespierre were determined to crush Danton, had he not addressed it to the Convention ? Danton might perhaps have been saved Why should we be dupes of the words, " unless, indeed, we wish to find evil in the simplest and most correct acts," when we have in mind the last phrase in his first letter to the Committee : " It is urgent that you indicate a course for us to follow, and the only method would in our opinion be a decree " ? By these words he obviously suggests a judicial method of preventing the defence. This would be a *decree*. Saint-Just did not need to be told twice.

---

[1] This was written after the 9th of Thermidor.

The decree was passed   It is possible that this single letter of Fouquier's may have caused his ruin some months later.

Fouquier was an agent of the law, but should all feeling of humanity, all pity, be abolished when it was a matter of applying that law? Why should he have no share in the responsibility for the atrocious condemnation of Madame de Lavergne, on the day before Danton's trial? The facts are these.   Louis François de Lavergne-Champlaurier, lieutenant-colonel, military commander of Longwy, had just been condemned for having delivered Longwy to the enemy. He was very ill and aged.   His wife had personally taken steps with the Committee of General Security to ask for a reprieve.   Madame de Lavergne was twenty-six, young and beautiful.   Amar, old Vadier (called "sixty years of virtue"), and Voulland received her banteringly, pretending to be surprised that "she wished to put off the moment that would rid her of an old and infirm husband."[1]   She went to the Vice-President of the Tribunal.   Dumas received her as Amar, Vadier, and Voulland had done   Then she understood there was nothing left for her to do.   She went to the Tribunal and seated herself on the ground in the middle of the crowd.   She waited until the hearing began. Then she saw the gaolers of the Conciergerie carry in her husband on a mattress, in a dying condition.   The writ of indictment was read, and sentence of death pronounced.

Suddenly a cry rose from the middle of the crowd in one of the halls adjacent to that of the Tribunal, a cry of "Long live the King!"—several times repeated.   It was Madame de Lavergne "*who wanted to be guillotined because they were going to murder her husband*," as she declared to the officials before whom she was immediately led by the police.[2] She had suddenly become mad from grief.   Questioned repeatedly, she could only say   "I have asked for a King. I want to be guillotined.   They are going to murder my husband   I want to go to bed."   And when her examination was read, she declared that she no longer knew what they had asked her, or what she had answered.   She was

[1] Campardon, I. 287.   [2] Archives Nationales, W. 342, dossier 643.

placed on the benches for the prisoners. It was Grébeauval, the Public Prosecutor's deputy, who pleaded against her. She was condemned to death. Herman, icy and impenetrable, presided over the sitting

The writ of indictment, which may be seen among the Archives, had been prepared by one of Fouquier's secretaries ; but the Public Prosecutor had signed it, and added in the margin some notes, " some exact statements." Can it be said that he had no responsibility for the death of Madame de Lavergne, who was guillotined at the age of twenty-six for having tenderly loved her aged husband ?

The consequences of Danton's death made themselves felt from the 16th of Germinal (April 5, 1794) onwards. It was necessary to keep the public mind occupied, to set public opinion on the wrong track, to prove that the Conspiracy existed, that it was not an invention of the police, that the patriots ran the greatest dangers, that they risked assassination. For this business the Committees of Public Safety and of General Security used one of their creatures whom they kept for some time in the house of detention of the Luxembourg. His name was Laflotte, " an ex-Minister of the Republic of Florence." Laflotte was a prison spy and an *agent provocateur*. It was he who lodged information against the Conspirators. He was the principal witness at the trial On the proposal of Billaud-Varenne his declaration was read by a secretary at the Convention on the 15th of Germinal It dealt with a plot contrived by certain prisoners at the head of whom were General Arthur Dillon and Deputy Philibert Simond. Dillon had written to the wife of Camille Desmoulins, offering her a thousand crowns to hire people, and to have the Revolutionary Tribunal surrounded during Danton's trial Chaumette's wife had passed through the Luxembourg , she had made signs of satisfaction to her husband by clapping her hands. Dillon claimed that in the Luxembourg prison there were 200 men willing to do his bidding ; Simond that he had forty. The blow was to be struck at night They would then go to the Committee of Public Safety, and " slaughter it."

First of all, to collect the prisoners and fetch them out, the alarm would have to be given in the prison. Dillon charged himself with leading the armed force. He claimed that he had on his side the writer and a turnkey who would compel the officer of the guard to give the pass-word. The conspirators had admitted Laflotte into their secret. The spy "passed a very agitated night, fearing that Dillon might take it into his head to execute his plan in the middle of the night." He got up at dawn and hastened to communicate with the Committee of Public Safety.

It is an obscure affair. How much truth was there in all this? Was the plot real? The information laid by the spy Laflotte came at a singularly opportune moment during Danton's trial. A pretext had been found. This same pretext was to serve, during their trial before the Tribunal from the 21st to the 24th of Germinal, against Chaumette, the national agent of the Commune of Paris; against Gobel, the renegade Bishop of Paris, "apostles of atheism"; against Arthur Dillon, the treacherous general; against Deputy Philibert Simond, and against twenty-one other prisoners in the Luxembourg, among whom were Lucille, the pathetic young wife of Camille Desmoulins, and Hébert's widow.

According to Fouquier-Tinville these prisoners, all of such different circumstances and origins, conspired together in the Luxembourg prison to replace the son of Louis XVI. on the throne of France. Their machinations were paid for by the Foreigner's gold. The Public Prosecutor saw in them, moreover, accomplices of Hébert and " of other *conspirators* already smitten by the sword of the Law."

In the spring of 1794, a shudder of terror shook France to her foundations. Alarm was everywhere. The "batches"[1] were beginning It was Saint-Just who denounced the slackness of the Provincial Tribunals. He carried the law of the 27th of Germinal (April 16). " Persons accused of

---

[1] *Fournées*, or batches of loaves for the oven, the name given to the groups of condemned persons tried at the same time and sent together to the guillotine.—TR.

PETER GASPAR CHAUMETTE

conspiracy will be brought before the Revolutionary Tribunal from all quarters of the Republic. The Committees of Public Safety and of General Security will promptly search out the accomplices of conspirators and cause them to be brought before the Revolutionary Tribunal." Denunciations were forwarded to the Public Prosecutor: denunciations voluntary and subsidised, made " in the name of the liberty and happiness of the French people " ; denunciations of servants against their masters, of clerks against their employers, of deserted women against their lovers, of debtors against their creditors, and *vice versa*, of soldiers against their officers. Billaud-Varenne, in his report to the Convention on the 1st of Floréal, depicts in blazing lines a project for national regeneration by means of the guillotine . " Vigorous action is necessary. . . . The inflexible austerity of Lycurgus became at Sparta the immovable foundation of the Republic , the weak and trusting character of Solon plunged Athens again into slavery. . . This parallel contained the whole science of government . . . The pretensions of Prussia and of England vanished with Brissot, Carra, Hébert, Danton, and Fabre d'Eglantine. . . ." War continued, however. Armies and generals were needed. Billaud-Varenne drew an " enchanting " picture of a France regenerated by virtue and justice that had been made the order of the day · instruction made universal ; purification of heart ; egoism destroyed , no more beggary , no more hospitals , charity bestowed in the dwellings , work for all , well-being for all , the triumph of citizenship and sensibility.[1]

On that day the Revolutionary Tribunal tried a large " batch " of twenty-five former members of the Parlements of Paris and of Toulouse, Lepeletier-Rosambo, Bourrée-Corberon, Bochart de Saron, Molé de Champlâtreux, Lefebvre d'Ormesson, Pasquier, etc They were accused of having protested against the decrees of the National Assembly. They appeared before " solid " jurors who were not " gentle-

[1] *Moniteur* of 2nd of Floréal, year II.

men " as they were—Gravier, the vinegar-seller, Brochet, the ex-lackey, Trinchard, the ex-dragoon and carpenter, etc.

Among the accused was Henry Guy Sallier, a former President of the Cour des Aides " You are mistaken," he protested, " for I was not a member of the Parlement, but a President of the Cour des Aides. The matter has to do with my son, Guy Marie Sallier, a Councillor in the Parlement." His protest was in vain He was guillotined. There was even an error regarding his person. At his examination, which took place in Fouquier's presence, he had declared that his name was Henry Guy Sallier and not Guy Marie. Fouquier had in his hands all the documents relating to the matter. He was not present at the actual trial, his deputy, Gilbert Liendon, pleading in his stead. But it is none the less true that Fouquier had carelessly issued a warrant for the arrest of the father instead of the son, and had equally carelessly drawn up his indictment against the father

Later, at Fouquier's trial, Sallier's son came forward to give evidence. His declaration was clear.[1] It should be noted that on this 1st of Floréal, Fouquier wrote to Hanriot, the commander of the armed forces of Paris, to tell him that " the verdict will be given at three o'clock." [2] Was he then sure of it beforehand ? It must be noted, finally, that the farewell letter of Honoré Rigaud, one of the Parliamentarians of Toulouse, written to his wife at the moment when he was starting for the scaffold, was never sent to the address it bore. It is still to be found in the bundle of papers pertaining to the Tribunal preserved among the Archives.[3] It is a sad letter, full of noble resignation, in which the unhappy man forgives his enemies, begs his family not to attempt to avenge his death, and sends to his wife and children his last thoughts. Fouquier-Tinville did not take the trouble to forward it. Herman had ceased to be President of the Tribunal some days before. In reward for his

[1] See page 244.   [2] Archives Nationales, A. F. II , 48, No. 200.
[3] Archives Nationales, W. 121, pièce 110

JOHN MAY ROLAND DE LA PLATIERE

attitude during Danton's trial, he had, on the 19th of Germinal, been appointed Minister of Justice in succession to Paré. Dumas, the Vice-President, had succeeded him as President. Fouquier was on bad terms with Dumas, a notorious drunkard, whom the Public Prosecutor spoke of as his "mortal enemy." Fouquier's position became difficult. Watched closely by the Committees, detested by his President, he often gave vent to sudden bursts of anger against his secretaries and the jurors [1] His violent character and his overbearing temperament were ill adapted to the limitations of his office

Herman, however, thought that "the law gave too much power to the Public Prosecutor and did not allow to the Tribunal so much supervision as was desirable" He considered that "Fouquier did his work somewhat in the style of a Procurator."[2] This ex-Procurator was impatient with the caprices of Dumas, with the abrupt, incoherent manner in which the presiding judge conducted the proceedings, and interrupted and silenced the accused. He opposed him; he insisted that certain witnesses should be heard. These two magistrates were in constant rivalry.

However, business kept coming in on all sides. On the 5th of Floréal (April 24) thirty-five inhabitants of Verdun were placed in the dock. They were charged with having given up Verdun to the King of Prussia. Several of them were old men of seventy, seventy-two, seventy-five, and seventy-six years of age. There were young girls, two of whom, Claire Tabouillot and Barbe Henry, were only seventeen.

These last were not condemned to death, but to twenty years' detention and to exposure on the scaffold for six hours.[3] On the 6th of Floréal (April 25), Anisson Duperron,

---

[1] He was snappish and rough to the jurors One day as he was coming away from a hearing, he said to them, "How could you declare that that man was guilty? He was not even brought to plead" On other occasions he would burst into a rage against them because they had acquitted

[2] Archives Nationales, W 501, 2nd dossier, p 78.

[3] Archives Nationales, W 352, No 718

the Director of the National Printing Office of the Louvre, was condemned to death. His magnificent estate of Ris became the property of the nation. Very generous in his district of Ris (re-named Brutus), he died the victim of an abominable attempt at blackmailing on the part of the Mayor and some other inhabitants who were jealous of his immense fortune. On the 9th of Floréal (April 28) Fouquier mistook two accused persons for one. And this fact tends to justify Herman's criticism when, as a witness in Fouquier's trial, he affirmed " that personally he regarded him as a bit of a blunderer, that is to say that his office was not orderly enough," and that " the Tribunal had often reprimanded him for want of accuracy and precision in his writs of indictment "[1] The two accused persons who were mistaken for one on this 9th of Floréal were Pichard-Dupage and Olivier-Despallières. Their names were mixed up into Pichard-Despallières In the " batch " for this day [2] there figured Denis François Angram d'Alleray, a former civil lieutenant at the Châtelet. He had rendered some services to Fouquier when he was a Procurator at the Châtelet. The Public Prosecutor of the Revolutionary Tribunal remembered the debt of gratitude contracted by the Procurator before the Revolution. He told Citizen Angram to deny everything.[3]

The latter was charged with having sent assistance to one of his children who had emigrated. He did not deny the fact, but openly declared . " I know the law. It forbids all communication with the emigrants But the laws of nature take precedence over the laws of the Republic." He was guillotined.

On the same day Fouquier asked the Committee of Public Safety for a remuneration of from fifteen to twenty thousand *livres* for Sanson, the public executioner. The Committee granted twenty thousand *livres* [4]

Among others brought before the Tribunal during Floréal

---

[1] Archives Nationales, W. 501, 2nd dossier, p 78
[2] Archives Nationales, W. 501, 2nd dossier, p 78.
[3] Campardon, I , p 312.
[4] Archives Nationales A F., 22, dossier 69, p 81.

were soldiers, *sans-culottes*, drunkards, cabmen, national guards, vine-growers, milliners, dressmakers, men of the Court and of the people, artisans and peasants. The grounds of offence were seditious cries, and, above all, that of " Long live the King ! " which continually issued from the mouths of the humble as the supreme expression of their misery and despair. On the 13th and 14th of Floréal the accused consisted of officers, non-commissioned officers, and soldiers of the battalions of the National Guard of the districts of the Filles-Saint-Thomas and of the Petits-Pères. On the 15th of Floréal, of aristocrats and *sans-culottes* guilty of counter-revolutionary utterances. On the 16th of Floréal, there was Claude Françoise Loisillier, " a maker of millinery," who had stuck up royalist placards on the walls in her district. Two other women, a hairdresser and a milliner, appeared in the dock with her. They were tried and condemned to death for seditious cries. A cook was acquitted. She, it appears, had not acted " knowingly." On the 17th of Floréal, there were " batches " of eleven and of thirteen accused persons ; on the 18th, " batches " of eighteen and of seven ; on the 19th, Lavoisier and the Farmers-General (to the number of twenty-eight). They were charged with falsifying their accounts , but this crime did not involve appearance before the Revolutionary Tribunal. A plot had accordingly been trumped up. In reality it was their property that was desired. They offered two millions out of this property. They defended themselves in long, carefully prepared, and very circumstantial Memorials It was lost labour. There was no time to take account of them. Speed was necessary. Fouquier-Tinville had made out his writ of indictment, and they were condemned to death.[1]

On the 21st of Floréal Madame Elisabeth was brought before the Tribunal with twenty-three other prisoners, including four members of the de Loménie family (François, Charles, Athanase, and Martial). Fouquier-Tinville affirmed, at the time of his trial, that he wished to divert the arguments, and to save Athanase de Loménie, a former Minister

[1] Archives Nationales, W. 358 to 362.

of War. " Imbued with veneration and respect for the ex-Minister," he said, " I had arranged to turn to account all that was memorable and advantageous for that worthy ex-Minister ; but, having foreseen my laudable intentions, Liendon, my deputy, anticipated me at the hearing ; he arranged to have the case tried before my arrival at the Tribunal, and I was not able to fulfil my good intentions." Then followed a eulogy of M. de Loménie, whose virtues he proclaimed, which brought upon him this reply from Cambon, one of the deputies of the Public Prosecutor. " I hold in my hand the writ of indictment presented by you and signed by you against Loménie." Cambon read this document and said · " You have just made a very pompous and well-merited eulogy on Loménie, the ex-Minister, and yet in your writ of indictment you make it out a crime that he captured votes to become the Mayor of his district, and that he asked for petitions from neighbouring districts. Why, then, do you shelter yourself to-day under his qualities in order to excuse a conviction that your eulogies now deny ? Did your heart formerly deny what your mouth utters to-day." We do not possess Fouquier's answer [1]

If we are to believe Madame Elisabeth's defender, Chauveau-Lagarde, Fouquier-Tinville was so perfidious as to deceive him by assuring him that her trial would not take place so soon, and he refused him authority to confer with her. On the following day, her lawyer saw her in the dock, and in a prominent position [2] Fouquier had been present at her examination. He was not present at the hearing of the case. It was Gilbert Liendon who occupied his place, and Dumas who presided. The beginning of the indictment is written in Fouquier's hand · " Elisabeth Capet, sister of Louis Capet, the last tyrant of the French, aged thirty, born at Versailles " The document is in Fouquier's style. He revised and signed it. This document lays it down that " it is to the family of the Capets that the people

[1] Buchez and Roux, XXXIV , p. 441.

[1] Chauveau-Lagarde , *Note historique sur les procès de Marie-Antoinette et de Madame Elisabeth*, p. 50.

owe all the evils under the weight of which they have groaned for so many centuries. It is at the moment when excess of oppression has forced the people to break their chains that all the members of this family united to plunge them into a state of slavery more cruel than that from which they were trying to emerge. The crimes of all kinds, the wicked deeds heaped up by Capet, by the Messalina, Antoinette, by the two brothers Capet, and by Elisabeth, are too well known to make it necessary again to paint here the horrible picture ; they are written in letters of blood in the annals of the Revolution, and the unheard-of atrocities perpetrated by the barbarous emigrants or the sanguinary satellites of the despots, the murders, the incendiaries, the ravages, and, finally, the assassinations, unknown to the most ferocious monsters, which they commit on French territory, are still ordered by this detestable family in order to deliver a great nation to the despotism and fury of a few individuals Elisabeth has participated in all these crimes."

The document is well known, and it is not necessary for us to reproduce it in its entirety. It is interesting to note that a blank death warrant must have been signed. In the original, which may be seen at the Archives, a considerable space separates the text of this warrant from the formula, " given and delivered," followed by the signatures of the judges. Many other warrants at this period show the same irregularity.

On the 25th of Floréal, Madame Douet, who appeared as a witness at the trial of her husband, Jean Claude Douet, an ex-noble and Farmer-General, was placed among the accused and guillotined along with them.[1]

On the 26th of Floréal, Fréteau (Emmanuel Marie Michel Philippe), ex-Councillor of the Parlement of Paris, was brought before the Tribunal among a " batch " of prisoners, and acquitted, but detained in prison Fouquier caused him to appear again before the Tribunal on the 26th of Prairial when he was condemned to death. This affair will be dealt with in the following chapter.

[1] Archives Nationales, W. 365, dossier 309

E

The connection between the Committee of Public Safety, the Revolutionary Tribunal, and the Prosecutor became closer and closer. The popular tribunals and commissions sent every day to the Committee of Public Safety a list of all the judgments given, so that the Committee might identify the persons tried and the nature of the cases. At the beginning of each *décade* [1] the Prosecutor sent in a memorandum of the business which he proposed to bring before the Tribunal in the course of the *décade*. Masses of papers arrived daily. The "nature" of some allowed of no delay, "owing to the character of the evidence." On the other hand, some presented "obstacles." The former went through as urgent, the latter waited. Often also "the business" was ready, but the accused persons had not arrived from the provinces, or the ushers had not found them in the prisons of Paris. At the last moment Fouquier filled up the vacancies in his own fashion from the list approved of by the Committee of Public Safety, and thus caused terrible blunders But the important thing was that the Tribunal must not be idle.

The indefatigable Public Prosecutor coped with this crushing task. Every day eighty to ninety letters left his office [2] Thierriet-Grandpré, a witness who came forward to give evidence at Fouquier-Tinville's trial, saw "a heap of letters and memoranda addressed to him by accused persons, which he neglected to open and which he took into his office without breaking the seals." Those letters can be read to-day by anyone who looks through the papers of the Revolutionary Tribunal among the Archives. Poor old papers, moving and pathetic, pages for the most part dictated by anguish, yet in a respectful or flattering tone, or a touch of familiar *sans-culottisme*! Most of them plead on behalf of their writers. Some intercede for a husband or a wife; some want to know the prison in

---

[1] In the Revolutionary Calendar a period of ten days, called a *décade*, was substituted for the week of seven days —TR

[2] Fouquier's declaration at his trial Buchez and Roux, XXXIV., p 310

which there is some dear one who has been arrested. Some hideous letters grovel and lodge informations. Some ask for places. Some are from prisoners who are ill and beg for attention Some, such as those of Claire Tabouillot and of Barbe Henry, the young girls of Verdun who were condemned to twenty years' detention, but who escaped death, express " eternal gratitude " to Fouquier ; but at the same time they entreat the Public Prosecutor to give orders for their repatriation. One feels that they are still far from being reassured. A certain number appeal to Fouquier's humanity, but in a tone that recalls Chabot's prayer to Robespierre on the 4th of Frimaire, from the Luxembourg prison · " You who love patriots, deign to remember that you have numbered me on their list." Finally, some are full of sincere cordiality towards the man who has done them a service.

Evidently, the Public Prosecutor had not time to read all those letters or to answer them. His day's work would not permit it. Every evening he went to the Committees of General Security and of Public Safety. Sometimes he did not get home until five o'clock in the morning. Very often he had not three hours' sleep, and, in order that he might be at his post without delay, a decree of the 2nd of Prairial granted him a suite of rooms in the Palace of Justice.[1]

[1] Archives Nationales, AF. 22, dossier 69, p. 90.

CHAPTER III

ON the 4th of Prairial in the year II., at half-past one o'clock in the morning, as he was going up the staircase into his dwelling, No. 4, Rue Favart, Deputy Collot d'Herbois found himself confronted by a man who attacked him, shouting out : " This is your last hour ! " and two pistol shots were fired at him. The first missed fire. Collot, throwing himself backward, avoided the second. His walking-stick fell. He leant down to pick it up. The man bounded upstairs. A door closed on the sixth floor. It was there that the assailant lodged.

The Deputy's housekeeper, Suzanne Prévôt, who, when she heard her master knock, had come down with a light, was standing, candle in hand, in front of the door of the flat, on the fourth floor, ready to open the outer door. She saw a man pass by her, with a pistol in each hand, which he kept lowered close to his thighs. She heard the cry and the report of the pistol. She rushed into the flat, opened a window, and shouted into the courtyard : " It is Admiral ! "

The outer door of the house remained open. Collot d'Herbois shouted into the night, " Help, they are shooting me ! " A patrol of the Lepelletier Section was passing through the square in front of the theatre.[1] The citizens saw the Representative of the people, bare-headed and gesticulating. Immediately three of these brave men entered the house and resolutely climbed the stairs. They were neighbours, belonging to the Rue Favart station, Nicolas Eloi Horgne, an architect and corporal of the guard; François Bion, a barber; and Geffroy, a locksmith.

The man was barricaded in his room, and heard them com-

[1] The National Opéra-Comique.

ing to arrest him. He shouted . "Come on, scoundrels, and I will kill you." They struck at his door. Collot d'Herbois went up with them, and, as he wanted to go in first, armed with a sabre that a volunteer had lent him, Citizen Geffroy prevented him   He seized him by the arm, and said to him   "I order you, in the name of the people, to remain here.   I shall either perish or place the assassin in the hands of the Section. When virtues are the order of the day, the first thing to do and doubtless the most useful to the country is to relieve the soil of liberty of such a monster."

The door opened   A shot was fired. Geffroy, the locksmith, was struck by a bullet, which passed through his right shoulder. The assailant was overpowered and led to the police-station in the Rue Favart, where he was searched. In his pockets were found three bad coins, two of two *sous*, one of one *sou*, four leaden bullets wrapped in two pieces of paper, one of them being a pass dated the 27th of Ventôse, made out in the name of Admiral, and a pair of spectacles.

A small, solidly-built man with a stern face, he was perfectly calm. "There was austerity in his attitude "[1]

His answers were clear, and given in a firm tone, in the cheerful, musical accent of his province. He came from the Puy-de-Dôme, and was a native of Auzolette in the Issoire district. His name was Henri Admiral, "a former employee in the former lotteries."

On the previous day he had waited for four hours at the Committee of Public Safety to assassinate Robespierre. Not being successful in this, he had determined to assassinate Collot d'Herbois   He was very sorry that he had failed   It would have been a fine day's work for him. All France would have admired him. He regretted that he paid ninety *livres* for a pair of pistols that missed fire.

Fouquier-Tinville was informed at once, and immediately sent to Dumas, the President of the Tribunal, the following letter :—

[1] Archives Nationales, W. 389, dossier 904.

" Paris, this 4th of Prairial of the Second Year of the
Republic, one and indivisible.

" Citizen and President,

" I have the honour to send to the Convention a
memorandum, drawn up to-night, which states that a man
named Admiral conceived the frightful project of assass-
inating Citizens Robespierre and Collot d'Herbois ; that all
day yesterday he traversed the terrace of the Feuillants and
the approaches to the Committee of Public Safety in order
to reach Citizen Robespierre , that about half-past one
to-night, as he lodged in the same house as Citizen
Collot d'Herbois, this madman waited on the staircase,
and at the moment when Citizen Collot d'Herbois was going
up to his flat, fired at him a pistol shot which happily
miscarried and thus saved his life.

" As soon as I was informed of this outrage, I had the
murderous ruffian brought to the Conciergerie, and I propose
to have him tried to-morrow at two o'clock.   Greeting and
fraternity.

" A Q FOUQUIER,

" Public Prosecutor of the
Revolutionary Tribunal." [1]

At nine o'clock in the morning, Dumas, accompanied
by Girard, the registrar's clerk, questioned Admiral at the
Palace of Justice. The prisoner answered simply and without
evasion.   He had been a messenger in the offices of the royal
lottery ; he had then been employed in Minister Bertin's
house.   He had served in Champagne as a volunteer in
the sixth Paris battalion.   He had left the Filles-Saint-
Thomas battalion   Dumas asked him who had given him
his appointment at the lottery.   It was the Marquis de
Manzuy, the Emperor's chamberlain and Director of the
Brussels lottery.   He saw him for the last time on October
6, 1789, with his wife, on the road from Versailles to Paris.
Why had he brought pistols ?   For the crime committed
yesterday.   What was his design ?   To assassinate Collot

<hr>

[1] Archives Nationales, W. 389, dossier 904.

d'Herbois and Robespierre. He had carried the pistols for three days in order to use them at the first opportunity. On the previous day he had gone out at nine o'clock in the morning. He had gone to the Rue Saint-Honoré, and had spoken to a fruiterer, asking him at what time Robespierre went to the Committee. " Ask at the back of the courtyard. He lives there," the woman had answered. He took ten steps in the courtyard and met a volunteer with his arm in a sling, and a citizeness. They told him that Robespierre was engaged, and that he could not speak to him He went away If he had met the tyrant he would have accomplished his design.

From there he had gone to Roulot's, a restaurant at the end of the terrace of the Feuillants, where he had lunched, and then to the Convention, to the gallery. He had fallen asleep there At the end of the sitting he had stationed himself in the gallery that leads to the Committee of Public Safety. Under the pretext of going for news, he had gone to the outer door of the Committee, where he had waited for Robespierre in order to assassinate him. It was in vain. He then stationed himself in the vestibule that separates the Hall of the Convention from that of the Committee. Some deputies passed through. He asked their names. They were not those whom he sought. He then went out.

He went to the Café Marie and to the Café Gervoise, where he played draughts with a young man. He supped at Dufie's eating-house at the corner of the Rue Favart. At eleven o'clock he went home. He waited until Collot d'Herbois came back. The rest was known.

Dumas asked him a last question in regard to the sums of money " over and above his known resources " which he had paid for his daily expenses. Those sums, he said, were the result of his savings and of the sale of his goods [1]

Without losing time Dumas drew up the following note ·—

[1] Archives Nationales, W. 339, dossier 904.

"Admiral's Attempt.

" It appears that the affair of the assailant of Robespierre and Collot d'Herbois ought to be investigated in the following respects

" 1. By all possible means to drag from the monster confessions which can throw light upon the conspiracies;

" 2 To consider this crime in its relations with foreign countries and with the conspiracies of Hébert, Danton, and all those that took place in the prisons;

" 3. To gain information as to his relations with persons who have belonged to or who may belong to the conspiracies;

" 4. Especially to gain information concerning the places he has been in and the persons he has associated with for the past fifteen days, and of the conversations in which he has engaged;

" 5. To gain information how it is that, being fifty years of age and having a situation, he went into Champagne with the sixth Paris battalion , how he behaved there, how and why he left the said battalion, and what his relations there were;

" 6. Whether he had been a guard at the Temple, and, if so, whether anything had been noticed in his conduct there;

" 7. To seek to discover whence the pistols came, and to know why a gun had been given to him by preference." [1]

An actual conspirator had thus been taken. Admiral's act belonged to the vast conspiracy which Dumas and Fouquier-Tinville were investigating He was, doubtless, an agent of the Foreigner, along with de Batz, the unseizable de Batz, the terror of the Committees; de Batz who had attempted to save Louis XVI. during the passage from the Temple to the scaffold, and who had tried to bring about the escape of Marie Antoinette, de Batz who at the height of the Terror walked about Paris, had five or six lodgings, and, when they came to arrest him, had gone from the place some moments before, leaving his bed still warm.[2]

[1] The gun which had been given to him three months before by his captain at the Lepelletier Section

[2] Campardon, *Le Tribunal Révolutionnaire*, I , p 363

Collot d'Herbois had been brought close to death by Pitt's old and royalist conspiracies. But " the destiny of the Republic watched over his life," as Barère said to the xcited and cheering members of the Convention. " This ime we have not to deplore the loss of a citizen nor to open he doors of the Panthéon   .   d'Herbois, the people's epresentative, is amongst you." [1]

That same evening, whilst Fouquier-Tinville, after a day pent in investigations among the persons with whom ιdmiral associated, was studying the report drawn up by wo commissioners of the committee of surveillance of the .epelletier Section, a young girl, Cécile Renault, presented erself at the house of Duplay, the carpenter, where Maxi-ιilien Robespierre lived, saying that she had been three ours looking for him.

It was nine o'clock.   Duplay's eldest daughter answered hat the Deputy was absent.   Cécile Renault showed ill-umour at this, and took an offended tone   She was sur-rised that he was not at home.   His duty as a public offi-ial was to answer all those who came to see him.   Suspicions 'ere aroused ;   the Committee of General Security was not ιr away, and she was taken there   On the way, she declared atly that when people presented themselves at the King's welling   under   the   old   régime   they   were   allowed   to ιter at once.   She was asked if she would prefer to have a ιng.   She answered ·   " I want a king, because I prefer ne tyrant to fifty thousand."   The Committee had her ιarched.   There were found on her only two small knives ιth tortoiseshell and ivory handles ;   but she spoke ι an excited fashion, and was locked up in the Concier-ιrie.[2]

The commissioners of the section immediately went) her house.   Her father was anxiously awaiting her. hey searched the young girl's room.   " We found there," rote the commissioners, " above her bed, a sort of banner ι which is printed a large crown surrounded with *fleurs*

---

[1] *Moniteur* of the 5th Prairial, year II
[2] Archives Nationales, W. 389, dossier 904

de lys and on which there is a cross of silver paper." Renault, the father, and all his family were arrested.

While investigations regarding the conspiracy were being made, Fouquier-Tinville was not idle. During this month of Prairial there were " batches " to be put on trial, " batches " that had come from the Departments, composed of people unacquainted with one another, aristocrats and *sans-culottes*, priests and ex-priests, notaries, notaries' clerks, traders, teachers, workmen and workwomen, accused of counter-revolutionary utterances and writings. The following are some examples from among the mass of those accused.

On the 2nd of Prairial it was a teacher, Gabriel Delignon, who had received an anonymous letter compromising him in a conspiracy, and who had brought it to the Commune Death.[1]—On the 3rd, a notary, Jarzoufflet, who had no confidence in the *assignats* (paper-money), and who had known a priest. Death.[2]—On the 4th of Prairial, the day of Admiral's attempts, it was the woman Costard, who in despair at the fate of Boyer-Brun whom she loved, had given utterance to her grief in a letter to the Committee of General Security, ending with these words : " Strike, since I have lost my lover ; end a life that is odious to me and that I cannot endure without horror. Long live the King ! Long live the King ! Do not believe that I am mad ; I am not ; I believe everything that you have just read, and I sign it with my blood." Death.[3]—On the 6th of Prairial, a fishmonger, his wife, and a washerwoman, Catherine Pérard, were condemned to death. The two women were drunk and shouted, " Long live the King ! " They were held to be aristocrats, although, according to Judge Masson's expression, " their external appearance was thoroughly *sans-culotte*." [4] On the 8th of Prairial, it was a dentist who said that he occupied himself with nothing but his business, and did not know what the National Convention was. Death.

[1] Archives Nationales, W. 369, No 824
[2] Archives Nationales, W. 370, No 832.
[3] Archives Nationales, W. 374, No. 835
[4] Archives Nationales, W. 372, No 840.

—A navvy who shouted out, " Long live the King ! Long live the Queen ! " [1] etc., etc.

On the 6th of Prairial, Collot d'Herbois and Robespierre appeared at the Jacobin Club. There was a prolonged ovation, and they were welcomed " with transport." As soon as they entered the hall, " all eyes were fixed on those precious men ; all hearts leaped at once ; cheers of the keenest joy proved to them the amount of interest they inspired. . . . The God of free men watched over them. . . . The people had not to shed tears on their funeral urns." Robespierre spoke " I am one of those whom the events that have taken place should interest least ; it is not, however, possible for me to refrain from dealing with them in their relation to the public interest. . . . Frenchmen ! friends of equality ! leave it to us to employ the small amount of life that Providence grants us in fighting the enemies that surround us We swear by the daggers stained with the blood of the martyrs of the Revolution and recently sharpened against ourselves, to exterminate to the last those scoundrels who would rob us of happiness and liberty." [2]

To " the plots of the Foreigner," Robespierre replied by the law of the 22nd of Prairial (June 10, 1794).

After having heard the report of the paralysed Couthon, " gentle in face and in language," the instrument of the Committee of Public Safety, the National Convention resolved :

" Article I.—There shall be in the Revolutionary Tribunal a President and three Vice-Presidents, a Public Prosecutor, four deputies for the Public Prosecutor, and twelve judges.

" Article II —The jurors shall be fifty in number.

" Article III.—These various functions shall be exercised by the citizens whose names follow : Dumas, President , Coffinhal, Scellier, Naulin, Vice-Presidents ; Fouquier-Tinville, Public Prosecutor ; his four deputies ; twelve judges, and fifty jurors.

---

[1] Archives Nationales, W. 373. No 843
[2] *Moniteur*, 10th of Prairial, year II.

" Article IV.—The Revolutionary Tribunal has been established to punish the enemies of the people.

" Article V.—The enemies of the people are those who seek to destroy public liberty, either by force or fraud.

" Article VI.—Those are to be regarded as enemies of the people who shall promote the re-establishment of royalty, or seek to degrade the National Convention and the revolutionary and republican government of which it is the centre, etc.

" Article VII.—The punishment for all offences that come within the scope of the Revolutionary Tribunal is death.

" Article IX.—Every citizen has a right to seize conspirators and counter-revolutionists, and to bring them before the magistrates ; he is bound to inform against them as soon as he knows them.

" Article XVI.—The law gives patriotic jurors as defenders to patriots ; it does not grant them to conspirators." [1]

In reality, there were to be no more preliminary investigations, no more examinations, no more pleadings. The accused were to be at the mercy of the jurors And it is known what the jurors were. Furthermore, not only were the accused refused a hearing at the preliminary investigation before the trial, but they were not even to be examined at the public hearing of the case. As an example, there was a case on the 6th of Messidor when three young Bretons of the Quimper district, Perron, Toupin, and Thomas André, were suspected of having amused themselves by cutting down the tree of liberty at Banalec, on the day in October, 1793, on which they were summoned to join the colours. There was no real evidence against them. Mathieu Toupin and Corentin Perron were condemned to two years' deportation, Thomas André to a year's imprisonment by the Quimper tribunal. The moderation of these sentences was denounced to the Minister of Justice at Paris. The prisoners were sent before the Revolutionary Tribunal by decree of the Convention.

They were condemned to death. The official report of

[1] *Moniteur*, 24th Prairial, year II.

the trial contains these words written by the registrar's clerk: "Note: It has been impossible to get the exact names of Perron, André, and Toupin, because they were from Lower Brittany and there were no interpreters." [1] This requires no comment

Fouquier's task was not simplified by the law of the month of Prairial. On the contrary, the mass of conspirators who had to be brought to trial increased to such an extent that the Public Prosecutor, forced to act quickly, no longer knew which way to turn. He would go into the office of the ushers whose duty it was to fetch the accused from the prisons, shouting and swearing, smashing the portfolios, threatening and frightening everybody. " If you don't make haste, I will lock you up. I will have you locked up," he would exclaim, and then shout out insults. Late in the evening after dinner the trembling clerks pointed out to him that they had not time to transcribe and serve all the indictments that he had ordered them to copy for the next morning. " Do as you like ! " he would answer. " There will always be enough of them! Make haste ! Things must move ! " If the indictments were signed by him alone, and not by the judges, his clerks would point this out to him. "Go on," was the reply, "their signatures shall be obtained." [2]

At first Fouquier had drawn up the indictments himself or in co-operation with his deputies Then he had employed a clerk, and finally two. As the number of conspirators increased the more they were guillotined, Fouquier became too much occupied, and left the task of drawing up the indictments to his clerks. [3] He contented himself with signing his name at the bottom of each page, adding some words on the margin or rectifying the text here and there. This is why we can prove to-day (his deputy Cambon did so at Fouquier's trial) that these indictments are full of spaces between the lines, erasures, unauthorised commitments, and blank spaces intended

---

[1] Archives Nationales, W. 395, No. 916, 2nd part, p 78.
[2] Contat's evidence at Fouquier's trial
[3] Toutain's evidence at Fouquier's trial

for the names of a greater number of victims, and that no
trouble had been taken to cancel these   Names of accused
persons had been added, in a strange hand, to the indictments after they were drawn up.   It is enough to open some
of the bundles of papers relating to the Tribunal for the
period comprised between the 22nd of Prairial and the 9th
of Thermidor to be convinced of all this.

These documents were served on the interested parties
only the day before the trial.   Fouquier did not deny this at
the time of his own trial.   He said that he always gave
orders to serve the writs of indictment in the evening.
Château, his former secretary, contradicted him on this
point, saying ·   " It often happened that at nine o'clock
in the evening we did not know the names of those who
would be put on trial the next day   How could we give
them their writs of indictment that evening ? " [1]

At the hearing, the accused were not given time to speak.
And there was no one to defend them, for lawyers had no
longer a right to do so.   The President would ask a prisoner :
" Did you do such and such a thing ? "   On his negative
or affirmative reply, the President would say ·   " Next."
If the prisoner insisted, Dumas or Coffinhal shouted at him.
" You have no right to say any more   You have no right
to say any more." [2]   In order to exonerate himself Fouquier
said   " That was the President's business, that did not
concern me.   I have pointed out several times to Dumas
and Coffinhal that they did not give the accused enough
latitude.   I have had altercations with Dumas on this
subject "   But at Fouquier's trial, Berthaut,[3] registrar of
the Tribunal of the Théâtre-Français Section, deposed that
at the hearing of the affair relating to the conspiracy in the
Carmelite prison, the Public Prosecutor (who was sitting
that day) said to a witness for the defence   " Are not you
and the prisoner both of the same Section ? "   " Yes."
Then Fouquier rejoined vehemently ·   " I have something

[1] Château's evidence at Fouquier's trial
[2] Brunet's evidence at Fouquier's trial
[3] Berthaut's evidence on the 2nd of Germinal in the year III.

against you. You are of the same Section. You stand up for one another" And he prevented the witness from being heard further.

The law of the month of Prairial had hardly been passed, when Fouquier, acting on the suggestion of Vadier, a member of the Committee of General Security, brought to trial eleven inhabitants of Pamiers, among whom were the two Darmaings (John Pierre Jérôme, a lawyer, and François, an ex-King's-Advocate). Vadier came originally from Pamiers He had a personal grudge against his compatriots. One of them, Cazès, had refused his daughter to Vadier's son. In two letters, one of the 4th of Prairial and the other of the 7th, Vadier had expressed to Fouquier the hope that they would be condemned. (" I point out to you that, if by any ill-fortune those men could be acquitted, it would be a public calamity.") The inhabitants of Pamiers were condemned to death on the 23rd of Prairial (June 11). [1]

On the 26th of Prairial (June 14) a " batch " of thirty Parliamentarians from Paris and Toulouse,[2] appeared before the Tribunal for having, on September 25 and 27, 1789, protested against the Acts of the National Assembly relating to the Parlements. There were no incriminating documents and no witnesses. The memorials drawn up by the prisoners had been left by Fouquier among the papers in the registrar's office. He had taken no account of them. All were condemned. Among them was Fréteau, an ex-Councillor of the Parlement of Paris, who had been acquitted on the 27th of Floréal. Fouquier had again seized him and sent him for trial. " Fréteau," say Fouquier's pleadings for the prosecution, " has shown himself to be an enemy of the people whose representative he was, and he has violated the laws, whose observance is of the utmost importance to the Empire, by confiding his son's education to a conspirator, to one of those men animated by the most cruel fanaticism, who had refused to take the oath due from every citizen

[1] Archives Nationales, W. 383, dossier 891. Among the condemned persons there was one, Larue, who was not even examined.
[2] W. 386, dossier 897

to the government under which he lives." [1]   At the time
of his trial Fouquier was rigorously taken to task on the
subject of Fréteau.   It will be seen how he defended himself.

On the 29th of Prairial (June 17) Admiral, Cécile Renault,
her father, her brother, her aunt, and forty-nine other
prisoners were brought before the Tribunal.   All were convicted of having made themselves " the enemies of the people
by participating in the conspiracy of the foreigner, and at-
tempting, by assassination, famine, the fabrication and intro-
duction of forged paper-money (*assignats*) and base coin, the
depravation of morality and public spirit, and insurrections
in the prisons, to promote civil war, to dissolve the national
representation, to re-establish royalty, or any other tyran-
nical domination."   The hearing lasted only three hours.[2]
The Tribunal condemned them all to the punishment of
death, conformably with Articles 5, 6, and 7 of the law of the
22nd of Prairial, which it caused to be read to them.   All were
to be brought to the place of execution and put on the scaffold
clothed in red shirts, as assassins of the Representatives of the
people.   Yet only one of them had committed an attempt
at assassination.

The execution of the fifty-four, who have been called the
" red shirts," took place at four o'clock in the evening at the
Barrier of Vincennes.[3]

Excluding Admiral, the fifty-three others who were condemned might be regarded as conspirators, not as assassins.
Why did Fouquier inflict on them the indignity of the red
shirt ?   At his own trial he answered this question.   " Because the sentence so provided," he said.   But Cambon,
the Public Prosecutor's deputy, denied this, and produced the sentence.   Fouquier continued .   " I claim that

[1] A priest who had not taken the oath to the Civil Constitution of
the Clergy.   W. 386, dossier 897, p 135

[2] Fouquier says five hours, but he was not sitting

[3] On the 21st of Prairial, the day following that of the Festival of
the Supreme Being, the guillotine had been transported from the
Place de la Révolution to the Place Sainte-Antoine in front of the site
occupied by the old Bastille   On the 26th, at the request of the
inhabitants of the district, it was transported to the Barrier of Vincennes.

this is a mistake of the registrar, for that was the sentence pronounced." He was contradicted by Harny, an ex-judge of the Tribunal, charged along with him : " I point out that the Tribunal did not pronounce that sentence. I was astonished when I heard the order to have red shirts made, I made some remarks about it, but was told it had nothing to do with me "

In reality, it was the Committee of Public Safety that had given this order to Fouquier-Tinville

The affair of " the red shirts " has often been related, and this is not the place to return to it. Let us only note that it is sufficient to examine the list of accused persons to have an idea of the strange ' mixture " compounded by Fouquier. Admiral, the man of Auvergne, rubs shoulders with people of all conditions whom he certainly had never seen, such as Madame de Sainte-Amaranthe, her daughter, her son, and the Comte de Fleury. The latter had been imprisoned in the Luxembourg. There had been no question of an investigation into his case. He went into the dock and was condemned for having written, on that day, the famous letter to Dumas " Courage, men of blood, invent conspiracies in order to send to the scaffold the remnant of honest men who, having nothing with which to reproach themselves, have remained passive beneath your blows. All my friends or intimate acquaintances, the Prince de Rohan, Bossancourt, Marsan, d'Hauteville, Lécuyer, etc., conspirators ! if ever they could have been that, join my name to theirs. Having always shared their opinions and their mode of life, I ought to undergo the same fate You tremble, souls of mud, when you meet magnanimous courage which, fearing nothing, reproaches you in crying tones for the crimes of which you make yourselves guilty every day, by pronouncing judgments dictated by hatred and vengeance. Tremble, vile monsters, the moment is coming when you shall expiate your crimes Signed The ex-Comte de Fleury, a prisoner in the Luxembourg." Dumas had shown this letter to Fouquier, saying . " Look here ! read this *billet doux*, I believe this fine gentleman is in a hurry." " Yes," Fou-

F

quier had answered, " he seems to me to be in a hurry, and I am going to send for him " He did send for him, and the Comte de Fleury was guillotined the same day.

This study is concerned with the responsibility incurred by Fouquier-Tinville as Public Prosecutor, and not with the history of the Revolutionary Tribunal. It is not necessary to give here as full an account of the affair called " the conspiracies in the prisons " as a complete statement of the matter would require. In the second part of this study the depositions made in the inquiry after Thermidor will be reproduced from the original papers preserved among the National Archives, and as the general effect of those depositions will enable us to understand Fouquier's activity in a vivid and striking manner, it seems sufficient to say here, in a few pages, what those conspiracies were, and what part was reserved for the Public Prosecutor by his chiefs.

At the beginning of Messidor there were in Paris forty houses of detention,[1] all of which were full   As new prisoners came continually from the Departments, it was necessary to find accommodation for them.   Room was made by emptying the Paris prisons of some " lots " of prisoners who were sent to the Conciergerie, then to the Tribunal, and then to the scaffold.   For this a motive, a pretext, was found in the Conspiracy of the Foreigner which gave rise to, 1st, the Conspiracy in Bicêtre (two " batches," one of 37 prisoners,

---

[1] M Wallon gives, following Proussinalle (*Histoire Secrète du Tribunal Révolutionnaire*, I , p 298), the list of the Paris prisons : La Grande Force, la Petite Force, Sainte-Pélagie, les Madelonnettes, l'Abbaye, les Capucins, Bicêtre, la Salpêtrière, la Mairie, le Luxembourg, la Bourbe, la Caserne, Rue de Vaugirard, Picpus, les Anglaises, Rue de Lourcine, les Anglaises, Faubourg Sainte-Antoine, les Ecossais, Saint-Lazare, la maison Belhomme, les Bénédictins Anglais, le Collège du Plessis, la maison de Répression, la maison Coignard, la maison Mallay, les Fermes, la caserne des Petits-Pères, la caserne, Rue de Sèvres, la maison des Oiseaux, la caserne des Carmes, le Collège des Quatre-Nations, Montaigu, Port-Royal, maison Escourbiac, Hôtel Talaru, Vincennes, maison Lachapelle, Hospice de l'Evêché, maison Brunet, les Anglaises, Rue Saint-Victor, maison Picquenot, Rue de Bercy, and la Conciergerie.   One ought to add the dépôts in the forty-eight sections   (Wallon , *Tribunal Révolutionnaire*, IV., p. 263)

tried on the 28th of Floréal, the other of 37, tried on the 8th of Messidor) ; 2nd, the Conspiracy in the Luxembourg (four " batches," the first of 60 prisoners, tried on the 19th of Messidor in the Year II , the second of 50 prisoners, tried on the 21st, the third of 46, tried on the 22nd, and the fourth of 18, tried on the 4th of Thermidor) , 3rd, the Conspiracy in the Carmelite prison (49 prisoners, tried on the 5th of Thermidor) , 4th, the Conspiracy in Saint-Lazare (three " batches," the first of 25 prisoners, tried on the 6th of Thermidor, the second of 26, tried on the 7th of Thermidor, and the third of 25, tried on the 8th of Thermidor). There were, finally, on the 9th of Thermidor, 25 prisoners at the hearing presided over by Dumas, and 23 at that presided over by Scellier. We can see clearly now that the idea of these conspiracies was nothing but a most outrageous fabrication.

Their true fomenters and agents were the prison spies— Valagnos, Beausire, Benoit, Boyaval, Dupaumier, Verney, Guyard, Manini, Coquery, Jobert (the Belgian), and some others. In the second part of this study it will be seen that Fouquier had relations with those scoundrels. A good deal of evidence given at his trial agrees in saying that he made use of them, that he encouraged them. They were his auxiliaries and those of the Committee of General Security.

It was Valagnos who invented the Bicêtre conspiracy. Valagnos was an ex-house-painter, and ex-member of the Revolutionary Committee of the Chalier Section He had been condemned to twelve years in chains for dishonesty in performing his duties as a commissioner of clothing. He had been imprisoned at Bicêtre. He confided to one of his fellow-prisoners [1] that he had " discovered a conspiracy, and hoped that this would shorten his twelve years in chains." In a first letter to his former committee, he denounced some prisoners who were convicts like himself. He represented them as determined to escape. This letter remained unanswered. He wrote another to the same committee, giving details. It was whilst going to the convict-prison,

[1] Guillot, a defender in the Tribunal.

during the journey from Paris to Brest, that the escape would take place. The committee of the Section sent this second letter to the Committee of Public Safety, which forwarded it to Herman, the President of the Commission for the Administration of Civil Affairs, of Police, and of Tribunals. By a resolution of the Committee of Public Safety, passed on the 25th of Prairial, the prisoners who had been denounced were brought before the Revolutionary Tribunal. The same resolution authorised the commission to bring before the Tribunal " all other individuals detained in the said house of Bicêtre who might be suspected of having taken part in the plot " On the 26th, Lanne, Herman's assistant, went to Bicêtre. Fouquier-Tinville accompanied him. Fouquier drew up a list, and sent it to Lanne with these words : " Citizen, enclosed is the account of the suspects found in our transaction. I request you to send me to-morrow, at ten or eleven o'clock at latest, all the documents of this business, in particular the resolutions." [1] On the 27th, Lanne copied out the list and sent it to Fouquier. He sent him at the same time the resolution passed by the Committee of Public Safety on the 25th, and the list of prisoners whom that Committee was sending before the Revolutionary Tribunal. In all, there were thirty-seven prisoners who appeared before the Tribunal. Fouquier's writ of indictment affirms that the aim of this *plot* was " to overcome the citizens forming the armed force of the house of detention of Bicêtre, to force the doors of the said house in order to go and kill the Representatives of the people, members of the Convention's Committees of Public Safety and of General Security, to tear out their hearts, to cook and eat them, and to put to death the most conspicuous of them in a cask furnished with spikes." No witnesses were heard, with the exception of Valagnos, the convict. The thirty-seven Bicêtre prisoners were condemned and executed. Fouquier, at his trial, said that they were criminals, that they were condemned to chains. A poor reason ! Had they conspired or not ? If they had only attempted to escape, they did not deserve

[1] Archives Nationales, W. 500, 1st dossier, p 8

the guillotine. Brunet, the chief surgeon of Bicêtre, a witness at Fouquier's trial, said . " The conspiracy that the murderers have imagined is a falsehood, I will even say, a calumny The law had seized the guilty. They ought, doubtless, to have undergone their punishment. But no power, at least unless a fresh crime had been *proved*, could strike beings who were expiating the punishment due to their crimes " Brunet, passing through the halls, the rooms, and the cells several times a day, doubtless knew what to think about the state of the prisons And Deschamps, the treasurer, deposed that when they came to take away the prisoners in order to bring them before the Tribunal, one of them, aged 79, was so frightened that he wounded himself in the belly with his razor

On the 17th of Messidor, the Committee of Public Safety resolved that the commission over which Herman presided should make a daily report to the Public Prosecutor on the conduct of those detained in the different prisons of Paris. The Revolutionary Tribunal was bound, in conformity with the law, to try *within twenty-four hours* those who attempted to revolt or excited any ferment.[1]

On the 18th, Fouquier wrote to Subleyras, the President of the Popular Commission, to the Museum (the Louvre) :

" I send you herewith a list of the conspirators of the house of detention of the Luxembourg whom I propose to have put on trial to-morrow I ask you in consequence to transmit to me all information you may possess about these individuals."[2]

On the same day he wrote to the Committee of Public Safety to inform them that he " would bring the conspirators of the Luxembourg to trial, the next day, in the Hall of Liberty."

At eleven o'clock in the evening on that 18th of Messidor, whilst the prison was asleep and everything quiet, a considerable armed force invaded the large court-yard. There was an alarm. Calls were heard in the rooms, hurried

---

[1] W. 500, dossier 3, p 79, and W 501, dossier 1, p 55.
[2] W. 501, 1st dossier, p 45

footsteps on the stairs   A hundred and fifty-six prisoners were transferred to the house of justice, counted, and crowded together at the Conciergerie while waiting for the hour of the sitting.   President Dumas had caused an enormous scaffolding [1] to be erected in the hall of the Tribunal, the benches of which rose as high as the cornices of the ceiling and filled a large part of the enclosure.   It was on this scaffolding that he intended to place the conspirators of the Luxembourg

But that night Fouquier went to the Committee.   He saw Collot d'Herbois, Billaud, Saint-Just, and Robespierre, and it was decided that instead of being tried in the mass (which might arouse too violent a feeling among the public) the hundred and fifty-six would be tried in three lots.   The scaffolding was accordingly demolished.

At nine o'clock in the morning of the 19th of Messidor, the prisoners of the first batch received their writs of indictment.   At ten o'clock they entered the dock, to the number of sixty.   At three o'clock they had all been tried and sent to the guillotine.   Madame de Boisgelin, as she was leaving the Tribunal and crossing the courtyard, said to those of the prisoners who had not been tried :   " We have not been allowed to speak.   It will be your turn to-morrow." [2]

At this hearing there had been condemned Jean Dominique Maurin, " 47 years of age, born at Barcelonnette, in the department of the Basses-Alpes   Before the Revolution he had been a book-keeper to different merchants, and since then a steward of the Duchesse d'Estissac's estate at Hallum, and an agent of the ex-Maréchale de Biron," says the judgment.   Now the writ of indictment has   " Jean Dominique Morin, *formerly quarter-master*, aged 47 years, born at Barcelonnette, in the department of the Basses-Alpes."   The

---

[1] It is this scaffolding (*échafaud*) that M Thiers confused with the guillotine in his *Histoire de la Révolution Française*, 9th edition, Furne, 1839, p 138, when he says ·   " It was necessary to order Fouquier-Tinville a second time to remove the *guillotine* from the hall of the Tribunal "

[2] Jobert's evidence at Fouquier's trial

accused man, hearing the statement for the prosecution read, and understanding that there was a mistake, protested : " It is not I." He was condemned. But Fouquier immediately claimed,[1] and the Tribunal ordered, that Louis Clerc Morin should also be brought to trial. The latter was guillotined three days after his namesake on the 22nd of Messidor. He formed part of the third " batch " from the Luxembourg. At Fouquier's trial a witness, Vauchelet, said that Morin " so far from being concerned in that alleged conspiracy, was not in the Luxembourg prison."

On the 9th of Messidor, the Tribunal had heard only five witnesses These were four police spies (Boyaval,[2] Meunier, Verney, Benoît), and a turnkey of the Luxembourg, Lesenne This latter declared that there had been no conspiracy. Fouquier immediately demanded his arrest.

The Swiss porter of the Luxembourg, Nicolas Strahl, and others gave evidence afterwards at Fouquier-Tinville's trial that no conspiracy had existed in the prison, and that everything was calm. " Those conspiracies," he said, " have only existed in the public prints."

A man who had a narrow escape was Jean Martin, a lawyer, included in the third " batch " of the alleged Luxembourg conspiracy, that of the 22nd of Messidor.[3] He

---

[1] " The Public Prosecutor claims, and the Tribunal orders, that there be given him a memorandum of the verbal indictment brought by him against Morin " Archives Nationales, W. 409, dossier 941

[2] Boyaval was, with Benoît, one of the great makers of the lists A tailor and a lieutenant of light infantry, a narrow-minded, chattering liar, Boyaval boasted that he was entrusted with making out the lists Sometimes he said he had orders from the police officials, sometimes from Robespierre, and sometimes from Fouquier He went to the Tribunal to give evidence as a witness against those he had denounced

[3] In the list of unfortunate beings taken off during the night between the 18th and the 19th was found the name of Pierre Charles Machet-Velye, an ex-Comptroller of Buildings to Monsieur, the king's brother Uncommunicative, always shut up in his room, living isolated, and perpetually occupied with a law-suit which he was carrying on against a former Procurator of the Parlement, Machet-Velye had received, in his prison, the news that he had won his suit. He was guillotined on the 22nd of Messidor as an accomplice in the conspiracy of Grammont, *who had been executed four months before*

was acquitted, perhaps because he said that he had known "the project of making a scene in the prison which Grammont carried out in part." After Robespierre's fall, he sent, on the 13th of Thermidor, to the Committee of Public Safety a very curious report in which he described in a striking manner the sitting of the Tribunal on the day when he appeared before it. Sceller presided Royer deputised for Fouquier-Tinville. Boyaval, the spy, was the first to give evidence, then Verney, a turnkey at the Luxembourg and an active informer, then Benoît, another spy.

Here, for instance, is a little dialogue between the President and Goursault, one of the accused

The President —" Why have you been arrested ? "—" I do not know."—The President —" Are you noble ? " " No, I am a labourer's son "—The President —" All right We know the moral sense of an administrator of lotteries ; you say no more."

his arrival at the Luxembourg [1] (Cf. Réal's evidence at Fouquier's trial)
On the 21st of Messidor, fifty prisoners appeared before the Tribunal charged with taking part in the Luxembourg conspiracy ; this was the second " batch " One of the accused, Pierre Louis Moreau, an architect and a chevalier of Saint Louis, was a brother-in-law of the poet, Ducis , the latter wrote the following letter to Fouquier to intercede with him on behalf of his relative —
" Paris, the 20th of Messidor of the year II. : Citizen, I do not solicit your justice, that would be to insult your well-known integrity, but I yield to my wife's tears The fate of her brother is to be decided to-morrow by the Revolutionary Tribunal he is Citizen Moreau, formerly architect of the City of Paris He has always been obedient and faithful to the laws of our country, he has paid all that was asked of him, in particular, thirty thousand *francs* for the war in La Vendée , nothing against him has been found among his papers, on which official seals have been placed both in the city and the country He was engaged in no plot , before his detention he was farming an emigrant's land, for which he paid rent to the nation ; he is a good father, tenderly loved by his wife and daughters , we hope, just and incorruptible citizen, that you will soon restore him to the arms and the eyes of us who are waiting for him We are sure that you will bring his innocence into full light Accept the assurance of my veneration and my entire confidence in your wisdom and virtue *Signed* Ducis, of the former French Academy " Archives Nationales, W. 93. Moreau was condemned to death. Campardon, I., p 382.

The examination of each of the forty-six prisoners was conducted in similar style.

On the 21st of Messidor, at the Jacobin Club, Robespierre returned to the affair of the conspiracies. He spoke of "the cabals secretly directed against the Revolutionary Government and the plottings of those traitors who are burning to sow dissension among the patriots" According to him, the recent victory of Fleurus threatened to lead the public mind towards leniency. "It is natural to slumber after victory. . . The true victory is that which the friends of liberty gain over the factions." It was necessary, therefore, that the extermination of the conspirators should continue.

It was as a conspirator that Jean-Claude Pelchet, an architect and ex-Chief Inspector of Buildings to the King, appeared before the Tribunal, on the 25th of Messidor, because a certain Dodin, who informed against him, declared that, during a journey they had made together from Versailles to Paris, the architect had expressed royalist sentiments opposed to the principles of the Revolution. Witnesses were not allowed him. Fouquier wrote to his deputy that their appearance did not seem to him indispensable, and that he ought to do all he could to prevent the prisoner's defence from being cut short. Fouquier's note is among the papers relative to the case.[1]

Those sixteen Carmelite nuns of Compiègne were conspirators who were charged with fanaticism, together with Citizen Mulot de la Ménardière, a townsman of Compiègne and a very indifferent poet, who had sent counter-revolutionary verses to one of the nuns, his cousin. He was married. Fouquier, in his indictment, describes him as "a rebellious ex-priest," though he had never been a priest. In the writ of indictment he becomes "the chief of a counter-revolutionary assembly at Compiègne, of a sort of Vendean focus. His correspondence with those women who were subject to his will gives evidence of the counter-revolutionary sentiments that animated him, and one sees in it especially that pro-

[1] Archives Nationales, W 414, No 949, 3rd part.

found knavery familiar to those hypocrites who are accustomed to give out that their own passions are the rule established by Heaven's will."[1] Documents were produced against him which were not in his writing Fouquier had no longer sufficient time to identify documents.

All the nuns were sentenced to death, even those against whom there was nothing, even the two non-cloistered sisters.

On the 1st of Thermidor (July 19, 1794), three generations of the same family were in the dock. This was what Fouquier called " the Magon conspiracy," comprising J. B. Magon de la Balue, a merchant and an ex-noble, 81 years of age , Luc Magon de Labélinaye, a merchant and an ex-noble, 80 years of age ; Erasme Charles Auguste Lalande Magon, his son ; Françoise Magon, his daughter, Saint-Pern's wife ; Saint-Pern ; François Joseph Cornulier, twenty-two years of age, and his wife (the same age) , Amélie Laurence Céleste, Saint-Pern's daughter—and others. Saint-Pern's son, aged seventeen, was brought before the Tribunal He protested, told his age ; his sister and his mother confirmed his statements. Then Dumas declared : " Citizen jurors, you see that he is conspiring at this very moment, for he is more than seventeen years old." [2] He was condemned ; *but the fact that he was seventeen years of age was allowed to remain in the sentence.* It was his father against whom the indictment was directed Here Fouquier's responsibility was directly involved. The indictment read · " No. 5, Saint-Pern—without Christian names or descriptions ; No. 6, Saint-Pern's wife " [3] In the questions propounded to the jury, we read : " No 5, Jean Baptiste Marie Bertrand Saint-Pern, aged seventeen, a native of Rennes, residing at Paris, an ex-noble, without occupation." The Christian names and the rest were added afterwards. The writ of indictment aimed at the father, but with such lack of precision was it drawn that it was the son who was condemned ! This was a criminal irregularity. But there was more to come. The daughter,

---

[1] W 421, No 956, p 125
[2] Ducray's evidence at Fouquier's trial.
[3] Archives Nationales, W 423, No 958, 2nd part, p. 41

young Saint-Pern's sister, was condemned on the indictment made out against her father.   Fouquier's responsibility is still graver in this case.   The indictment states that : " Cornuillier, son-in-law of Saint-Pern *and his wife was* also an accomplice in the Magon conspiracy and one of the assassins of the people on the day of August 10."

Madame Cornulier was six months gone with child.   Her execution was postponed.   Eight days later Robespierre's fall took place.   She was set at liberty and came to give evidence against Fouquier.   Her evidence will be given in the second part of this study.   The official report of the sitting at which her family was condemned did not contain the names of the jurors , but she had them always in her memory—Prieur, Châtelet, and Renaudin, who were afterwards accused in their turn.   And she furnished an irrefutable proof against them in the paper in which her husband had sent her a lock of his hair before he died, and which was nothing else than the list of the jurors of the 1st of Thermidor.   Fouquier exclaimed   " I was not sitting " ; but the writ of indictment was his, and Lohier, a juror, charged along with him, said . " The writ of indictment has nothing to do with me."

Together with the Magons, a genuine *sans-culotte*, a lawyer, Citizen Duchesne, called Duquesne, " a member of the Versailles society of *sans-culottes*," was impeached as a conspirator, although his hairdresser, an influential man, had certified that he was " the warmest friend of the Revolution."   But there is some mystery here, for he was condemned to death

It is to be noted also that, with the Magons, there was Legris, the registrar's clerk, the sad accomplice of so many irregularities, so many blank warrants, Legris, in whom Fouquier saw " the conspirator Havré's agent with Magon la Balue." [1]

[1] " Legris, calling himself the conspirator Havré's steward, was his agent with Magon la Balue in order to procure for him the funds necessary for the execution of his liberticidal plots   He procured for him in the month of March, 1792, a sum of thirty-two thousand three hundred and seventy-five francs.   He is known to have left French

He was arrested at his house at five o'clock in the morning while in his bed, and brought at seven o'clock to the Conciergerie. At nine o'clock his writ of indictment was served on him; at ten o'clock he was in the.dock before the Tribunal; at two o'clock he was no longer alive [1] This summary execution terrified the clerical staff. It found itself threatened. Whose turn would be next? Neither the registrar nor the surviving clerks forgave the Public Prosecutor. We shall see the terrible and precise accusations made by Pâris and Wolff at his trial.

On the 4th of Thermidor the last "batch" from the Luxembourg appeared. In this "batch" were the Noailles ladies, "deaf and worn with age" The President asked them their names. They did not hear him. They were brought nearer. At last they understood, gave their names, and were sent back to the benches on which the prisoners sat [2] They were condemned and guillotined. Joseph Meynard-Mellet (17 years old) was taken for young de Maillé and guillotined in his place. A mistake in the name. Moreover, young de Maillé himself was also guillotined on the 6th of Thermidor. He had flung a rotten fish at the head of the purveyor of food during a meal in the prison. Who were the witnesses at this trial? Always the same— Boyaval, Benoît and Beausire.

This is how Benoît afterwards gave an account of his evidence at the Tribunal on that day

" On the 4th of Thermidor an usher came with a policeman to the Carmelite Prison to take me again to the Tribunal.

territory to go to Mons and confer with Havré on the execution of his plots Finally, he is known, in the months of February, March, April and May, 1792, to have been lavish in attributing the feudal and counter-revolutionary titles of duke and duchess to those infamous conspirators, and to have described himself, at the end of his letters, as M le duc d'Havré's steward, the mask of patriotism which he has assumed and the audacity he has shown in daring to claim the confidence of a Tribunal which punishes conspirators without distinction will only render more terrible the punishment that awaits him and serve as a lesson to those who dare to imitate him " (Signed, A. Q. Fouquier) W 423, No 958, 2nd part

[1] Tavernier's evidence at Fouquier's trial.
[2] Julien's evidence at Fouquier's trial.

On this occasion I was not made to repeat what I knew of Grammont's conspiracy ; I was only asked if I knew the accused   I knew three of them.   I said what I knew of them, without hatred as without fear, and I urged the Tribunal not to trust to my evidence alone, but to send for their room-mates, who would bear witness to the same truth.   In regard to the others all I knew of them was that they were staying at the Luxembourg.

"How were those prisoners examined who were not charged with belonging to this new conspiracy ?   They were only asked if they had any acquaintance with a conspiracy that had existed in the Luxembourg, and still existed at that very moment, and if they had given information about it.   On a negative or affirmative answer, they passed on to the next."

He adds (let us not forget that this was written after Thermidor, when he was in prison and defending his life) :—

"What a manner of trying men !   How the jurors ought to reproach themselves for the deaths of those whose defence they did not listen to ! "

"I remember," Benoît also writes, "that on each occasion when we went to give evidence, Boyaval spent a good deal of time alone in the room of the Public Prosecutor.   Everything leads to the presumption that he was well acquainted with all that was happening.   As we were returning from the Tribunal on the 4th of Thermidor, I asked Boyaval about a room-mate of his who had also been mine.   'We shall have him guillotined soon,' Boyaval answered.   'He is for the first " batch " as well as Fossès and his father-in-law.   I have been twice to the Committee of Public Safety during the last few days, I was there yesterday, and it is I who am entrusted with that.   We are going to hurry them up   We leave some like him as bait for the others and we pick them all up in a lump.' " [1]

Benoît sought, in writing these lines, to clear himself of responsibility , but letters, such as the following, from him to Fouquier-Tinville are to be found among the Archives —

[1] W 501, 2nd dossier, p 146.

" Citizen, I have a declaration to make to you which will perhaps be to the public advantage, for the hydra of aristocracy must be overthrown at all points BENOIST. This 21st of Messidor of the year II. of the Republic one and indivisible." [1]

Benoît had passed the 23rd of Messidor at the Carmelites.[2] He occupied in that prison a private room where he could write. At the Carmelites he did the same work as at the Luxembourg The janitor, Roblâtre, a brute who tormented the prisoners in order to drive them to exasperation, received an order to treat him with consideration. In order the better to gain the trust of the prisoners and to incline them to make confidence, Benoît told some that he came from the Department of Eure-et-Loir, others that he came from Calvados, or from the Eure, whilst as a matter of fact he came straight from the Luxembourg prison. He had liberty to go and come, to enter and to leave ; he had a seal bearing the arms of the Nation.

Another police spy at the Carmelites was Citizen Manuel.[3]

[1] This also is a letter from Benoist (there are others in the same portfolio) .—

" (To the Citizen Public Prosecutor of the Revolutionary Tribunal at Paris)

" This 25th of Messidor of the Year II of the Republic one and indivisible.

" Citizen,

" I believe I ought to denounce to you all the scoundrels who seek to humiliate the Convention. An individual about whom I gave information, on the 23rd of this month, to the janitor of the house of detention of the Luxembourg has said in the presence of two citizens whom I pointed out to him, that the Committees of Public Safety and of General Security had caused scoundrels to be shut up in the Luxembourg in order to rid themselves of honest people so that they might govern alone and despotically. I only write this letter from a fear that he may not have informed you or the Committee of General Security. Greeting and fraternity, Benoist. I have many other things of which I ought to inform you, but at the moment when I was writing to you I was transferred to the Carmelites and I have been ill since then, but to-day I hope to be better and to inform you as well as the Committees of General Security and of Public Safety of all that I know " W 501, 1st dossier, p 33.

[2] That is the day following the third Luxembourg " batch." This comparison of dates is significant

[3] See the evidence of Gouget-Deslandres at Fouquier's trial.

Fouquier, at the trials, would say to him "Come, patriot Manuel, enlighten the Tribunal regarding the perfidious intentions of these scoundrels." Then Manuel, looking at the accused on the benches, would disclose what he had noticed in prison regarding the conduct of each of them Fouquier, according to Gouget-Deslandres, "rubbing his hands in token of the fullest satisfaction."

In reality, the so-called conspiracy in the Carmelite Prison seems to have been absolutely imaginary. It owed its origin only to a plan of escape attempted by five or six prisoners who had found a rope in the belfry, and who with the help of this rope, which they transformed into a ladder, had tried to escape Faro and Arbeltier, officers of police, went to the Carmelites on the 30th of Messidor. They questioned the prisoners. Virolle, a surgeon, suspected of being the principal "conspirator," denied the remarks that were attributed to him in regard to Robespierre and the Committee of Public Safety Another, Champagnier, was also denounced. A list of forty-nine conspirators was drawn up. Virolle, the surgeon, in desperation, threw himself out of a window and was killed. He was replaced by another, Bourgeois, an ex-lawyer. The forty-nine appeared before the Tribunal on the 5th of Thermidor (July 23). Three only were acquitted Fouquier's indictment is drawn up with visible carelessness and haste. He furnished no proof. " Virol, a prisoner in the house of the Carmelites, was the head of this new conspiracy, which coincided with those in the houses of detention of Bicêtre and of the Luxembourg It *appears* also that the conspirators in the first two houses had an understanding and a secret correspondence with those in the Carmelites " [1] There are all classes in the list of accused—ex-nobles, a merchant, a teacher, ex-priests, an ironmonger, a cutler, a shopkeeper, a haberdasher, a lawyer, an upholsterer, sailors, a domestic servant, a prince —Louis Armand Constantin de Montbazon-Rohan, ex-

[1] Except for Virolle and Champagnier, none of the accused were examined at the inquiry There is no report of an examination among the papers

Vice-Admiral. The official report of the hearing bears the name of Fouquier-Tinville as present at the pleadings.[1] We shall see from the evidence of witnesses at his trial that he spoke several times against the accused.

In spite of the extreme credulity of the public, the system of Dillon conspiracies, Grammont conspiracies, etc., became worn out. "One blushed," says Réal, "at returning to this commonplace method." A conspiracy at Saint-Lazare was imagined. The informers were Manini, an Italian "man of letters," and Coquery, a locksmith According to their statements, "the prisoners were to escape and massacre the members of the Committee of Public Safety." In order to give a material proof of the plot, Coquery sawed through the bar of a window On the 23rd of Messidor, the day following the third "batch" from the Luxembourg, Faro was commissioned to hold an inquiry at Saint-Lazare. He heard Manini, Coquery, Desisnards, Allain, Gauthier, Scelle, and Semé, the janitor. Semé was replaced by a safe man, Verney, the former turnkey of the Luxembourg, who boasted of "despatching the prisoners at Saint-Lazare as he had done at the Luxembourg" To these hired plotters were joined Jobert (the Belgian), Pépin Dégrouhette, Roger La Pointe, Lepêcheux, Robinet, and Horace Molin. They made out lists, and acted as witnesses at the sessions of the Tribunal. Pépin Dégrouhette especially distinguished himself. He had been a judge of the Tribunal established on August 17, and had afterwards been sent to prison for dishonestly using his position to enrich himself He would return drunk from the Tribunal, and boast that he had been embraced by Fouquier, that he was all-powerful at the Tribunal He was hated and feared

The indictment for the Saint-Lazare conspiracy contains eighty names, two of which are erased. It was dealt with on the three occasions (the 6th, 7th and 8th of Thermidor). In the "batch" of the 6th, there was included young Fortuné Charles Louis François de Maillé (17 years of age), who had thrown at the purveyor's head a rotten fish that

---

[1] Archives Nationales, W 429, No 965, 2nd part, p 95.

had been served up to him.   Young Mellet, who had been
mistaken for him, had, as we have seen, been guillotined on
the 4th of Thermidor.   In this " batch " of twenty-five
prisoners, tried on the 6th of Thermidor, and all condemned,
we may also mention the Abbess of Montmartre, Marie
Louise de Laval Montmorency, aged seventy-two, and young
Isabelle Pigret de Meursin, aged twenty-one, paralysed in
her legs.   They were condemned as accomplices in the
plan to escape.   How could this woman of seventy-two
and this paralysed girl have escaped through the window
which Coquery had sawn ?

Mesdames de Meursin, Joly de Fleury, and Saint-Aignan
declared themselves pregnant.   Madame de Saint-Aignan
alone was recognised to be so by the officers of health.   She
was detained along with her husband   As for the others, " it
is impossible," wrote Coffinhal on the revised memorandum
of the sentence, " for men to communicate with women in
the house of detention of Lazare."   But, all the same, they
were prosecuted and condemned for having conspired with
them !

On the day of the 7th of Thermidor there were twenty-six
accused, twenty-five of whom were condemned.   Here also
there is an error of name and of person   Madame de Mayet [1]
was brought to trial instead of the Vicomtesse de Maillé.
None the less Madame de Mayet was condemned to death
and executed.   As for the Vicomtesse de Maillé (she was
thirty-nine), they returned two days later to look for her
in her prison.   She was led to the Tribunal.   She appeared
as No. 23, the last on the list, at the session presided over
by Scellier on the 9th of Thermidor.   As she entered the
hall of audience she saw the benches on which her young son
had sat three days before.   She fainted.   The people—if you
can call " the people " those who enjoyed attending the great
sessions of the Tribunal—the people murmured and made
a display in her favour.   The judges adjourned her case
to a later session   She was transferred to the Hospice de
l'Evêché.   The next day was the 10th of Thermidor   She

---

[1] Louise Elisabeth Gabrielle Mathy-Simon, Mayet's widow

G

was saved. She will be heard giving evidence at Fouquier-Tinville's trial

It was at the session of the 7th of Thermidor, at the head of the list, that Antoine Roucher, man of letters, and his friend, André Chénier, the poet, made their appearance. Everybody knows their story and how they went to their execution. The verses written by André Chénier are also known, those splendid, vehement verses of the *Jeune Captive*, that immortal cry of rage uttered by an honest man, powerless before his executioners .

> " Mourir sans vider mon carquois,
> Sans percer, sans fouler, sans pétrir dans leur fange
> Ces bourreaux barbouilleurs de lois,
> Ces vers cadavéreux de la France asservie,
> Egorgée ! . . . . . "

Let us also note on the list of the twenty-five condemned on the 7th of Thermidor, Louis Sers, fifty years of age, a captain of infantry, commandant of Chandernagor. Coffinhal, when revising the list of accused in order to propound the questions to the jury, wrote on the margin before the name of Louis Sers, these words " *Captain of infantry, commandant of Chambarnagot.*"

At this session only three witnesses, three police spies, were heard—Manini, " an author-artist," Pépin Desgrouettes whom we know, and who styled himself official defender, and Coquery, the locksmith

In the third " batch," that of the 8th, there were twenty-five accused and twenty-three condemned, among them the two Trudaines, Charles Louis, twenty-nine years old, and Charles Michel, twenty-eight, and Jean Simon Loizerolles, condemned in mistake for his son, François.[1] Here the error was not due to Fouquier. Coffinhal, who presided at the session on that day, and the registrar's clerk must alone bear the responsibility for the additional words that exist on the page of questions pro-

---

[1] M Louis Comber gives an entirely different account of the Loizerolles trial Cf *Episodes et Curiosités Révolutionnaires,* p 307 —TR

pounded to the jury, and which were employed for drawing up the verdict The first document in this bundle[1] is a general list of the prisoners at Saint-Lazare, numbered in the Public Prosecutor's hand. We read there : " No. 18, Loizerole, the son." This is not a reference to the father. On the indictment, signed by Fouquier, there is, in the list of accused persons . " No. 5, François-Simon Loizerolles, the son, aged twenty-two, born in Paris, residing at No. 82, Rue Victor." This is not a reference to the father. In the body of this indictment · " Loizerolles, Primpin (one of the accused), and others, the priests Brognard and Broquet, have not ceased since the Revolution from displaying the most pronounced aversion and hatred for the sovereignty of the people and for equality." That is all. Yet at the moment the questions were propounded to the jury, Coffinhal's hand had corrected and written *Jean* instead of *François*, *father* instead of *son*, *sixty-one* years instead of *twenty-two*. Coffinhal's hand had also added the words " a former lieutenant of the bailiwick of the Arsenal, an ex-noble," which apply to the father. The official report of the session and of the verdict[2] reproduce the form adopted and imposed by Coffinhal

The father sacrificed himself for his son without protest, and he stoically allowed himself to be guillotined in his place. Fouquier, when brought to trial after the 9th of Thermidor, defended himself against the charge of having committed this criminal error by saying · " After the odious law of the 22nd of Prairial, there was no longer any examination in order to procure the Christian names and descriptions of the prisoners brought before the Tribunal , it was necessary to send to the different houses of detention where they were, and the man who went to Lazare to take the Christian names, the age, and the description of Loizerolles, the father, did not take care to ask if there were several Loizerolles, and he took the Christian names and description of the son, who

[1] Archives Nationales, W 431, No 968
[2] They are in the handwriting of Jacques Derbez, registrar's clerk. W. 431, No 968

presented himself instead of the father, although his note bears the name of Loizerolles, the father, those names, descriptions, and age were filled in by the secretary of the prosecutor's office just as they were brought back."

Fouquier blunders here. For on the general list of the Saint-Lazare prisoners selected to be sent to the Tribunal, can still be read, under No. 18, the name of Loizerolles, the son, and nowhere is there a reference to that of the father. But where Fouquier is right is when he incriminates Coffinhal and the registrar's clerk " This omission and this crime, if they really exist, are due to President Coffinhal and to the registrar's clerk who was responsible for the session, and not to the Public Prosecutor's deputy, who, no more than the latter, ever signed the minutes of the verdicts and could in no way be responsible for them." We shall hear the evidence of Loizerolles, the son, at Fouquier's trial.

In conclusion, let us recall that on the 7th of Thermidor (July 25), at six o'clock in the evening, at the Oiseaux, a tranquil prison where the prisoners paid very highly for their board, and where it seems that until then there was a desire to forget them, a noise was heard in the street. An immense chariot, drawn by four horses, had stopped before the door. Four gendarmes and an usher of the Revolutionary Tribunal entered the prison. The janitor had to ring the bell. At this summons, the prisoners assembled in the courtyard.[1] The roll was called. Eleven prisoners were chosen to enter the chariot. Among them were the Princesse de Chimay, the Comtesses de Narbonne-Pelet and Raymond-Narbonne, the Comte de Clermont-Tonnerre (74 years old), the Marquis de Crussol d'Amboise, and M. Simeon de Saint-Simon, Bishop of Agde (70 years old) When these eleven had entered, the chariot started off and went to Port-Libre and to Plessis. It was at Plessis that it " loaded " Thérèse-Françoise de Stainville, Princesse de Grimaldi-Monaco (26 years old), she whom Fouquier called " the woman Monaco," in a letter of the same date addressed to the

---

[1] *Mémoires sur les Prisons*, II., p 189.

members of the Popular Commission, claiming from them documents against a certain number of persons such as "Crussol d'Amboise, Clermont-Tonnerre, the woman Chimay, Saint-Simon, the woman Quérrohen, the woman Monaco," etc., for he had not received the said documents, and " those persons will be brought to trial to-morrow."[1]

The Princesse de Monaco declared herself pregnant. On the following day she withdrew her statement. She had only wanted to gain time to write to her children and to send them her hair. The decision which declared her not pregnant and which ordered her execution is dated the 9th of Thermidor.[2] She must have formed part of the last cartload.

To sum up the Public Prosecutor, overworked and broken down, was no longer able to draw up his writs of indictment himself He had them drawn up by his secretaries. Those documents no longer contained even the semblance of a proof. Entire families were sent to the guillotine. The motive ? They had conspired Where ? When ? How ? There was no answer.

Each evening Fouquier-Tinville arranged that " batches " of accused persons should be put on trial next day. Quantities of documents were lacking. He claimed them. He wanted them at once But time pressed, and he had received an order to draw up the case for the prosecution for the next day. Mistakes as to persons were made, criminal, irreparable mistakes, since there was but one penalty—the guillotine. So-and-so was charged in mistake for so-and-so, condemned in mistake for so-and-so, guillotined for so-and-so. All this is easy to verify to-day. The documents exist among the Archives

Fouquier-Tinville was in close touch with those hirelings, the police spies of the prisons These wretches gave evidence at the pleadings, if one can call pleadings sessions of some hours at which sixty prisoners are tried in an afternoon and condemned to death. Moreover, at some of the

[1] Archives Nationales, F⁷ 4, 436, liasse T , p 9
[2] W., 432, dossier 971, 2nd part, p 47.

sessions, only the police spies appeared as witnesses. Take for example the session of the 19th of Messidor (the first "batch" from the Luxembourg) when there were sixty accused, all of whom were condemned, and only five witnesses, of whom four were spies, and the fifth a turnkey, Lesenne, who, not having the heart to lie, said he had not known of a conspiracy in the prison. Fouquier had him arrested before the session ended. Take another example —the second "batch" from Saint-Lazare, on the 7th of Thermidor. There were three witnesses, three spies, Manini, Pépin Desgrouettes and Coquery.

On the official reports of the sessions, the jurors were no longer even designated by their names Did they fear future responsibility if the form of government were to change ? Was there not time enough, or did no one take the trouble to inscribe their names ? The matter remains a mystery.

That Fouquier, devoted as he was to his task, hardened as he may have become, should feel himself exhausted ; that he should recognise that he and his staff were worn out beyond the limits of human strength , that he no longer saw clearly in that atmosphere of fever and blood in which he lived ; that he declared himself overwhelmed ; that he said to the attendants in the refreshment-room of the Tribunal, the Morisans, in a moment of communicativeness and disgust : " I would rather dig the ground ! "—all this is reasonable and human. None the less, he remained at his post and was anxious to remain at it.

Did he reflect, did he think, did he meditate on what had been accomplished in sixteen months ? All that blood ! All that red frenzy ! All those heads that " fell " ! All those human existences cut off ! Those young women ! Those young girls ! Those old men ! Those young men ! So many human lives for an imaginary, or at least a doubtful plot !

But that he reprobated his task, that he understood that too much was too much, and that the hour was near when he must give account—for everything has to be paid for, and violence attracts violence—this does not appear. Nothing in his attitude as a tenacious official, exact and firm at his post, indicates this.

The political drama is at its last act. We have reached the 9th of Thermidor.

CHAPTER IV

ON the night of the 9th of Thermidor, Fouquier-Tinville was late in returning home to the Palace of Justice.

He had been to deliver to the Committees of Public Safety and of General Security the two lists it was his duty to furnish to them; one containing the names of prisoners tried during the past ten days; the other those of the "conspirators" to be brought before the Tribunal during the following ten days.[1]

At ten o'clock on the morning of the 9th of Thermidor, he had taken his place at the Tribunal in the Hall of Equality. Dumas presided over the session, assisted by Antoine Marie Maire, Gabriel Deliège, and Jean Baptiste Henry Antoine Félix as judges.

The court was open to the public. Nine jurors entered, whose names on this day were given in the official report of the session—Specht, Magnien, Potherat, Masson, Devèze, Buttin,[2] Gauthier, Fenaux, and Laurent.

The accused were led to the bar. There were twenty-five. Four old men of from seventy to seventy-five, beside young men, and others in the prime of life, and there were three women. A lamentable spectacle presented itself before the

---

[1] It was by a resolution of the Committee of Public Safety that Fouquier had to hand in these lists. He continued to furnish them up to and inclusive of the 9th of Thermidor. Buchez and Roux, XXXIV., p. 239.

[2] Buttin is mentioned on this particular day in the two official reports of the sessions held at the same time, one in the Hall of Equality, the other in that of Liberty. This demonstrates once again the haste and carelessness with which the judicial documents were compiled during Messidor and at the beginning of Thermidor in the year II.

public, a public, however, surfeited by these exhibitions, which had now lasted for sixteen months. One of the accused, an old man, deaf, blind, and in his second childhood, was carried in by the gendarmes and placed on the prisoners' bench. On the previous day he had been transferred from the Luxembourg to the Conciergerie. Three gendarmes and Budelot, the coachman of the Tribunal, helped him down from the carriage. The state he was in when he arrived was such that the whole of his clothing had to be changed. Too stupefied to know where he was, his eyes deprived of light, his ears not hearing the questions, and his palsied tongue incapable of articulating any intelligible sound, he was unaware of the terrible Tribunal. He was the ex-Accountant-General, M. Durand Puy deVérine. His wife appeared with him, she also was charged, then her name erased, and finally re-inserted

The Public Prosecutor's witnesses were introduced. To twenty-five prisoners there were only five witnesses,[1] and even those five witnesses had only to do with three of the accused.

Dumas had the jurors sworn. These then took their seats in the court, facing the accused and the witnesses. The President told the accused that they could be seated, and then questioned them on their names, ages, professions, residences, and places of birth. The registrar read the writ of indictment. Drawn up, on the previous evening, under Fouquier's supervision, this writ at first contained fifteen names. But as it was impossible for him, in his rapid task, to identify twelve of those names, the Public Prosecutor had crossed out the twelve following—those of a stonemason, an innkeeper, a seller of lemonade, three soldiers, a major and his wife, those of three other persons, and, lastly, that of a woman whose identity was not sufficiently established by two masculine Christian names, doubtless those of her husband.[2] Then making out a new list, Fouquier rapidly drew up a writ of indictment against twenty-one other prisoners. But here again a difficulty arose. One of the accused, Louis

---

[1] W 433, dossier 973.
[2] Those twelve persons were saved by the 9th of Thermidor.

Clair Maurin, whose place of birth was unknown, was affirmed to be dead Fouquier wrote on the margin *condemned*. Dumas wrote *dead*. As a matter of fact, Louis Clair Maurin, who had been confused with Jean Dominique Maurin, guillotined on the 19th of Messidor, had himself been guillotined on the 22nd Another, Jean Baptiste Lafond, 37 years of age, an ex-priest, whose place of birth was also unknown, and whom Fouquier has described as " an intriguing ex-canon, a frequenter of gambling dens, a gambler in the funds," could not be found He was mentioned under the heading of *absent*. Was it in order to replace these two who were missing that the Public Prosecutor " reinserted " on his list Perronnet Brillon-Bussé and Jérémie Saint-Hilaire, " at first omitted as having been mistaken for others " ? Here they were at the session. Fouquier's list is complete— there are twenty-five accused in all [1]

The system of *amalgams* was working better than ever. At this session, in the Hall of Equality, a lawyer and former agent of Condé's, was arraigned with an ex-Treasurer of France , an ex-Mayor with a captain of cavalry of Condé's regiment ; an architect with an ex-justice of the peace. Who were the others ? An ex-noble, an ex-cashier of a glass factory, a teacher of astronomy born at Oppenheim in the Palatinate, an upholsterer of the Rue Mouffetard, an ironmonger of the Rue Saint-Martin ; the divorced wife of a commissary, an ex-legislator and an ex-noble, a merchant born at Villeneuve-d'Agen ; two poor chimney-sweepers, whom the indictment described as ex-nobles, and who actually were the Loisons, husband and wife, managers of the marionette theatre of the Champs-Elysées ; a private in the 17th battalion of infantry ; a captain of a mounted regiment ; a clerk in the administration of public lands ; an upholsterer to " Capet's aunts " ; a bailiff of the Haute-Marne , finally, Pierre Durand Puy de Vérine, ex-Accountant-General, and his wife, Marie Marguerite Barcos, a sad and dismal couple already marked with the immobility of death.

All those accused persons are mentioned by Fouquier-

[1] W. 433, dossier 973.

THE NIGHT OF THE NINTH

ERMIDOR, IN THE YEAR II.

Tinville as "suspected of having engaged in operations tending to excite trouble, of having passed and signed resolutions tending to favour and propagate the system of federalism and to impede the circulation of provisions, of having held communication and correspondence with the internal and external enemies of the Republic, of having caused help in money to be sent to them in order to facilitate their invasion of French territory."

Care must be taken not to be deceived by the formulæ dear to Fouquier, Dumas, and Coffinhal In reality, the first three prisoners, Jean Antoine Lhuillier, Sébastien Alaroze Labrenne, and Gabriel François Sallé, were the only ones against whom there exist the elements of proof in the portfolios of the Revolutionary Tribunal. Vainly were proofs sought against the others. And what proofs! The facts are that on August 4, 1793, the municipal officers of the seven municipalities forming the canton of Chevagne, in the district of Moulins, in the Department of the Allier, assembled at Chevagne, were confronted by a menacing dearth of provisions, and had proposed to have recourse to mutual union and assistance in all that concerned the means of subsistence. They proposed to aid the adjoining districts with their surplus of corn, if there were any. They showed themselves, besides, determined to defend the necessary and indispensable products of their own district by all legal means. Could that be made out as a crime ? Very prudent and wise measures were taken with a view to realise this aspiration. But on August 13, the executive council of the Department of the Allier had decreed that this deliberation bore all the marks of illegality and anarchy, that it "tended to give the idea of federalism," and was "an attempt against unity and indivisibility" and against "the distribution of provisions" Out of fifteen who had signed the proposal, four had been arrested—Lhuillier, Labrenne, Sallé and Durand, the President. Then the President had been set free. The three others were to be tried in the revolutionary style. On the 30th of Floréal they had appeared before the director of the *jury d'accusation* of the tribunal of the district of Moulins

They had to answer this question · " What had been their views and for what motive had they proposed on August 4, 1793, in the canton of Chevagne, to prevent the distribution of grain necessary for the existence of their fellow-citizens who ought to be as dear to them as themselves, and to whom they owed, according to natural law and humanity, every assistance even to the exhaustion of the product of their harvests which the Supreme Being had preserved and destined for all their fellow-citizens as well as for themselves. The territory of France belongs to the whole Republic. Consequently all individuals inhabiting it have equal rights. If they were imbued with these truths, they would not have fallen into the illegality of anarchy that could not but give the idea of federalism " On the 6th of Messidor of the year II , a judgment of the criminal tribunal of the Allier ordered all the documents in the case to be sent to Fouquier-Tinville. He was to " consider in his wisdom whether he ought to cause those accused to be brought before the Revolutionary Tribunal."[1] The Public Prosecutor of Moulins having asked his colleague of Paris if there was ground for issuing a warrant only against the three accused persons indicated as ring-leaders, or if it were necessary to include the fifteen signatories to the measure, Fouquier-Tinville had answered by the following note · " Warrant against the three chiefs only." That was why Jean Antoine Lhuillier,

---

[1] " While uncertain as to the line you will take," the Public Prosecutor of the Allier wrote to Fouquier, on the 9th, " I think I am anticipating your wishes in telling you that the general opinion of the patriots of the district is that almost all the signatories of this proposal are good ignorant citizens, as are our rural inhabitants, whose signatures have been tricked from them, that they did not know they were being made to commit an act of liberticide, and, on the contrary, believed they were only labouring for the public good which they have not ceased to love. It is thought also that the author of this whole business is Lhuillier, a former agent of the traitor Condé, and that Labresne and Sallé, formerly privileged persons, had a great deal to do with it " *It is thought !* Everybody did not think thus For one can see among the papers a certificate and a fervent petition from the citizens of the commune of Chezy in favour of Alaroze Labresne, "a magistrate necessary to their commune," signed by " the small number of those who can write."

Sébastien Alaroze Labrenne, and Gabriel François Sallé appeared before the Revolutionary Tribunal on this 9th of Thermidor, in the Hall of Equality.

As for the others, nothing in the documents indicates what really was their crime.   There is no material evidence.

The reading of the writ of indictment had ended.   The voice of Pesme, the registrar, ceased.   In the court five individuals got up and went out.   These were the witnesses brought forward by the Public Prosecutor and summoned at his request.   It was about noon.   The weather was heavy and thunder-laden   Through the open windows the great hum of Paris was heard.   A name rang out, called by the usher.   It was that of the first witness, Dupont, a member of the revolutionary committee of the Beaurepaire Section. He knew Loison, the director of the theatre of marionettes. He made his declaration.   One after another there entered and gave evidence the spy Jobert (the Belgian) ; an engraver who knew the prisoner Lavoisien ; Lambert, a trader ; Descaffé, without profession, and Aubert, an innkeeper, who knew the prisoner Marche, an usher.

Fouquier-Tinville then began to speak, and expounded his writ of indictment.   He described the means by which he would prove his case.   No defender answered him, the defence having been suppressed by the law of Prairial.

Then the jury were invited to retire to their room to deliberate.   The President caused the prisoners to withdraw.   The Tribunal remained in session.

Suddenly there was a thunderbolt.   The President of the Revolutionary Tribunal had just been arrested whilst sitting. An order of the Committee of Public Safety !   He was led away.   Citizen Maire, one of his assessors, replaced him, and the session went on amid general amazement [1]

---

[1] The judgment on Lhuillier and others, to the number of 25, condemned to death, ends thus —

" Given and pronounced on the 9th of Thermidor of the second year of the Republic, at the public session at which sat René François Dumas, President, Antoine Marie Maire, Gabriel Dehège, and Jean-Baptiste Henry Antoine Félix, judges, who have signed this present judgment with the registrar's clerk, and at the moment of the

Nothing in Fouquier-Tinville's attitude betrayed emotion or anxiety. He was master of himself Did he suspect the causes of the brutal arrest of the President ? Did he know of the violent speech delivered by Dumas on the previous day at the Jacobin Society during the tumultuous session when Robespierre defined the political situation in these menacing terms " It is easy to see that factious persons are afraid of being unmasked in the people's presence ; moreover, I thank them for having distinguished themselves in so pronounced a manner, and for having made me better acquainted with *my* enemies and those of our country " ?

Did Fouquier know that Dumas, mounting the tribune, had denounced the *conspiracy* as by no means doubtful, and the Government as counter-revolutionary ? Did he know that, addressing those who, at the beginning of the session, had quarrelled with Robespierre about the right to speak, Dumas exclaimed " It is strange that men who for several months have kept silence, ask to be allowed to speak to-day, doubtless to oppose the expression of the crushing truths that Robespierre has just made. It is easy to recognise in them the heirs of Hébert and Danton. I prophesy to them that they will also inherit the fate of those conspirators."[1]

Towards half-past one, a report was current at the Tribunal that the Faubourg Saint-Antoine was in an uproar,

delivery of the jury's verdict, the President having retired, Citizen Maire has performed his duties as President (Signed) Maire, Dehiège, Félix, Pesme." (W 433, No. 973) On the margin of the third page of this judgment (on the back) Pesme, the registrar's clerk, has written, " Note This judgment was given on the day of the arrest of the traitor Dumas, and it was impossible to procure the names of some of the birthplaces and residences —M P." " Dumas was arrested on his seat at noon." Robert Wolff's evidence at Fouquier-Tinville's trial. W. 500, 3rd dossier, p. 10.

[1] Dumas when arrested was transported to and imprisoned in Sainte-Pélagie, at 4 o'clock. " Several individuals came to take him away The weakness of the janitor is the reason that he got out. Immediately on learning this fact, we (the Committee of General Security) had the janitor of Sainte-Pélagie arrested " (Voulland at the Convention. Session of the 13th of Fructidor, year II. See the *Moniteur*)

that grave trouble was to be feared, that drums were beating to arms.[1]

The session continued, or rather the sessions   For in the Hall of Liberty, at the same hour, twenty-three prisoners were on trial. Scellier presided , Grébeauval, Fouquier's deputy, occupied the seat of the Public Prosecutor. Fouquier had revised and signed the indictment on the previous day, the 8th of Thermidor

But the jurors in the Hall of Equality caused Maire to be informed that they were ready to give their verdict.   They entered and each resumed his place.   One after another the President called on them, and asked them to give their " vote " on each of the questions propounded to them, and in the order in which they appeared in the memorandum they held in their hands.   It was a memorandum drawn up by Dumas before the trial, that morning or on the previous evening, the terrible brevity and the embarrassing formula of which deserve to be recorded   It is to those enigmatic and evil questions that men incapable of judging in cold blood or possessing a knowledge of the case were going to give answer.   From the way in which Dumas made out this list of questions they were certain to be completely bewildered   Yet, on their " yes " the lives of twenty-five accused persons depended [2]

[1] W 500, 3rd dossier, p 10

[2] Here are some of the questions propounded, as Dumas made out the minute —

" Are they convicted of having declared themselves enemies of the people, that is to say —

1, Charpentier , 2, Valot , 3, Durand (*sic*) , 4, the woman Durand (*sic*) , 5, Larcher (*sic*) , 6, Brillon Bussé , 7, Saint-Hilaire , 8, Vrigny , by keeping up a correspondence with the internal enemies of the State, tending to favour the invasion of French territory and to destroy public liberty   9, Soumesson , 10, Lavoisien ; 11, Gillet , 12, Loison , 13, the woman Loison , 14, Legay ; 15, Duval , 16, Mongelchot ; 17, Guérin , 18, Foicier , 19, Vatrin , 20, Coqueau , by joining the coalition of conspirators leagued against the people, seeking to corrupt the public mind, to repress patriotism, employing trickery, menace, and violence to favour the tyranny of Capet, the triumph of the factions, and the destruction of liberty. 21, the woman Coriolis, by instigating the humiliation and dissolution of the national representation. 22, Lhuillier , 23, Alarose La Brenne , 24, Sallé,

The jury's declaration was affirmative in regard to all the prisoners except the woman Coriolis, who was acquitted. The other twenty-four were condemned to death in conformity with the provisions of Articles IV., V. and VI. of the law of Prairial. Their property was declared confiscated to the Republic to be used for the subsistence of widows and orphans, " if they have no other resources."

The session ended. In the courtyard of the Conciergerie was already heard the rumbling of the carts which Fouquier caused to be prepared to carry away the condemned. There were six of them, and none too many ; for the other session, that of the Hall of Liberty, had decided well also. Twenty-one had been condemned, and there was also the Princesse de Monaco, whose death-warrant Dumas had signed that morning in the council chamber.[1] Total . forty-six heads doomed to fall before night at the Barrier of Vincennes.

It was half-past two o'clock. At the Convention, Maximilien Robespierre had just flung at his opponents, who were shouting, " Long live the Republic ! " the bitter retort, " The Republic ! It is already ruined, for the brigands are triumphant."

Three days before, on the 6th of Thermidor, Fouquier had dined at the house of Citizen La Jariette, in the Rue Meslay, with Deputies Goupilleau de Fontenay, Cochon de Lapparent, Morisson, and some members of the Revolutionary Tribunal, Scellier, Coffinhal, and Grébeauval. A friend of La Jariette, Jean Baptiste Vergnhes, a man comfortably off, living on his income, was at the dinner. Coffinhal, his neighbour in the Ile Saint-Louis,[2] had said to him · " You ought to invite to your house to-morrow the members of the Revolutionary Tribunal who are here this evening." Vergnhes had said " yes," and given the invitation. Fouquier, saying he had

by, on August 4, 1793, instigating the formation of illegal assemblies and passing resolutions tending to prevent the distribution of provisions and to excite civil war by famine 25, Maréché, by instigating through his speeches and proceedings the dissolution of the national representation and the re-establishment of tyranny
[1] Archives Nationales, W. 432, No 971, 2nd part, p 47.
. [2] Coffinhal lived in the Rue Le Regrattier

engagements on the 7th and 8th, proposed the 9th, which was adopted.

They had then arranged to meet on that day between three and four o'clock, at the house of Vergnhes, at the western end of the Ile Saint-Louis (Ile de la Fraternité) at No. 1, Quai Egalité, formerly Quai Bourbon.[1]

Accompanied by Coffinhal, the Vice-President, and the juror Desboisseaux, a member of the General Council of the Commune of Paris, Fouquier-Tinville was about to leave the Palace of Justice to keep this invitation when one of the executioner's assistants approached him. He informed the Public Prosecutor that trouble had broken out in the Faubourg Saint-Antoine through which the carts must pass on their way to the Barrier of Vincennes. The same observation was made to him by two employees in the ushers' office, André Contat and Etienne Simonnet They told him that " things were going to happen in Paris ,[2] that it would be prudent not to go on with the executions, that it might endanger the guard, etc." Fouquier stopped and listened to them. For a moment he paused to think. A tragic moment, during which the fate of forty-six human beings was to be decided ! For a moment he pondered, and turning to the executioner's assistant said : " The course of justice must not be stopped. Proceed ! "

A little farther on he met Adnet, the captain of gendarmes, who told him that Hanriot had given orders to arrest Botot-Dumesnil, the commander of the gendarmes attached to the Tribunals. Ought the carts to start ? This news should have been enough to give pause to Fouquier. But nothing could do that. " I cannot stop the course of justice," he answered Captain Adnet.

The carts started, carrying the unfortunate persons, who twenty-four hours later would have been saved , carrying the paralytic Durand Puy de Vérine and his wife, the Loison couple, the charming and heroic Princesse de Monaco The carts started, and Fouquier departed to sup with Vergnhes.

---

[1] W. 500, 3rd dossier, p 46.   [2] W. 500, 3rd dossier, p 58.

II

During the meal there was no discussion of the events of the day, neither of the arrest of Dumas, which, however, " had struck the guests who were members of the Revolutionary Tribunal, and Fouquier[1] in particular, with consternation," nor the tragic facts of which at that very hour the Convention was the scene. Fouquier ate little.[2] His host, " who saw him only for the second time," asked himself whether this consternation was " the result of astonishment or of complicity."[3]

From the windows of the house in which Vergnhes lived it was easy to perceive what was taking place in the Communal House   About five o'clock, at the moment when this melancholy repast was ending, loud noises and a prolonged clamour were heard, and some one cried :

" Look at the crowd in the square.   They are workmen. It might be a riot "

Vergnhes's servant came to say that they were workmen protesting against the law of the maximum.   The noise increased.   A quarter of an hour afterwards this servant, who had been out for news, returned to say that Robespierre and his friends had been arrested, and that the crowd was rushing towards the Commune.   Coffinhal, a member of the General Council, rose, and, sending for his sash, said · " I am going there ! "   " My post is in my office where I might receive orders at any minute," said Fouquier.   " I am going there "   Vergnhes, " a little agitated by these disturbances," listened to the advice of one of the guests, Tampon, a judge of the Tribunal of the Third Arrondissement, and went to his Section, and Tampon started for his.[4]

Fouquier, accordingly, returned straight home.   Proceeding along the Quai aux Ormes, he encounted Oudart, the President of the Criminal Tribunal [5]   They walked together to the Palace.   Beside them, quite close, on the Place

---

[1] W 500, 3rd dossier, p. 46.
[2] *Ibid*
[3] *Ibid*
[4] W 500, 3rd dossier, p 64.
[5] The Criminal Tribunal tried crimes and offences against the common law.

de la Maison Commune, the riot raged. They did not stop. They edged past the riot, which ignored them. They were in a hurry to get back, Fouquier above all.

At the Palace of Justice, in this company of Terrorist officials, now terrorised, everybody was trembling for himself. And here came the "chief." Usually violent and morose, he was this evening silent, dejected, circumspect. He was desirous of knowing what was going to happen. He sent out for news.

He called for Adnet, the police officer, who gave him an account of the different events of the day from the time of his departure Commander Botot-Dumesnil had been arrested at four o'clock, in the midst of his troop, by order of Hanriot, Lescot-Fleuriot, and Payan,[1]

Fouquier said "I remain at my post"[2] At six o'clock in the evening he was with his wife,[3] doubtless to reassure her, whilst in his own mind there sprang up and increased an anxiety that he did not wish to show.

At eight o'clock, Dubesne, the lieutenant of gendarmes, called to give him an account of his mission The execution of the condemned had taken place "with the usual calm." Fouquier at this hour was at home, "in his domicile," with Scellier, the Vice-President of the Tribunal, and Grébeauval, one of his deputies.[4] He left his apartments, and went to the place where he usually spent his evenings before going to the Committee, to the refreshment-room of the Tribunal, where he was to remain throughout this long evening of the 9th of Thermidor. There he was to be seen and heard. Witnesses were afterwards able to say how correct was his attitude, how "pure" his conduct, how irreproachable his utterances. The "scoundrel" Dumas, his enemy, was doubtless going to pay with his head for his audacity in having conspired against the Convention He, Fouquier, the executant of the law, the vigilant and indefatigable purveyor of the guillotine, remained at his post, and, unshaken, awaited the orders of the Convention and the Committees.

A melancholy evening, this spent with the Morisans, the

---

[1] W. 500, 3rd dossier, p. 46.   [2] *Ibid.*   [3] *Ibid.*   [4] *Ibid.*

attendants in the refreshment-room of the Tribunal. The tocsin was heard sounding An enormous clamour, like gusts of wind, rose through the night, and died away against the walls of the Palace of Justice. Groups formed in the sweltering streets, and, in the depths of the gaols, prisoners, who had resigned themselves to an early execution, were astounded and attentive.

The man who, for sixteen months, had appeared as the all-powerful exterminator, as the axe and rods suspended over human existence, this man was to the Morisans a *customer*, regular in his habits, a good and homely fellow. Several times they heard Fouquier complain that his trade was a cruel one, that he would prefer " to dig the ground." Several times they heard him ask " Were there many people at the executions ? " and when they answered, " Yes," he would say : " It is frightful ! What a wretched trade ! " And he would shrug his shoulders.[1] Several times, after the 22nd of Prairial, they had heard him say · " The times are very cruel ; it cannot last." They often heard him complain of Dumas, his rival.

The heat was stifling. About nine o'clock Fouquier descended to the refreshment room and ordered a bottle of beer. He had just learned that Botot-Dumesnil had been set at liberty by the Committee of General Security. He sent for him, desirous of knowing what was happening. Botot-Dumesnil despatched orderlies for news. Fouquier also sent out Malarme, the secretary of the prosecutor's office. On several occasions he said : " Whatever is done, I remain at my post "

One after another fragments of news came to him. Maximilien Robespierre, his brother Augustin, Couthon, Saint-Just, and Lebas had been unanimously impeached by the Convention. Lebas had been sent to the Conciergerie ; Augustin to Saint-Lazare and then to La Force ; Saint-Just to the Ecossais, Couthon to La Bourbe, Maximilien to the Luxembourg. But the janitor of that house had, it appears, refused to receive him by virtue of an injunction

---

[1] W. 500, 3rd dossier, p 45 *bis*.

THE ARREST OF ROBESPIERRE

of the police administrators not to admit any prisoner without their orders.[1] Robespierre insisted on being imprisoned. In vain. He was then led to the offices of the police administration on the Quai des Orfèvres. The General Council of the Commune had appointed a provisional executive committee composed of nine members—Payan, Coffinhal, Louvet, Lerebours, Legrand, Desboisseaux (the Desboisseaux with whom Fouquier had dined at the house of Vergnhes some hours before), Châtelet, Arthur, and Grenard, Hanriot had been arrested and replaced by Giot, of the Théâtre Français Section, who had taken an oath to serve the country. Coffinhal and Desboisseaux, about ten o'clock, both wearing national sashes, sabre in hand and at the head of a body of artillerymen, forcing all the doors of the Committee of General Security at the Tuileries, calling for Robespierre with loud cries, had invaded the Committee, gone over the whole building, and carried off Hanriot by force [2]

But the drama continued. On Voulland's proposal, the Convention, sitting at night, had outlawed Robespierre, his brother Augustin, Saint-Just, Couthon, and Lebas as traitors to the country Their friends rescued them from the prisons. They were at the Commune.

Fouquier, on learning this news, said . " I remain at my post even if I perish there."

On several occasions emissaries of the rebel Commune came to him and tried to induce him and the members of the Revolutionary Tribunal to come " into its bosom," and to make common cause with the refugees and the outlaws.[3] They invited him to the Hôtel de Ville. He sent them back He answered that he recognised the Convention alone. Twice during the evening he sent Malarme to the Committee. He was anxious to make it known that he was at his post, at the Tribunal Malarme, coming back, found him at supper with Morisan, the attendant in the refreshment-room, his wife, their daughter, and their son-in-law, Gillier,

---

[1] W 500, 3rd dossier, p 39   [2] W 434, No. 975, p 23.
[3] Fouquier's Memorial for his defence

the secretary of the prosecutor's office.[1] It was past midnight

At this moment a torrential shower fell upon Paris, flooding
the streets, and dispersing the crowds and even the delegates
from the Convention, who, by the light of torches, had
just proclaimed the decree of outlawry A sort of lull, an
abatement, took place A long silence. Then, suddenly
on the other bank of the Seine, there was a volley of cannon
and the trampling of troops The Convention, on Voulland's
proposal, had ordered Barras to lead his armed force against
the Hôtel de Ville, against the insurgent Communal House.
Barras and Léonard Bourdon had put themselves at the
head of the columns of the Convention, divided into two
sections—one proceeding along the quays with Barras, the
other along the Rue Saint-Honoré with Bourdon. It was
one o'clock in the morning

The Public Prosecutor, accompanied by Deguaigné,
the usher, Budelot, the Tribunal's coachman, and Demay,
left the Palace of Justice, crossed the Pont-Neuf, and went
to the Committees of Public Safety and of General Security,
which had assembled together He was anxious to be seen
steadfast at his post. There he heard from Thuriot and
Merlin (of Thionville) of the victory of the Convention.
Maximilien Robespierre was grievously wounded. The
Commune was beaten.

Early morning approached. The gray dawn lit up the
victory of Thermidor A new task was preparing for the
Tribunal and for Fouquier. He returned with his three
companions to the Palace of Justice He had a right to a
well-earned rest. His conscience testified to him that it
would be difficult to have shown " purer behaviour " than
his It was half-past three, and he went to bed.

But his sleep was of short duration At five o'clock he
was awakened by Léonard Bourdon, the Representative of
the people, who brought him orders

[1] W. 500, 3rd dossier, p 45 *ter.*

CHAPTER V

SUSPENDED at six o'clock in the morning, the session of the Convention was resumed at nine. The Department of Paris came to congratulate the Assembly on having saved the country. The Revolutionary Tribunal was afterwards admitted to the bar One of its members spoke [1]

"Citizens, representatives," he said, "you have just covered yourselves with glory ; we come to join our congratulations to those you will receive from the whole of France , we come to glory in our own immovable confidence—and it will always be the same—in remaining attached to the national representation in spite of the efforts the conspirators last night did not cease to make to associate us with their crimes. Some traitors had crept into our bosom , you have known how to distinguish them, and soon they shall feel the punishment due to their crimes For our part, entirely devoted to the national representation and to our duty, we come to take your orders for the trial of the conspirators." (Applause.)

Fouquier-Tinville then made an observation —

"There is a difficulty," he said, "which checks the progress of the Tribunal. The municipal officers are included among the great offenders whom you have outlawed. Now, in order to execute the decree against the rebels, it is only necessary to verify the identity of their persons. But in this respect I point out that there exists a decree requiring that this identity should be verified in the presence of two municipal officers of the accused Commune , now, it is

---

[1] The *Moniteur* only calls him "the orator."

impossible to perform this formality in the present circumstances when the municipal officers are themselves charged. I ask the Convention to remove this difficulty." [1]

Thuriot answered "The Convention ought to take measures in order that the conspirators may be punished without delay; any delay would be to the prejudice of the Republic. The scaffold must be erected immediately, and with the heads of his accomplices must fall the head of that infamous Robespierre who proclaimed to us that he believed in the Supreme Being, and who only believed in the power of crime. The soil of the Republic must be purged of a monster who was in a position to have himself proclaimed king. I demand that the Tribunal withdraws to the Committee of General Security to take its orders and that it returns to its post."

This proposal was carried. [2]

On the same day, at one o'clock in the afternoon, the Revolutionary Tribunal held a public session with open doors Scellier presided He had as assistant-judges Foucault, Bravet, Maire, Félix, Laporte, Harny, Deliège, and Garnier-Launay [3]

Fouquier-Tinville, assisted by his deputy, Liendon, was in his place, and demanded the appearance at the session of the twenty-two "conspirators," all decreed to be guilty of rebellion and outlawed. They had been identified by witnesses, and, moreover, all of them had confessed.

One by one the prisoners were introduced The first was Maximilien Robespierre, carried on a stretcher, his head bandaged, and dying. His age ? Thirty-five. His identity had been attested by Pierre Vincent Augustin Lecoin, an employee at the Commission of Relations, residing in Paris, at the Rue du Bac, and by Jean Fabre, an employee in the office of the Revolutionary Tribunal, residing in the Rue Jacob. —2. Georges Couthon.—3. Louis Jean Baptiste Lavalette, brigadier-general of the army of the North —4. François Hanriot, ex-general of the armed forces of Paris.—5. René François Dumas, ex-President of the Revolutionary Tri-

---

[1] *Moniteur*, 12th of Thermidor, year II.   [2] *Moniteur, Ibid.*
[3] Archives Nationales, W. 434, No. 975.

PEINT PAR DAVID

SAINT-JUST

membre du Comité de Salut public

bunal —6. Antoine Saint-Just, ex-Deputy of the Convention, 26 years old.—7. Claude François Payan, ex-juror of the Revolutionary Tribunal, ex-agent of the Commune of Paris. —8. Jacques Claude Bernard, ex-priest, member of the General Council of the Commune, and chief clerk in the Mayor's Office.—9 Adrien Nicolas Gobeau, provisional deputy to Fouquier, member of the Commune of Paris.— 10. Antoine Gency, cooper and ex-member of the General Council of the Commune.—11. Nicolas François Vivier, ex-lawyer and judge of the Tribunal of the Third Arrondissement, outlawed by the Convention. He had presided at the Jacobin Club the night before.

Fouquier-Tinville rose and, laying down his hat and cloak, left the court He did not wish to prosecute his friend, Lescot-Fleuriot, the ex-Mayor of Paris His deputy, Liendon, took his place [1]

The roll-call went on —12. Jean Baptiste Edmond Lescot-Fleuriot, artist, ex-Mayor of Paris, 43 years old, born at Brussels —13 Antoine Simon, shoemaker, ex-member of the General Council of the Commune, residing in Paris at No 32 Rue Marat (the Simon of the Temple, the Dauphin's tormentor).—14. Denis Etienne Laurent, municipal officer. —15. Jacques Louis Frédéric Wouarné, an employee at the Commission of Commerce and Provisions —16. Jean Etienne Forrestier, smelter, member of the Commune.— 17 Augustin Bon Joseph Robespierre (the younger), ex-Deputy of the Convention —18 Nicolas Guérin, member of the General Council of the Commune.—19. Jean Baptiste

---

[1] But, as Public Prosecutor, Fouquier had demanded the appearance of his friend before the Tribunal Here are the terms in which he did so —

"Citizens and representatives,

"A decree of to-day, providing that the Mayor and ex-General Boulanger, both outlawed, shall be executed without delay, both being at the Committee, I request you to give orders that the gendarmes bearers of this present shall immediately bring them before the Tribunal, the judges being in session to execute the law.

"Greeting and fraternity

"The 10th of Thermidor of the Year II. of the Republic one and indivisible. A Q FOUQUIER."

Mathieu Dhazard, hair-dresser and ex-member of the Commune.—20 Christophe Cochefer, formerly an upholsterer, member of the General Council of the Commune.—21 Charles Jacques Mathieu Bougon, an ex-messenger at the stamp office, ex-member of the General Council of the Commune —22. Jean Marie Guenet, timber merchant, member of the General Council of the Commune.

The Tribunal ordered that the twenty-two abovementioned conspirators should be at once handed over to the executioner of criminal judgments, the execution to take place on the Place de la Révolution By five o'clock on the 10th of Thermidor, they were dead.

On the following day, the 11th of Thermidor, seventy *outlaws*, members of the General Council of the rebel Commune, were handed over to the executioner of criminal judgments.[1] Fouquier had, on the previous day, asked for ten or eleven carts to be sent to the Conciergerie for this execution. We know this from the evidence of Etienne Desmorest, the executioner's assistant But the official report of the session has no mention of the Public Prosecutor's name. He is represented by Liendon and Royer, his deputies

On the following day a last " batch " of twelve members of the General Council of the Commune went to the scaffold. They were " convicted of having taken part in the liberticidal and rebellious deliberations of the Commune of Paris on the ninth day of the present month, and on the night between

---

[1] Charles Huant Desboisseaux, the juror of the Revolutionary Tribunal and member of the Commune, who had sat with Fouquier in the Hall of Equality on the 9th of Thermidor, and afterwards went with Fouquier to dine at the house of Vergnies—this Desboisseaux was included among the 70 *outlaws*

During the tragic night he had gone out of the Commune between midnight and one o'clock Wandering about, he had been at different eating-houses, he had supped with Coffinhal, at the Ecu, in the Rue d'Enfer, then had gone home to see his wife, he did not find her, saw the seals on his house, and again wandered about until six o'clock in the evening, and finally entered the house of Citizen Martin, a lemonade seller, on the Quai aux Ormes Information was lodged against him, and he was arrested there, and brought to the Conciergerie.

the ninth and tenth, and of having participated in the said deliberations whilst it (the Commune) sheltered in its bosom traitors ordered by the National Convention to be arrested." [1]

At the session of the Convention on the 14th of Thermidor, Lecointre (of Versailles) demanded the repeal of the law of the 22nd of Prairial, relating to the organisation of the Revolutionary Tribunal.

" It is a veritable martial law," he said.

The saying was true It met with success There was applause. The Convention unanimously repealed the law.

But the Tribunal, whose reconstruction the Committee had proposed at the Convention, was about to be revived. And at the head of the list presented by Barère, we read " Public Prosecutor, Fouquier-Tinville."

An unexpected and striking event then happened. Fréron the journalist, a violent man, " the saviour of the south," Fréron, who on the 9th of Thermidor, had demanded the arrest of Couthon, Saint-Just, and Lebas, made a speech denouncing Fouquier.

" All Paris demands from you the richly merited punishment of Fouquier-Tinville. You have sent to the Revolutionary Tribunal the infamous Dumas and the jurors who, along with him, shared the crimes of the scoundrel Robespierre. I am going to prove to you that Fouquier is as guilty as they were, for if the President, if the jurors, were influenced by Robespierre, the Public Prosecutor was equally influenced by him, for he drew up the writs of indictment with the same intention. I demand that Fouquier-Tinville be sent to stew in the hell of blood which he has shed I demand a decree for his accusation "

Tumult. Applause on all sides. Cries of : " Put the decree of accusation to the vote "

Turreau opposed the decree. " It would be honouring that scoundrel too much I demand that he be simply put on trial before the Revolutionary Tribunal "

This proposal was carried, applause breaking forth several times. By virtue of this decree, the Committee of General

[1] Archives Nationales, W. 434, No. 978.

Security passed a resolution the same day that Fouquier-Tinville, the Public Prosecutor of the Revolutionary Tribunal, be arrested immediately and taken to the prison of the Conciergerie ; that he be brought to trial without delay, and that seals be placed on his papers. Two officers of the Committee, Chandelier and Limage, were charged with the execution of these measures.

The victory of the men of Thermidor was complete. Thus, the man who, four days before, went into the prosecutor's office in the Revolutionary Tribunal, garbed in his short cloak and wearing his raised Henry Quatre hat, who pleaded against Maximilien Robespierre, against Saint-Just, against his own enemy, Dumas, who " performed their toilet and fitted them out for kingdom come," was to learn at his own expense that, in its continuous evolutions, Humanity sometimes displays a sudden and pitiless abruptness.

On the afternoon of that 14th of Thermidor, about half-past two o'clock, the news reached Fouquier that he was to be brought to trial. He was in the refreshment-room of the Tribunal, drinking his usual glass of brandy, and talking over the events of the day with his colleagues. Two men entered and went up to him. One of them was a small hunchback, Jean Feuilles, a secretary in the prosecutor's office, and devoted to the Public Prosecutor, the other was unknown to him ; both were deeply moved.

Feuilles approached Fouquier and taking him aside said :

" Here is a citizen who comes from the Convention. He has been a witness of all that has just happened there. You are to be put on your trial and are about to be arrested. This citizen is Cauchois, Poincarré's uncle."

Fouquier knew Poincarré, a secretary in the prosecutor's office, well. He had confidence in him, for the prosecutor's office had not ceased to be favourable to the Public Prosecutor, while the registrar's office was hostile to him since the arrest of Pâris, called Fabricius, the chief registrar of the Tribunal, and since the execution of Legris, the registrar's clerk.

" Did you hear the decree for arresting me ? " inquired Fouquier.

" Yes, I heard it."

" I am quite easy in my mind. I am not guilty. I will wait until they come to arrest me."

And he swallowed his brandy

But a few moments afterwards, he left the refreshment-room, went up to his office, and spoke of the decree that had just been passed against him, adding that he feared nothing. He afterwards went to warn his wife, the gentle and loving Henriette Jean Gérard d'Aucourt, whom he married as his second wife twelve years before. Having reassured her, he proceeded to the Tuileries, to the Convention.

For the last time he pursued the way he had so often travelled during the past sixteen months—over the Pont-Neuf, and along the Quays. The heat of the August afternoon was overwhelming. It was three o'clock. The murmur of the city boomed in his ears. But he did not hear it. He did not see the familiar spectacles of the streets. He walked on, in a maze, in a dream that would not end. The Committees would listen to the evidence. He was not guilty. He was easy in his mind. Yet it was not long before that, returning one evening from the Committee of Public Safety, as he was crossing the Pont du Change, he seized his companion, and, pointing to the Seine, exclaimed · " Look how red it is ! '' Was he drunk that evening ? Or was he overwhelmed by fatigue, by the weight of his work, his colossal labour, he who, during the last sixteen months, had frequently not slept three hours a night ? To-day, this 14th of Thermidor, the Seine was not red Its changing waters flowed on, dancing in the light. With his hat pulled down over his face, he proceeded along the quays. He paused before the Louvre of the Valois, his vigorous, thick-set form wrapped in his blue frock-coat. He continued his way to the Tuileries.

At that hour, Chandelier, Limage, and five members of the Committee of General Security, accompanied by Debreaux, the police-officer, presented themselves at his dwelling. They found there only a woman and children. They called upon Citizeness Fouquier-Tinville to tell them where the Public Prosecutor was.

" At the Convention, at least that is what the messengers of the Tribunal have said."

" What has he gone to do at the Convention ? "

" I don't know, at all."

" You are deceiving us, for you knew that a warrant had been issued for your husband's arrest and trial."

" Yes, I knew "

" Who told you ? "

" He, himself ; but I do not know who told him. All I know is that the news was brought to him at his office ; but I do not know the bearer. The office attendants might tell you."

They immediately asked of the first attendant they saw, Simon Malparti, if he knew who warned Fouquier.

" A private citizen who is the uncle of Poincarré, a secretary in the prosecutor's office."

Malparti offered to take Chandelier into the offices to look for this uncle in the presence of Derozière, the policeman. Cauchois was found in the refreshment room.

He was put through the usual cross-examination. He told how he informed his nephew, and how, when he heard it, " the little hunchback " as he was called at the Tribunal, said that Fouquier ought to be warned immediately. He had taken the Public Prosecutor aside and had told him that there was a warrant for his arrest ; that he had heard the decree pronounced. Fouquier had answered, in the presence of Deliège, the Vice-President of the Tribunal, that he was quite easy in his mind, and was waiting until they came to arrest him. It was Malparti who told Limage and Chandelier that, when he left the refreshment-room, Fouquier went up to his office, and afterwards to the Convention

It was the little hunchback's turn to appear before the members of the Committee.

His name was Jean Feuilles. He was twenty-seven years old. He was born at Viviers, in the district of Coyron, in the Ardèche. He was an employee in the prosecutor's office of the Revolutionary Tribunal, and resided in the City, at No. 14, Rue Lanterne. He confirmed the statements of Cauchois. They overwhelmed him with questions.

" From whom did you hear that a warrant had been issued for Fouquier-Tinville's arrest ? "

" I heard it from a citizen of whom I know nothing except that he is a friend of Citizen Poincarré."

" Did you not say that the Public Prosecutor should be warned at once ? "

" I said so along with several others who were present, as to who spoke first, I do not remember. All I know is that the news was brought to the witness-room, that Poincarré communicated it to those who were in the Council Chamber, and that it was when Poincarré came down from the Chamber that it was said warning ought to be given to Fouquier-Tinville, who was then in the refreshment room "

" Could you give the names of those who were present and who said with you that Fouquier ought to be warned ? "

" I cannot be certain of any of them. I know that Poincarré was present , I went up with him to the refreshment-room. Poincarré did not come up."

" You are afraid of giving the names of citizens, but the truth will come out "

" If I were sure, I would give the names, but I am afraid of speaking at a venture."

" Yet a witness declares that it was you who spoke."

" Certainly, I spoke."

" With what intention ? "

" I had none "

" Did you say that some one ought to go up to the refreshment-room to warn him ? "

" I said so, and as a matter of fact I went up with several citizens whose names I do not remember and with the man who brought us the news."

" Did you not take him to the refreshment-room ? "

" I went with him there , that is all I can say."

" Who spoke in the refreshment-room ? "

" I said to Fouquier : ' Here is a citizen who comes from the Convention and who has been a witness of what has just taken place ' After which, that citizen, Poincarré's friend, informed Fouquier of the decree which ordered his arrest."

" Yet a witness states that it was you who took him by the arm, brought him to the refreshment-room, took Fouquier aside, and told him what you had just heard."

" I do not remember exactly what took place , as regards what I said to Fouquier, I refer you to my previous answer."

" Knowing that this decree was in existence, instead of warning him, why did not you, yourself, arrest him ? "

" I was not certain about it."

Cauchois and Feuilles were searched and their papers examined, but nothing suspicious was found. The two employees of the prosecutor's office were arrested, and taken to the Committee of General Security as suspected of having helped in Fouquier-Tinville's escape

A long search then began of the premises of the Revolutionary Tribunal and the Public Prosecutor's apartments. All the documents found in the prosecutor's office and the registry were kept there under the guard of Captain Adnet and his lieutenant, Bernard. Sentries were placed at all the doors of the registry and the prosecutor's office. The papers in Fouquier's apartments were collected and placed in a cupboard near the door, to the right of the entrance-hall. Citizens Courtier and Derozières, the gendarmes, were appointed their guardians. Those which the commissioners found in " Citizeness Fouquier's " portfolio were placed under seal.

The windows of the apartment opened on a little balcony overlooking the Quai de l'Horloge. In the course of their search, Courtier and Derozières, who had gone to the window, noticed a bundle of papers that had fallen or been thrown on the balcony. This the agents of the Committee of General Security seized, and it was found to contain six documents which were placed in an envelope to be sent to the Committee.

These judicial operations were not finished when Captain

Adnet and Lieutenant Bernard announced an important piece of news to the commissioners. Fouquier-Tinville had just gone back to the Conciergerie, where he had surrendered himself as a prisoner Botot-Dumesnil, commander of the police attached to the Tribunal, placed him under arrest.[1] Richard, the turnkey, inscribed his name on the prison registrar. The doors of the gaol closed upon him.

But the Conciergerie was full of those " counter-revolutionaries " and those " conspirators " whom the Public Prosecutor was reserving for the " batches " of the following days. Two days previously, on the 12th of Thermidor, if we are to believe an usher of the Tribunal, he had said : " The people must be satisfied. The guillotine is busy. It will be busier still " [2] Fouquier was recognised. Hoots and shouts of rage echoed all about him. " Wretch ! Scoundrel ! " hostile and desperate voices called out. He was surrounded and driven into a corner. He was on the point of falling when the janitor and his assistants intervened. To protect this extraordinary prisoner, they shut him up in a dark room, under the guard of a gendarme.

There, at the mercy of his own thoughts, in the dark, like a wild beast shut in his den, he waited and thought.

What hatred he had unloosed ! What a cursed, execrated name was his ! How all those people detested him ! And yet he asked himself whether he deserved such a fate. Day and night he had worked " to lay the foundations of the Revolution " so far as it lay in his power. Ah, why on the 22nd of Prairial, had his name not been erased from the list of those who composed the Tribunal ? Why would they

---

[1] " Paris, 14th of Thermidor of the year II of the French Republic, one and indivisible

" Citizen President,

    " I inform you that in conformity with the decree of the Convention of to-day's date, I have had Fouquier, the ex-Public Prosecutor of the Revolutionary Tribunal, placed under arrest, and that he is now detained at the Conciergerie.

" Greeting and fraternity,

    " Major commanding the Gendarmerie of the Tribunals,
                                                    " B. DUMESNIL "

[2] Joly's evidence at Fouquier-Tinville's trial.

I

regard him as the creature of Robespierre and Saint-Just?
Why treat him as a conspirator, as an enemy of the country,
he who " prided himself on being known as having always
succoured oppressed innocence, the poor and the patriotic"?

The night was passing. From hour to hour the vision of
his past work grew clearer before him. His methodical mind,
accustomed to the quibbles of legal procedure, began to
classify the charges that were to be brought against him,
which he had learned that afternoon at the Committee. Was
he thinking of his loved ones, of his wife and children who
were in their rooms in the Palace of Justice watching in
suspense? Doubtless, but he seemed to have been neither
softened nor dejected. He was coolly preparing for the
struggle, just as he coolly performed the duties of his
terrible magistracy. He was going to set to work on his
defence

As the night drew to an end, he was still writing, drawing
up his first memorial. This he sent to the Committee of
General Security, with a short note to Louis (of the Bas-
Rhin).

" Paris, this 16th of Thermidor of the second year of the
Republic, one and indivisible.

" Citizen Representative,

" Deign to oblige me by presenting to the Committee of which you are a member the enclosed memorial
which I send you ; I am innocent, I ask for justice.

" Greeting and fraternity,

" A. Q. FOUQUIER."

The entire memorial should be read to show Fouquier's
state of mind at the moment following his arrest. The
lawyer, the subtle Procurator, aimed at proving that he
was not guilty. He wished to appear free from anxiety.
He thought it necessary to destroy one by one the prejudices
and the imputations against him. He would invoke in his
favour humanity and justice. He claimed to be innocent,
a victim even, and seemed to believe that he would soon
be free.

" *Memorial for the Defence, to the General Committee of Public Safety of the Convention.*"

" *On behalf of Antoine Quentin Fouquier, ex-Public Prosecutor to the Revolutionary Tribunal, who surrendered himself voluntarily at the Conciergerie, and was brought before the Revolutionary Tribunal by a decree of the 14th of Thermidor.*"

" 1. I am charged with having made out writs of indictment against patriots. An examination of the registers refutes that charge ; for by inspecting them one can see that for the most part the indictments have been directed against acknowledged conspirators. It is possible, however, that among the informations lodged by malevolent persons, there may have been some directed against patriots. It was my great anxiety to protect myself from such scheming ; and if such a thing has happened, it is certainly a misfortune that renders me guilty ; for, since informations and charges came into existence, the law imposes on the Public Prosecutor the duty of ordering the proceedings against the suspects indicated. It is for the jurors to determine in their wisdom the value of the charge , and the conduct of the Public Prosecutor in such a case is to bring forward the prisoner's defence. Now, it is notorious that at the Tribunal I have never neglected this glorious task. I pride myself on being known as having always succoured oppressed innocence, the poor, and the patriotic.

" 2. I am charged with having been one of the creatures of Robespierre and Saint-Just. I have never been in the latter's house. I was even ignorant of where he lived. As for Robespierre, I have only been at his house once, the day of the attempt on Citizen Collot d'Herbois, just as I presented myself at the house of the latter. I have never been there since. I defy anybody to prove the contrary.

" 3. I am suspected of having had knowledge of the conspiracy which broke out on the ninth. On my honour I protest that I had no knowledge of that conspiracy until the moment of its discovery by the Convention ; I protest similarly that no overture was made to me by any of the conspirators, and that if one of them had presumed to do so, I should have had the courage to inform against him as I have had the courage to fill the perilous post I occupied since the creation of the Tribunal. If any of these scoundrels had made overtures to me in any way whatever regarding that horrible conspiracy, should I, on the 10th of Thermidor, have asked in court, as I did, for the law to be applied against the Robespierres, Saint-Just, Fleuriot, Payan, Hanriot, and Dumas, all acknowledged heads of that conspiracy ? Should I not have rendered myself liable to be pointed out by them, if, in truth, I had been their accomplice ? I have fulfilled my duty towards those monsters, as towards all others, because I have a pure conscience and have never been implicated in any plot.

" In support of that conduct, I point out that, when dining about four months ago at the house of Citizen Lecointre, the Deputy, with several others, in particular Citizen Merlin (of Thionville), I had a conversation with him that doubtless he will remember, which will prove how much I detested Robespierre's despotism.

" A few days before the last reorganization of the Tribunal, being informed that it was desired to reduce the number of jurors from nine to seven, I believed it my duty to represent to the Committee of Public Safety that the Tribunal having up to that time enjoyed public confidence, this reduction would infallibly cause it to lose that confidence. It would provide an opportunity for saying that the change was only contrived because those responsible for this reduction had not found enough creatures devoted to them. Robespierre, then on the Committee, shut my mouth by saying that it was only aristocrats who could speak in such a way.

" Several other members of the Committee were present. This remark caused my name, as I have since been told, to be erased several times from the list of those appointed by the decree of the 22nd of Prairial. I do not know to what I owe the misfortune of having been restored to the list, for.

but for that restoration, I should not to-day be groaning in chains.

" As for the provisions of the decree of the 22nd of Prairial, I have several times spoken of their rigour to the Committee of General Security ; several members must remember it ; they themselves acknowledged the severity of the provisions. They must have asked daily for their reform ; but, as for me, I could not refuse to execute the decree without being regarded and even treated as a counter-revolutionary   The members of the Committee of General Security must also remember that I have frequently spoken to them of the persistent opposition of Robespierre to the execution of the decree relating to Catherine Théot,[1] and that it was agreed that Citizen Vadier should make a supplementary report.   As a result of this I sent him all the documents, and they are now in his possession.

" For about a month the increased work of my post has not allowed me to go to the Jacobin Club.   I have not, in consequence, heard any of the speeches or denunciations of Robespierre's conspiracy, or the diatribes of the scoundrel Dumas.   I have heard them spoken of, and it is known how severely I censured them.   Citizen Martel, the Deputy, is also in a position to attest how, in a conversation I had with him about eight days before the conspiracy broke out, I blamed the despotism that Robespierre exercised over the Committee of Public Safety.

" My conduct on the 9th of Thermidor is easy to establish.   I was in court until half-past two o'clock.   I dined with several colleagues, and returned to my office at the Palace about half-past five in the afternoon.   The clerks, attendants, and other persons employed at the Tribunal are in a position to attest this fact   They are also able to prove

---

[1] The visionary whom Vadier had represented, in his speech in the Convention on the 27th of Prairial in the year II , as keeping, at her dwelling in the Rue Contrescarpe, " a primary school of fanaticism," and whom he gave out to be an agent of Pitt   She was reported to the Revolutionary Tribunal   But Robespierre caused an order to be conveyed to Fouquier-Tinville to postpone her trial. See Vilate's memoirs, *The Mysteries of the Mother of God Unveiled.*

that, in spite of the many emissaries sent to me by the Commune to induce the members of the Tribunal and myself to enter its bosom, and to acknowledge it alone, my answer was that I acknowledged only the Convention, that I would remain at my post, as I did until one o'clock in the morning of the 10th, and that, accompanied only by Citizens Desgaigné the usher, Beudelot, and Demay, I went to the assembled Committees of Public Safety and General Security, where I was seen by a great part of the members and by Citizens Thuriot and Merlin (of Thionville), the Deputies, who went there I returned to the Palace, where Citizen Léonard Bourdon found me on the 10th at half-past five ; all these facts are notorious and easy to prove It is difficult to show a purer conduct

" Yet I am summoned before the Tribunal, charged with having vexed and persecuted the patriots, although, at the same time, I am called a *wretch and a scoundrel* by all the counter-revolutionaries who are detained at the Conciergerie. I am forced to stay all day in a room without windows in order to keep myself from their rage, notwithstanding all the efforts of the janitor.

" However, consulting my conscience, I have done nothing to bring me to such a fate During the sixteen months that I have performed the painful duties of Public Prosecutor I have drawn up the writ of indictment against Marie Antoinette, and caused all the great conspirators to feel the sword of the Law. I, who would not find in any country an inch of ground to lay my head, I, who am the born enemy of all counter-revolutionaries, who would hew me in pieces if they could, I, who have spent night and day in laying the foundations of the Revolution so far as it lay in my power , I, who have never acted save according to the laws emanating from the Convention ; I, who *do not fear* the severest examination of all my papers even though I should have *to remain the longer in chains!* The greater part of the members of the Committees of Public Safety and General Security know my principles, my actions, and my thoughts , it remains therefore for me only to submit myself entirely to their justice. My memorial has been written without pretension and even with a sort of negligence in style which comes from the sad position in which I find myself ; but it expresses the truth.

" A. Q. FOUQUIER." [1]

" Paris, this 16th of Thermidor.

[1] Archives Nationales, W 500, 1st dossier, p. 111

PART II

THE PRISONER

CHAPTER VI

THOUGH a prisoner at the Conciergerie, the ex-Public Prosecutor was not kept in solitary confinement. News from outside reached him. He knew through the vigilant agency of his wife what was happening at the Convention and at the Jacobin Club. She wrote to him and kept him acquainted with what was said and what preparations were being made against him.

He was neither downcast nor demoralised. He was tenacious, shrewd, and apparently calm. His defence engaged all his attention. It may be summed up in this : that during the past sixteen months, he had *provoked* (it is his own expression) the trials of more than two thousand four hundred accused persons. He claimed that he had acted only according to the decrees of the Convention, in conformity with the laws " of justice and humanity." He was tireless in furnishing proofs of this with a sort of unconscious obstinacy.

His first memorial for his defence was dated the 16th of Thermidor. On the 17th, in a second memorial, he proceeded to insist upon certain isolated facts, giving them a special importance, discussing them, refuting complaints. He had just learned that the imputation made against him of having summoned patriots before the Revolutionary Tribunal had taken a more precise form, that those patriots had been named, that they were the inhabitants of Strasburg, who had been tried and guillotined less than two months before, on the 29th of Messidor (July 17). He hastened to reply to the Committee in a " supplement " to his memorial for the defence of the day before. He proceeded to set out the facts. "Deprived of all documents," he wrote from memory, yet his memorial was excellent

Lebas and Saint-Just, sent on a mission to the Departments of the Upper and Lower Rhine, had caused the arrest of Euloge Schneider, " the executioner of Alsace," who had been convicted of exactions, extortions, violations, crimes of all sorts Euloge Schneider was none other than the Public Prosecutor of Strasburg, Fouquier's provincial colleague

The Strasburg patriots in question, Yung, a shoemaker, Michelot,[1] a paymaster of the army of the Rhine, Monnet, a teacher, Frédéric Edelmann, a musician, and Louis Edelmann, a musical instrument maker, were, according to Fouquier, Schneider's partisans They declaimed to such an extent against his arrest and the doings of the representatives of the people, calling them " disorganisers " and " cannibals," that Leban and Saint-Just had caused them to be arrested and sent before the Revolutionary Tribunal. Fouquier thus exculpates himself

" The documents relating to the affair were sent to me by the Committee of Public Safety. I made out the indictment from those documents. In the course of the pleadings, I took care to remark that these suspects had given great proofs of patriotism since the Revolution. I laid stress, for this purpose, on all the attestations that they produced for me But several of those attestations were contradicted by later retractations from the regenerated society of Strasburg, all of which are attached to the documents in the registry of the Tribunal One of the accused has been proved innocent. Where, then, is my crime in this business ? Could I refuse to make out an indictment or to bring to trial individuals sent to the Tribunal by representatives of the people in the course of their mission ? I could no more do that in their case than in the case of those sent by the Convention The Law imposed that duty on me. . . ."[2]

What he does not say, what he cannot say, is that when

---

[1] Michelot was acquitted.
[2] Archives Nationales, W. 500, 1st dossier, p 110.

ANTOINE QUENTIN FOUQUIER-TINVILLE
From a contemporary lithograph

the representatives of the people on mission to the army of the Rhine had recovered from their prejudices and were convinced of the patriotism and innocence of the accused persons, they had caused them to be set at liberty. The documents of the Revolutionary Tribunal[1] contain instructive certificates given to those Republican patriots by the administrative body of Strasburg Suddenly, on the night between the 12th and 13th of Prairial, they had again been arrested by order of the Committee of Public Safety. It was impossible for them to guess the motives for this arrest. Was it that, under the sway of informers and of terror, " the regenerated society " of Strasburg denied the good certificates which the administrative body had given ? Vainly may one search the documents of the Tribunal for those denials.

Fouquier says that he took care, " *in the course of the pleadings*, to remark that the suspects had given great proofs of patriotism since the Revolution." But this observation in favour of the accused persons was made *orally*, and nothing concerning it exists among the documents in the registry. What did exist and what still exists there are, on the contrary, these lines of the indictment, made out and signed by Fouquier, and copied by one of his secretaries

" The two Edelmanns are charged with having been the associates and principal heads of the faction of Schneider whom national justice has struck with its sword . . . They have become instruments of the counter-revolutionaries and partisans of the suspected persons in custody." Each of the jurors could have read those lines in the copy of the indictment that was provided for him. They clearly marked out the brothers Edelmann for the guillotine

In his " supplement " of the 17th of Thermidor, Fouquier also lays stress, for his defence, on the fact that the pleadings of the Tribunal, in regard to the Strasburg patriots, "in spite of the rigour of the law of Prairial, lasted nearly three hours " Now on that day, 34 accused persons, 34 *arraigned persons* as Fouquier called them, 34 prisoners

---

[1] W 421, dossier 956, 3rd part

grouped by him in a single " batch," in one and the same indictment, had appeared at the hearing. The five men of Strasburg sat on the prisoners' benches beside a freeholder of the Charente-Inférieure, a courier of the Committee of Public Safety, a wheelwright and locksmith of Vaugirard, a man from the Ardèche, a syndic from the Abbey of Andlau (Bas-Rhin), a secretary of the popular tribunal of Marseilles, a farmer of the Department of the Rhône, a hair-dresser of Bar-le-Duc, a former merchant, the President of the Revolutionary Committee of Clichy, accused of having had the impertinence to ask " whether his ass was not in the Commune," the wife of the cook of the English ambassador at Paris, a teacher of mathematics of the Rue de la Verrerie, Mulot de la Ménardière, a citizen of Compiègne, and sixteen nuns and Carmelite sisters. Out of 34 accused persons, 30 were sent to the scaffold on that 29th of Messidor.

It is possible that the pleadings in regard to the Strasburg patriots—one of whom, Michelot, was acquitted—lasted nearly three hours. Fouquier affirms that *the fact is known.* It remains, none the less 1st, that the brothers Edelmann, the shoemaker Yung, and the teacher Monnet were executed ; 2nd, that those Alsatians were despatched to the Barrier of Vincennes with 26 other male and female companions in misfortune who had come to Paris from the four corners of France ; 3rd, that they were treated as conspirators although they were not even acquainted with one another. It was doubtless to avert the charge of so monstrous an abuse of power that Fouquier took care to end his *Supplement* with these lines :

" There is an important reflection, Citizen-Representatives, that I invite you to make in your wisdom. That is that during the sixteen months that I have occupied this rigorous office of Public Prosecutor I have *provoked* the trials of more than two thousand four hundred counter-revolutionaries, each more furious than the other. Neither fortune nor consideration could stop me. The execution of the laws, justice and humanity, such has always been my rule of conduct. This firm and invariable course has made me an incalculable number of enemies among aristocrats and others. That is the source of the imputations that are made against me. Ought I to expect such a fate, I, who for the last sixteen months have often not slept three hours a night ? Never was a request for pardon made by me to the Committees except on behalf of patriots and unfortunate persons How, after such conduct, can I be taxed with having instituted proceedings against patriots ? I rely always on your justice. A. Q. FOUQUIER. This 17th of Thermidor." [1]

On the same day he wrote to Louis (of the Bas-Rhin), a member of the Committee of General Security and a Deputy of the Convention. He requested him " to give orders " that the gendarme stationed in his room should be withdrawn He asked for a little air, hoping that the Committee would authorise the gaoler of the Conciergerie to place him in a room adjoining his own apartments.[2] He would be better off there. He could devote himself effectively to his work.

Two days later, on the 19th of Thermidor, he had drawn up a fresh document of considerable length which he entitled, *General Memorial for My Defence.* He addressed it to the Convention.

On many points this *Memorial* is a repetition of its predecessor. But in it Fouquier gives his defence a development all the more interesting as it is only from these documents that we know to-day how the ex-Public Prosecutor faced his judges.

Meanwhile, the reorganisation of the Revolutionary Tribunal was conducted rapidly, in a new spirit and with new men. The sanguinary law of the 22nd of Prairial was repealed. The question of intention was restored. This was the accession of a new form of jurisprudence.

Fouquier then adopted another course with the Convention. Towards the end of the session of the 21st of Thermidor (August 8, 1794), presided over by Merlin (of Douai), when Lakanal had just given an account of the state of public

---

[1] Archives Nationales, W. 500, 1st dossier, p. 110.
[2] W 500, 1st dossier, p. 108

feeling in Dordogne and the neighbouring departments, a secretary read the following letter

" Citizen President, I have matters of importance to the public interest as well as necessary for my own justification to communicate to the Convention I solicit, in consequence, from the Convention the favour of being admitted to the bar in order to expound them before it. Signed : A. Q. FOUQUIER, ex-Public Prosecutor to the Revolutionary Tribunal, and under arrest."

Lecointre (of Versailles) immediately addressed the House

" I convert into the form of a motion Fouquier-Tinville's petition, not in order that he may escape the sword of the law, but in order that the Convention may learn from his own mouth what were the levers that moved him "

There was applause. The Convention resolved that Fouquier-Tinville be brought to the bar and there heard.

Pocholle [1] : " Fouquier-Tinville can only come to speak of himself or of others. He ought not to speak of himself except before the Revolutionary Tribunal (Murmurs.) It seems to me that no different measures ought to be taken in regard to him than in regard to other accused persons."

One of the secretaries then read the decree passed against Fouquier.

Lefiot [2] · " It does not seem to me possible to grant the request made by Fouquier-Tinville He is an immoral man and has been condemned by public opinion. It is clear that he can only come here to throw the firebrand of discord, in continuance of the system which he adopted while filling his office. He can come here to kindle hatred (Murmurs.

---

[1] Pierre Pomponne Amédée, Deputy for the Seine-Inférieure. He, along with Charlier, caused *Commune affranchie* to be given back its name of Lyon on the 4th of Fructidor of the year II. (August 21, 1794)

[2] Jean-Alban, Deputy for the Nièvre, distinguished himself by his opposition to the course which the Convention followed after the 9th of Thermidor of the year II , and, above all, after the 1st of Prairial of the year III. He was arrested on the 21st of Thermidor of the year III. (August 6, 1795) and remained nearly three months in prison.

Several voices · " There is no hatred among the members of the Convention ") I say that parties have existed. I say that it is to be feared that this person may come to revive them. (Further murmurs.) I mean that if he were referred back to the Committees it is possible that he would accuse the Committees and that the truth would not be known. Well, then, appoint a Commission from among yourselves. (Murmurs) I had to say what was in my mind."

The President · " The observation not finding any support, I put it to the vote that the resolution be carried."

The resolution was carried. Shortly afterwards, the President announced that Fouquier-Tinville had arrived. The Convention ordered him to be admitted He entered and the President gave him permission to speak

Fouquier-Tinville " Having been informed that the warrant of arrest that has been issued against me was based chiefly upon presumed conferences with Robespierre, because I went every evening to the Committee of Public Safety, I considered that I ought to ask to be heard by the Convention so as to give it an account of the facts and motives of those proceedings.

" Until the advent of the Revolutionary Government, the Tribunal and the Public Prosecutor had no intercourse with the Committee of Public Safety, unless when they were summoned to it. Their intercourse was closer with the Committee of General Security, to which is entrusted the supervision of arrests and the revolutionary police of the Republic. However, they did not go even to this Committee, unless they were summoned. Fifteen days after the establishment of the Revolutionary Government, I was summoned to the Committee of Public Safety. When I reached the room outside that in which the Committee deliberates, Robespierre came to me and made a violent scene because I did not keep the Committee acquainted with what was taking place at the Tribunal. I told him that it was not usual for me to do this, that I had as yet received no orders to do it, but that I would do so if that was the wish of the

κ

Committee. He answered me, in that despotic tone that is known, that *the Committee so desired*. After that I went every evening to the Committee and on several days I saw him alone in the same room where I met him the first time, and where he heaped very bitter reproaches on me because I did not cause such-and-such generals and individuals to be brought to trial.

" Finally, one day I was brought into the Committee, and I gave it an account of all the doings of the Tribunal. At the period of Hébert's trial, closer relations were established. I acquainted the assembled Committee with the whole of the information which gradually came to the Tribunal connected with that faction.

" Before the law of the 22nd of Prairial was passed, I was informed there was a project for reducing the number of jurors to seven or nine, I regarded that project as dangerous I was at the Committee, and, in the presence of several members, I said that it was impolitic to reduce the number of jurors in a Tribunal that had hitherto enjoyed public confidence, it would create a belief that the number was diminished because a sufficient number of subservient creatures could not be found Robespierre said to me that it was only aristocrats who could reason thus. I have since been told that those remarks caused my name to be erased from the table of members of the Tribunal, and it would have been well if it had been so I was further told that Robespierre had a project for causing my arrest. It appears that he could not attain either of his ends, for I was retained.

" When I read the law of the 22nd of Prairial, I found it frightful. I did not speak of it at the Committee, because Robespierre was always there to close my mouth. I only testified my regret to some members of the Committee of General Security, and Citizens Amar, Voulland and Vadier told me that they were engaged in getting some of its articles reformed. Robespierre's despotism rendered it impossible to execute this project, for he extorted all the decrees he wished.

" At Danton's trial I wrote to the Committee to know

whether I ought to grant the demand of the accused that the witnesses whom they summoned should be heard For answer I received a decree which closed my mouth, and I obeyed the law.

" After examining an affair in which Citizen Gayvernon, a brother of the Deputy, and an adjutant called Barthélemy were implicated, I saw that there was nothing against them, and proposed to ask that they should be set free. Robespierre said to me ' *I have learned that you have a project for liberating those two individuals. I order you in the name of the Committee to bring forward the documents.*' I answered him that it was for the Tribunal to inquire into the matter, and to pronounce their liberation, if there was ground for it. Citizen Gayvernon came and asked me why I did not cause his brother, who was not guilty, to be set free I answered that my hands were tied, that he could inform the Convention of the fact, and that I would support him. This was also at the Committee, for I never saw him in private, either at his house or elsewhere.

" He wished to know the names of the Deputies who had given evidence for Kellerman's defence. I said that I did not remember them. He insisted and asked me · ' Was it not Dubois Crancé and Gauthier ? ' I excused myself, alleging my defective memory He asked me the same thing about General Hoche It was always in the name of the Committee that he spoke to me If I had followed the orders that he gave me, the trial of those citizens would have ended long ago

" It has been said that 1 furnished Robespierre with lists of the persons who were to be tried I should have been very guilty if I had done so, and I declare that I have had nothing to do with it But Robespierre had spies and agents in the Tribunal, and President Dumas was his accomplice

" He made the Committee of Public Safety pass a resolution, which is still in my drawer, and of which I was given notice lest I should forget it This resolution ordered that I should be bound to furnish to the Committee each *décade*[1] a statement of the persons who were to be placed on trial during the following *décade*. Every evening, in order to conform to another resolution of which I was also given notice, I furnished the list of persons who had been condemned or acquitted during the day, and it was then that Robespierre indulged in angry observations to the bearer of that list

" Never have I had any secret conference with Robespierre. Never have I received any order from him when alone. Citizen Merlin (of Thionville) can also tell you that, at a meal where Citizen Lecointre was also present, I spoke of Robespierre in a manner far from flattering. That caused me to be denounced to Robespierre's secret cabal as conspiring with the Deputies against him. I have never had any communication with him I groaned under his despotism. I acted only in accordance with the laws and the decrees. I would not have taken a step beyond them."

Merlin (of Thionville) · " I demand that Fouquier explain his conduct in regard to the conspiracy of the foreigner and that of the Luxembourg "

Bréard[2] : " I demand that he explain his conduct in regard to Catherine Théot."

Several voices " No discussion."

Tallien · " The Convention ought not to subject Fouquier to a cross-examination. He has asked to be heard on very important matters, and, up to the present, I have heard nothing worth listening to. Robespierre's conspiracy contained an infinite number of threads which are still hidden, and which will soon be disclosed. But it is not for the Convention to question Fouquier on particular facts. If he has declarations to make for the safety of the country, let him make them spontaneously A man such as he, who has been initiated into the mysteries of iniquity, ought to have valuable information. I also could bring facts against him. But it is useless to accuse him, since, for a long time,

---

[1] *Cf* note p 66

[2] Jean-Jacques, Deputy for the Charente-Inférieure, had spoken against Robespierre, and, on the 3rd of Thermidor, had opposed the printing of his speech.

Masquerier, pinxt.

MADAME TALLIEN.

W. Ward, sculpt.

France has been accusing him   I demand that he be not cross-examined at the bar "

Merlin   " I demand that he be heard "

Fouquier-Tinville   ' I am going to relate the facts as they occurred.   It was Lanne, Robespierre's agent, who was sent to the Luxembourg to discover if there were a conspiracy there   It was upon his report that I received from the Committee the list of persons implicated in that conspiracy.

" Dumas wanted 160 prisoners to be put on trial at once. He said that the Committee had ordered it   I did not believe him, and wrote to the Committee   I learned that my letter had been opened by Robespierre, who did not want to make any reply   I was at the Committee that evening   I found it assembled, and remember that I saw there Citizens Collot, Billaud, Saint-Just, Robespierre, and another of whose name I am not certain, but whom I believe to be Citizen Carnot   And it was decided that the 160 persons would be put on trial in three lots

" As for Catherine Théot, I received an order to bring the documents to the Committee in accordance with the resolution ordering her trial   I went there   In the first room I found Dumas, to whom Robespierre had doubtless given instructions   The Committee were assembled   I placed the documents on the desk   Robespierre took possession of them   And when he began to read them, every one went out, so that I was left alone with him and Dumas   He ordered me to leave the bundle   I obeyed and reported the matter to the Committee of General Security, which was especially entrusted with the supervision of the Tribunal "

After this declaration, Fouquier was, by order of the President, taken back to the Conciergerie   Merlin (of Douai) submitted for discussion a project for a decree on the organisation of the new Revolutionary Tribunal   At three o'clock the session was adjourned [1]

On the 12th of Fructidor (August 29), the ex-Public Prosecutor's case was before the Convention   Lecointre

[1] *Moniteur*, session of the 21st of Thermidor.

(of Versailles) had, on that day, undertaken to attack seven of his colleagues and to prove that Billaud-Varenne, Collot d'Herbois, and Barère, members of the Committee of Public Safety, and Vadier, Amar, Voulland, and David, members of the Committee of General Security, were guilty of and responsible for the crimes of the Terror, and for the excesses committed by the Revolutionary Tribunal. Before the Assembly, at first astonished and then hostile, he had read twenty-six charges which he had formulated. These complaints seemed to be based on certain articles in Fouquier's memorials for his defence.

A Deputy, Goujon, exclaimed · " What credit does Fouquier-Tinville deserve, that man whose interest it is to plunge a sword into the bosom of the Convention in order to save himself ? "

Billaud, " the rectilinear patriot," raging at Lecointre's accusation, asked · " Who does not see that this is an infernal intrigue contrived by Fouquier-Tinville to divert upon us all the odium of his conduct ? "

This session of the 12th and that of the 13th ended in the confusion of Lecointre, who could not prove his charges, and whose speech was continually interrupted by the cry : " Proofs ! Proofs ! " whilst he could not furnish any serious evidence When he ceased reading, there was, in the Assembly, an outburst of murmurs, invectives, and hootings.

There were shouts of, " Send him to the Petites Maisons ! "

It must be admitted that he had no evidence. Fouquier-Tinville's *Memorials* alone had furnished him with arguments.[1] Elie Lacoste demanded that a warrant be issued for Lecointre's arrest, and Cambon concluded thus :

" To-day when everything is made clear, when no evidence worthy of credit has been presented to you, and when you are convinced of the falseness of the accusation brought against several members of the National Convention, you ought, by a solemn resolution, to declare that it is a calumny."

[1] Lecointre, to whom Fouquier had not sent his *Memorials*, could have become acquainted with them through their having been communicated to him by Merlin (of Douai), Moyse Bayle, or Louis (of the Bas-Rhin).

This crushing proposition was voted unanimously in the midst of the most eager applause. A bad omen for Fouquier !

In the course of these debates, Billaud-Varenne and Legendre had made two mistakes, the one in affirming that, to reward Fouquier for the documents he had furnished, he had been transferred to Sainte-Pélagie, *without an order from the Committees* ; the other in stating that the precaution had been taken of placing him in solitary confinement there.

Now, Fouquier had been transferred by an order of the Committee of General Security, as we have seen. He was not in solitary confinement, since, on the 14th of Fructidor, he wrote the following letter to Moyse Bayle and to Louis (of the Bas-Rhin) " from the depths of the prison into which he ought never to have been thrown " :

" Not reading any newspapers, for they are not brought into the houses of detention for some not very obvious reason, I have just been informed that Citizen Lecointre, at the session of the 12th, has formulated twenty-seven (*sic*) charges against several Deputies, in particular Citizens Amar, Vadier, and Voulland   1st, that Amar and Voulland had said to the Public Prosecutor when handing over to him the decree concerning the affair of Danton and the others : ' *You ought to be easy now. This is something to bring them to reason,*' and Amar, Voulland, and Vadier, when there was a rumour in the Tribunal that the majority of the jurors were voting for the innocence of the prisoners, *had passed through the refreshment-room and had induced President Herman* to employ *all possible means* to get a sentence of death passed and that this was done by Herman, who spoke against the accused, and who urged the jurors who had voted for death to threaten the others with the vengeance of the Committees, and that these two charges were signed by me.

" I am ignorant whether those facts have been set forth at the Convention by Citizen Lecointre. But what is certain is that it is impossible to have based those two charges on my memorial or on any writing that has emanated from me. For, were I to perish a thousand times, independently of the improbability of those two charges, they are absolutely strange to me, and have not been *communicated by me either verbally or in writing to Citizen Lecointre*. I do not even remember that Citizens Amar and Voulland handed me the decree in question. As for Citizen Vadier, I only knew long afterwards that he came to the Tribunal. *He did not come into my office*, nor did I see him at the hearing of the case.

" Yet, by an error of journalists or others, here am I brought before the public as an informer against Deputies whose testimony I invoke in my memorials to justify myself. Is there a sadder or more unfortunate position than mine, after having spent days and nights in the public interest ?

" I cannot explain my conduct in regard to accusations that have reached me only in a very imperfect form. Perhaps if the Committee would inform me of the charges, I might have another answer to make to them. But it would be necessary for me to be heard. I shall never depart from the truth, even were I to suffer what I do not deserve. I therefore expect everything from its justice."

The publicity given a little later to the crimes of Joseph Lebon at Arras, and of Carrier at Nantes, must have warned Fouquier that his hour was near, and that his turn to be tried was coming. On the 28th of Fructidor, he wrote to Claude-Emmanuel Dobsen, a former judge of the Tribunal of the Terror,[1] and now the President of the new Revolutionary Tribunal ·

" To Citizen Dobsen, President of the Revolutionary Tribunal. At the Palace of Justice.

" Pélagie, this 28th of Fructidor of the second year of the Republic, one and indivisible.

" Citizen President,

" Informed that I am to be brought to trial on one of the *sans culottides*,[2] I have not too much time to collect all the documents necessary for my defence, the greater

---

[1] Dobsen had been cashiered on the 22nd of Prairial.
[2] Complementary days in the Republican Calendar.—Tr.

part of which are in the hands of the Deputies who have proceeded to the examination of the papers at the Popular Commission. As all the documents can only be collected by the defender whom I shall choose, I inform you that yesterday I invited Citizen Lafleutrie to the Tribunal to undertake my defence, which he has promised to do.

" But it is necessary for him to have permission to consult with me. I request you to give him this permission, unless indeed you consider that the cross-examination should take place first; in that case I pray you to let it take place at Pélagie, as was the case with the men of Nantes and others who were here, if you do not judge it suitable to transfer me to the Conciergerie there to await the day of my trial. I have received none of the papers that it had been agreed should be given me in order that I might know of what I am accused.

"A. Q. FOUQUIER"[1]

On that 28th of Fructidor, the ninety-four inhabitants of Nantes had just been acquitted by the Tribunal after a hearing lasting seven days. They had waited ten months for their trial.[2]

When Fouquier-Tinville heard of the verdict in his prison, he must have congratulated himself on it. It was through him that the piteous victims of Carrier, of Chaux, and of Gouillin, were still alive. When Public Prosecutor, he had protracted their trial, not wishing to plead against them, considering that the evidence sent to his office by the

---

[1] Archives Nationales, W 500, 2nd dossier, p 39.

[2] They were charged with " federalism, conspiracy against the Republic, having communication with the rebels in La Vendée, and monopolising merchandise " They left Nantes on the 7th of Frimaire in the year II (November 27, 1793), to the number of 132, escorted by a detachment of the 11th Paris battalion. Their journey from Nantes lasted forty days Thirty-five of them perished or had to remain on the road Three died in prison at Paris. During the journey they had suffered terribly, led from cell to cell, from empty church to empty church, from stable to stable, sleeping on innumerable pallets of rotten straw, eaten by vermin, worn out with fatigue, and unable to take off their clothes (Archives Nationales W. 449, dossier 105).

Revolutionary Committee of Nantes was insufficient. Five times he had written to that Committee to demand proofs and official documents The answer to his last letter only reached him on the 5th of Thermidor, nine days before his arrest, four days before Robespierre's fall.

It is true that, on that 5th of Thermidor, the order had been given to transfer the ninety-four inhabitants of Nantes in a body to the Plessis prison, a gaol of sinister reputation which the populace called " Fouquier's store-house." During the blood-stained opening of Thermidor, the Revolutionary axe struck with such fury that it may be asked what would have happened to these men of Nantes if Robespierre, Dumas, and Coffinhal had not succumbed. When we reflect on the 342 sentences of death that were passed at Paris between the 1st and the 9th of Thermidor ; when we know how, during those nine days, the prisons of Carmes, of Bicêtre, of Saint-Lazare were emptied by the guillotine's agency, it is permissible to ask whether the inhabitants of Nantes who were detained at the Plessis would not have ended by being also placed on trial and executed as were so many others.

But the 9th of Thermidor came. They still lived. They were saved, and without any doubt they owed their lives to Fouquier-Tinville, who, in this affair, had known how to show himself just and humane. Humane, because, knowing that since their arrival in Paris the men of Nantes had been attacked by a sort of epidemic disease of which several of them died, he had caused them to be distributed among three hospitals, that of Petit-Bercy, the Hospice de la Folie-Régnault in the Rue des Amandiers-Popincourt, and Doctor Belhomme's house, No. 70, Rue de Charonne. Just, because he had withstood the monstrous demands of the Revolutionary Committee of Nantes ; had refused, on the authority of simple notes and without any evidence or official documents, to treat these wretches as " brigands of La Vendée " or as " the head-quarters staff of the Catholic army," as a section of public opinion at Paris called them.

Ready to appear before his judges, the ex-Public Prosecutor, learning that the men of Nantes had been acquitted, could congratulate himself thereon He could remember this verdict, and be able, justly, to confront his accusers with this fact "Ninety-four French citizens owe their lives to me."

CHAPTER VII

THE year II. was ending. For Fouquier-Tinville bad news followed on bad news. In his own mind, it was evident that his trial would be that of one of the patriots who had occupied "a place in the Revolution." This harsh and sombre man suffered in his affections as a husband and a father. He meditated; he reflected and told himself that his family would die of starvation.

"Citizen President," he wrote on the 25th of Thermidor to the President of the National Convention, "allow the unhappy father of a numerous family to remind the Convention that the rigorous exercise of the functions of Public Prosecutor of the Revolutionary Tribunal of the Republic has given him as enemies all the enemies of the Republic; yet, in everything, he has exactly executed the decrees of the Convention and the *resolutions of the Committees of Public Safety and of General Security*. Firm in his innocence, he dares to claim from the Convention the justice that it alone can render him.

"A. Q. FOUQUIER." [1]

He corresponded with his wife through the agency of their faithful servant. Citizeness Fouquier-Tinville sent her husband, food, linen, and the books he required. His letters, which are very interesting, have been preserved, but they are not dated. The earlier ones were written from the Conciergerie when the ex-Public Prosecutor was drawing up his long memorials for his defence. The others date from

[1] Archives Nationales, F⁷ 4436, liasse T., p. 9.

156

after his incarceration in Saint-Pélagie.   Some of these letters have been copied at the Historical Library of the City of Paris.[1]

FIRST LETTER

" I ask you again, *ma bonne amie*, to hurry on the printing of my memorials, to correct them as you have seen me do, and, above all, to distribute none to anybody unless I tell you ; you ought to guess the reason.   I am engaged in making out a list of those among whom I think they ought to be circulated ; I rely enough on your regard to have no doubt that you are fulfilling my intentions on this point

" You remark to me that Citizen Asselin told you that he thought my eldest brother would come for my trial , I wish he would, but what can he do, except spare you some journeys ? for you must be very tired.   My innocence gives me some tranquillity, but the prospect does not console me, especially as I am always abandoned to myself   I give myself up to a crowd of reflections, each more sinister than the other.   Who would have thought that by doing my duty as I have done, I should be reduced to this sad position on account of monsters with whom I have never rubbed shoulders ?   Time is a great teacher, I know , so it is on that alone I count

" Again, no memorial to anybody, not even to Viefville nor to anybody else ; but you can send some through Asselin to my brothers, advising them to keep none of them, and

---

[1] It was from reading the second series of M Lenôtre's *Vielles Maisons, Vieux Papiers*, published in 1907 (the article on Madame Fouquier-Tinville), that we learned of the existence of *Notes et Documents sur Fouquier-Tinville*, published by M George Lecocq At that period we had copied out the manuscript letters reproduced here, which are preserved in the Historical Library of the City of Paris.   " When Madame Fouquier-Tinville died in want and hunger in Paris," says M Lecocq, " when the family had refused her estate, the State caused everything that composed the fortune of that unhappy woman to be sold   All the furniture, including the manuscripts referred to, was knocked down for some hundreds of francs   A celebrated amateur, M Walferdein, bought the autographs and some precious documents for his collection "

not to give them to anybody to read   We must wait some days before we distribute them.   As for the last, let them not be sent to anybody until a decision is come to ; of course your aunt can read it at home.   Impress on the printer that he must not give any away , I am more afraid of that than of anything else.

"Try and go to the Jacobin Club this evening and send me the result to-morrow with other news.

"No distribution of copies to the Tribunal either at present.

"I again embrace you, keep acquainted with the news of the day.

"Did you receive the ninety copies I sent you this morning? You tell me nothing about them. I will make out a list of the persons to whom they should be given.

"P.S.—Yes, I should like some eggs."

SECOND LETTER

"Good-morning, *ma bonne amie*, you were not expecting news from me so early , you have doubtless inserted in my memorial the various additions I sent you, especially that ending with the words, ' the great conspirators, *ex-nobles and priests* '

" I should like you to add after the words, ' ex-nobles and priests,' the following   ' from actual circumstances, there can remain no doubt as to the true motives of the author of the declamation and denunciation directed against me.'

" And instead of the words, ' as without pretension in the art of eloquence,' it would be well to substitute, ' without malice as without passion.' This passage is at the end of the last part of my memorial

" Those changes are necessary ; my request ought to prove to you that my trial occupies my attention more than anything else.

" In the course of my memorial and towards the end of it there is mention of the Luxembourg conspiracy, especially there should be this phrase, ' which was exactly executed on the 19th, 21st, and 22nd of Messidor '

" I should like, in the margin by that phrase and in the form of further information, these words to be placed, ' there ought to be among the Archives of the Popular Commission sitting at the Louvre a letter I wrote to it on the night between the 18th and the 19th, in which I inform it that in accordance with the decision of the Committee of Public Safety, the matter of the Luxembourg conspiracy will be tried in three sessions ; I asked the Popular Commission to send me on the morning of the 19th the notes, documents, and information it may have had relating to those who are to be placed on trial, and whose names I sent with my letter for this purpose ; I have acted similarly in all other affairs.'

" This note can be written at the foot of the page if it is obvious that there would not be room enough in the margin.

" When one composes a memorial in sections, it is only on reflection and with time that one recollects various important facts.

" P S.—If you pay the messenger give him 25 *centimes* and put it down to my account "

THIRD LETTER.

" I am pleased with your letter, *ma bonne amie*. In the hope of being transferred this evening or to-morrow morning, I am sending you back a shirt and the two volumes of Prudhomme's *Révolutions*. Find out where is the resolution that authorises me to *amalgamate* (the prisoners) ; I do not remember ; moreover, my affair is unfortunately embarrassing on this point as on everything else. Send to-morrow at eight o'clock in the morning. If I am transferred, I shall take what I can with me. Be always on the alert, above all prepare Fréron's numbers for my defence.

" Good evening, good night, and good health "

FOURTH LETTER.

" You are right, *ma bonne amie*   To affix my signature to my memorial is the only method to adopt to avoid forgeries   that is very practical, for what is more necessary for me to do than to avoid the snares that are laid for me ?

Thanks for the news you give me , send a dozen copies of my memorial, and more if you can, to-morrow so that I may sign them, and you will distribute them only among the persons I tell you. I see and know nothing · the officials yesterday gave us reason to hope that we would soon have newspapers, I hope so Continue to send me what you think best. You know that I am not particular about food, I eat because it is necessary. Send me some salt, and pepper, and uncork the bottle, for I have neither knife, scissors, nor a corkscrew.

" I am sending you some silk stockings, two dusters, a shirt, a handkerchief, and a bottle.

" I kiss you, our children, and your aunt.

" Till to-morrow.

" I am keeping the oil for the fricassée "

Fifth Letter.

" I wish, *ma bonne amie*, that you could send me some copies of my memorial with my dinner, for I have not one left. I have left you power to dispose of my memorial as you think, so act for the best. Do you know if the memorials you sent to the Convention have been distributed, do you know if they are being sold, of course, for the printer's profit ? I asked you for a copy of Marat's letters ; send with the originals those of Montanet. Brochet lives in the Rue Andrée des Arts near the Rue de l'Eperon. I mention this as it is essential to keep my memorials, it is important not to let the stock become exhausted. I have neither spoon nor fork, as we are only provided with wooden spoons and a fork like the broken spoon that I send you. Send me to-morrow two spoons and a fork, for this spoon does not belong to me, and I must return it to the lender.

" I am terribly wearied by my position, which I could endure with more patience if I had deserved it. Be always attentive to what is said about me, for things must come to an end. Good evening, good health, I kiss you, your aunt, and the children.

" I have had no brandy since yesterday."

SIXTH LETTER.

" I received your letter, *ma bonne amie*, and it gives me all the more pleasure as it assures me that you are well, I have also received my memorial, I am going to arrange everything so that you can have all this afternoon

" Greeting, etc."

" I kiss you, your aunt, and the children. I should like a bottle of brandy, for nothing keeps me up but taking a little."

SEVENTH LETTER.

" I send you, *ma bonne amie*, the list of witnesses who I think ought to be called for my defence with the facts that are personal to each of them ; it is important that you should send it to Lafleurie, after having read it and caused it to be read by those persons who are acquainted with what has taken place, and in whom you have confidence.

" It would be to the purpose to cause some memorials to be given to *Martin*, a former juryman, Rue de Savoye, Section Marat.

" I see that you are having a great deal of trouble, I wish I could rid you of it ; but we must submit to fate, we must hope that a happier time will come It is six o'clock. I have not yet been cross-examined, it is not certain that I shall be to-day, and I cannot be to-morrow on account of the festival. Good evening, good health, more details to-morrow."

EIGHTH LETTER.

" It is eight o'clock, *ma bonne amie*, and I have not yet had any news from the Tribunal or elsewhere, so that I cannot tell you if at dinner-time I shall be at Pélagie or elsewhere [1] If I go to the Tribunal and remain there, I will have you told ; if I am transferred elsewhere the maid at Pélagie will know the place that is the perplexity in

---

[1] On the 4th of Fructidor in the year II. Fouquier had been transferred from the Conciergerie to Saint-Pélagie On the 9th of Brumaire in the year III. he was transferred from Sainte-Pélagie to the Plessis.

L

which I find myself ; so I am always waiting as usual. As to the matter of the *amalgamation*, I have my answer ready : it is a poor resource for my enemies. If you learn anything send me word immediately. Be always on the alert either in your own person or through those who still take any interest in me. For instance, you could send to the Tribunal about ten o'clock to know whether I have reached there, or whether they are arranging to have me brought there. Kind messages to Citizen de Vitry and to all others Good day to everybody."

NINTH LETTER.

" I pity you, *ma bonne amie*, for the fatigue you must have experienced during the whole day that you remained at the Convention without having taken anything there. You must indeed have suffered greatly. You are right in thinking that matters are going very badly. What is happening must remind you that I anticipated these events when I remarked to you at the time of the affair of the Revolutionary Committee that an attempt would be made to stir up people's minds against Carrier and afterwards against me. You see that this is the course taken. One can say that there never was a more grievous position than that in which I find myself. The hope of making my innocence triumph alone sustains me, and my sole grief is for you and my unhappy family. Once again I am sure of my innocence ; but in this state of things, what means are there of getting my defence listened to ? That is my uneasiness, lest I be sacrificed and not judged.

" I send you in my portfolio a letter containing my feelings towards you, and two others which you will deliver, in time, if there is an opportunity. Do not grieve, they are the feelings engraven on my heart that I send you, and that, perhaps, I may not have another opportunity of conveying to you Shall I, perhaps, be happier ? Shall I display them in person ? I hope so ; but at such a juncture we must expect anything. That is why I have arrived at this decision Once more, do not be troubled.

" You must take the greatest care that my creditors do not seize everything from you to the last shirt, in addition to the property ; thus the first thing will be for you to disclaim community of property with me, and to take away as many as possible of the portable articles. The chicken will do me for to-day and to-morrow.

" I kiss you with all my heart. Keep well. I kiss aunt and the children."[1]

These are singularly moving letters. His part played, the mask has fallen. He is no longer the Public Prosecutor, he is a man, a husband, a father. The thought that remains with him is that of the amazing misfortune of the beings for whose existence he has done his work of blood. Now he is hemmed in, put in a cage, like a hunted animal ; he belongs to the men of Thermidor. His life is in their hands.

During the first days of his detention, he was preparing for the contest. He did everything for his defence. He wrote letters, drew up his *Memorials* at Sainte-Pélagie, in the midst of the prisoners, ex-jurors of the Revolutionary Tribunal or other officials of the Terror, such as Vilain d'Aubigny, Audouin, Guyard (the former janitor of Saint-Lazare), he spoke out, saying that he was having printed a memorial against the Committees. He briefed Lecointre for his sensational denunciation at the Convention.[2]

Now he had nothing more to do but wait until his fate was decided. And what an ordeal ! " That is my uneasiness, lest I be sacrificed and not judged ! " He knew that Carrier[3] and the Revolutionary Committee of Nantes were to be placed on trial. His turn was coming to mount the benches of the Tribunal.

---

[1] These letters have been published by M Lecocq (*Notes et Documents sur Fouquier-Tinville* Paris Jouaust, 1885, 61 pages) with eight other letters of which we do not know the originals

[2] So, at least, Riston, an agent of the Committee of General Security, reports

[3] Carrier's case was taken on 7th of Frimaire The trial lasted sixty sessions. Carrier, Pinard and Grandmaison were condemned to death on the 26th. The thirty others who were charged were acquitted

During the preceding month, and part of Brumaire, Judge Forestier, assisted by his registrar, Josse, conducted a prolonged inquiry. He heard a great deal of evidence, almost all in accord, from people who were well acquainted with Fouquier while he exercised his terrible magistracy. Certainly, there were some of those depositions, such as that of Pâris, the registrar, and his subordinates, which should be carefully examined, for, as is known, the registry of the Revolutionary Tribunal was Dantonist, and it did not forgive the Public Prosecutor either Danton's death or the sudden arrest and condemnation of Legris,[1] a clerk at the registry. And yet what precision, what clearness there were in the affirmations of Pâris, of Wolff, of Tavernier!

There were, moreover, other depositions, such as that of Château, Fouquier's former secretary, which seem to bear all the marks of frankness and impartiality, and which, though favourable to the accused on many points, none the less established very grave charges against him on other points

The writers who have studied the history of the Revolutionary Tribunal have, to this day, chiefly made use of two publications which we can condemn as being often inexact or partial. These are · 1st, *Fouquier-Tinville's Printed Trial*, published by Maret, bookseller at Paris, at the Cour des Fontaines, in the Palais-Egalité, and catalogued in the National Library under the classification Lib. 41, 1798; and 2nd, the *Histoire Parlementaire* of Bouchez and Roux, the 1837 edition, Volumes XXXIV. and XXXV., in which the pleadings in the trial are reproduced.

Without systematically setting aside those two publications, we think the time has come—since apart from all political ideas and preconceived notions, the reader requires to form an exact idea of the part that Fouquier played, and the responsibility he incurred—to have recourse only to the

---

[1] The evidence of Pâris is interesting But, when reading it, we ought to remember that Nicolas Joseph Pâris, called Fabricius, Danton's friend, and appointed, thanks to Danton, chief registrar of the Tribunal, had been dismissed and imprisoned six days after Danton's execution, on the 24th of Germinal in the year II

original documents, that is to say to the depositions of the witnesses preserved in the portfolios of the National Archives, and to analyse those depositions, a work that has not yet been done Just as we have felt bound to reproduce in full, the original *Memorials* of Fouquier, *written in his own hand*, in view of his defence, so we think that only the original depositions, preserved among the Archives, ought to be taken into consideration

Let us listen to the witnesses examined by Judge Forestier. We shall hear Fouquier afterwards

At noon on the 5th of Vendémiaire in the year III. (September 26th, 1794), a month and twenty days after the Public Prosecutor's arrest, the first witness appeared before Pierre Forestier, and Josse, his registrar. Nicolas Tirrart, 33 years of age, an usher of the Tribunal, residing at 281 Rue Saint-Honoré, stated

" Since the terrible law of the 22nd of Prairial, I have heard Fouquier say ' In this *décade*[1] there must be three hundred to three hundred and fifty tried.' On certain days when several citizens were acquitted, Fouquier would say with warmth · ' What ? have they acquitted those people ? I must have the names of the jurors.' Sometimes, when he returned in the evening at about ten or eleven o'clock, rather heated, Fouquier used to change the lists of the cases that had been prepared in the course of the day and of the accused who were to be tried the next morning. In the same way, when the day of the hearing came, he sometimes had everything changed, the cases and the accused Sometimes also he would call an usher and say to him : ' You must not summon the jurors whom I do not tell you.' He would then ask for the list and choose, at his own fancy, such a section for such a hall, although it was not the turn of that section to sit. It sometimes happened that he added the names of certain jurors who were not authorised to serve— Desboisseaux, Lumière, Trinchard, Renaudin, Girard, and Vilate. Sometimes, in the morning, before the hearing, I have seen Fouquier go up to the assembled jurors in their

[1] *Cf* note, p 66

hall where they deliberated. I declare that Fouquier has a very hard, violent, and menacing character, with that tone that only belongs to a despot."

The next witness, Jean Baptiste Benoît Auvray, aged 45, an usher of the Tribunal, of No 37, Rue de Provence, had heard Fouquier say several times, and in particular since the law of the 22nd of Prairial · " In this *décade* there must be 250, 300, to 350 prisoners tried " When the accused were acquitted, Fouquier would say . " What ? Give me the list of jurors ! What sort of jurors are these ? " He used to speak with incredible warmth : " Can one not count then on these people ? " The witness had also noticed that sometimes when Fouquier came in, at ten or eleven o'clock in the evening, he was very heated, and caused the list of cases prepared during that day for the day following to be changed, as well as the list of accused persons.

In regard to the modification of the jurors' turns, the depositions of the usher Auvray, were the same as those of the usher Tirrard. There is also agreement between both the depositions concerning the visits made by Fouquier to the jurors before the trials

" I should add," the witness declared, " that Fouquier is a very sharp, very petulant man , that he often threatened the ushers and fell into frightful rages, above all, when it was a matter of answering him about searching for the prisoners who were designated to us only by their family names. It was on this that he threatened me once, in a moment of fury, telling me that I should remember it. However, it is right to remark that when his anger had passed, he did not bear malice, and admitted that it was unfortunate for him to be like that, and that he knew well he could not but be disagreeable in the eyes of those to whom he spoke."

Auguste-Joseph Boucher, aged 51, a clerk to the registrar of the Revolutionary Tribunal, residing at No. 1036 Rue Saint-Dominique, knew that several times, when accused persons had been acquitted, Fouquier said to him ill-humouredly " Give me the names of those who compose the jury." Another remark of Fouquier's, made in the presence of the witness, who was then an usher, was " You are not making headway, gentlemen, you are not making headway ! Henceforth two hundred must pass through it every *décade*." One day, when commissioned by Fouquier to go to a prison to find the ex-Duchesse de Biron, he pointed out to him that there were two Duchesses de Biron. " Well," replied Fouquier, " bring both They will both pass through it." They did *pass*, in truth, and both mounted the scaffold the next day. Another day, when entrusted with a warrant for the arrest of a count or viscount de Castellane, the witness remarked to him that he desired to know which of the two it was for, the count or the viscount. Fouquier answered that he was to arrest all those who bore the name of Castellane.[1]

Robert Wolff, aged 38, clerk to the registrar of the Revolutionary Tribunal, residing in the Rue de Buci, declared that he had seen in Fouquier a very violent character, and a despotic, unbearable temper, " showing itself towards subordinate officials such as registrars, ushers, and other clerks." He was continually threatening to have them put in prison.

" As it seldom happened that he did not take too much wine at dinner, it was in this state that he would come to the ushers' office oftener than anywhere else to vent in fury the vapours that during dinner had mounted to his brain. None the less, when fasting, he gave way equally to the same transports. The whole Tribunal, not even excepting the judges, trembled before him, some through fear of prison, others through the credit he had with the Committees."

This deposition of Robert Wolff was a regular speech for the prosecution, clear, precise, implacable It was, on most of the important points, in full accord with the evidence we have just read, as well as with that which we are going to read. Let us not forget, however, that this deposition is that of a declared enemy of Fouquier-Tinville.

" It is not true, as Fouquier advances in his printed

[1] W 501, 2nd dossier, p. 83

memorial," Wolff goes on, "that he appeared against, and demanded the despatch to the scaffold of Mayor Lescot-Fleuriot, notoriously known as his most intimate friend; but the fact is that he only appeared against the first seven or eight who were tried on the 10th of Thermidor. When it was Fleuriot's turn, he gave place to Liendon, one of his deputies, who finished that hearing, which lasted until six o'clock in the evening, and at which twenty-two conspirators were condemned to the scaffold. After Fleuriot's condemnation, he reappeared at the hearing, wearing a light-coloured coat, and remained there for part of the time that was spent trying the others. I performed the duties of registrar at that hearing In consequence, I was a witness of the fact. Fouquier was so far from sending his friend Fleuriot to the scaffold that he violently reprimanded Tavernier, the usher who was present at the execution of the twenty-two on the 10th of Thermidor, for having caused his dear Fleuriot to be executed the last , he added that the usher had only acted thus because he had taken the opinion of his Section, which was also Fleuriot's Section (the Museum Section).

"On the 9th of Thermidor, when Fouquier dined at the house of Verghnes in the Ile de la Fraternité, although he pretends that he was ignorant of the troubles, as he says in his memorial in order to palliate his associating with the infamous Coffinhal, it appears from the following fact that he is trying to deceive. About one o'clock on the afternoon of that very day, Citizen Simmonet (one of the clerks to the ushers of the Tribunal) came to announce that there was trouble in the neighbourhood and in the Faubourg Saint-Antoine, that the drum had beaten to arms there, and that Hanriot had at the point of the sword rescued the pretended patriots from the hands of the gendarmes. An hour before, Dumas had been arrested while actually sitting in the Tribunal, and at two o'clock the whole Tribunal knew of the troubles which Robespierre's accomplices were beginning to arouse. About half-past three, Fouquier, with his hat on his head, went out to attend that famous dinner. He was then oppo-

site the prisoners' room, a few steps from the door out of the
Hall of Columns. Sanson, the executioner of criminal
judgments, in the presence of Desmorest (or another
relative who helped him to carry out the executions), of the
usher (who was to be present at them), and of myself, remarked that there was trouble in the Saint-Antoine quarter,
through which he must pass, and in the suburb where the
execution was to take place. He asked Fouquier whether
he did not think it prudent to postpone the execution.
Fouquier answered with a little emotion · ' Proceed in any
case. Nothing ought to stop the execution of judgments nor
the course of justice And, moreover, there is a force to protect the execution.' Fouquier then proceeded on his way to
dine with his companions It is correct to say that a
batch of six carts was waiting only for this order to set out
for the Barrier of the Faubourg Saint-Antoine. This was
immediately done.

" In regard to the humanity which Fouquier affects, and
the bitterness he feels about the sanguinary law of the 22nd
of Prairial, his conduct is not found to be in accord with the
sentiments of humanity which he parades, since it is notorious that in my presence and in the presence of several others
attached to the Tribunal, Fouquier, being at luncheon with
several jurors, worthy executors of that law of blood, coldly
calculated, as he picked his teeth, the number of victims
who were to be despatched. ' Things must move,' said he.
' There must be 400 or 450 this *décade ;* for the next one, so
many are always to be had.' And the cannibal jurors,
before whom he made such barbarous calculations, applauded.
The fact is so notorious that there are few among those
attached to the Tribunal who did not share those atrocious
sentiments who are not in a position to affirm it , moreover, his later conduct had only too well verified his
calculations. It is, for the honour of humanity, only too
notorious that he put on trial as many as seventy persons
at once, and charged them with taking part in the alleged
conspiracies in the prisons, especially in the first batch from
the Luxembourg when a scaffolding was erected which

reached to the top of the hall. Sixty-nine persons were tried before three o'clock, and executed the same day. That was in the case of the girl Renaud, her family, and Admiral All the people of Paris have seen or learned from public conversation in what manner, in less than four hours, sixty-nine persons were tried and condemned to death as accomplices of Renaud and Admiral. Things were hurried so much that, in order to avoid the time that would have been occupied by asking the names and descriptions of so great a number of persons and having them written down by the registrar, the judges' and the jurors' lists were made in the registry the evening before. This is how the proceedings enlightened the consciences of the jurors. An accused person would be asked : 'Are you acquainted with the conspiracy that existed, etc. ? ' The accused would answer in the negative. Then he was asked this other question which would seem to have been answered by the preceding one · ' Have you taken part in that conspiracy ? ' The same negative answer. If the accused wanted to enter into any details to demonstrate that he could not have taken part in that conspiracy, as soon as he opened his mouth the pitiless Dumas would say to him ' You can be heard no longer Gendarmes, do your duty.' And if the accused still wanted to speak, he was not allowed to take part in the proceedings When the questions had been repeated sixty-nine times and the laconic answer, ' No,' had been returned sixty-nine times, the Prosecutor summed up for a quarter of an hour, the President read out the questions which the jury were to answer, and the legion of accused persons had to retire. The jurors retired as a matter of form to their room, where they remained for half-an-hour, then came back, and handed in their declarations. The Public Prosecutor made a final speech. Judgment was pronounced, and the registrar was sent to tell the victims that within half-an-hour, that is to say within the time it took to cut off their hair and bind their hands, they would start for the scaffold This first trial is a type of those that followed it. And it was on that occasion that the custom began of thus playing with justice, and transforming into a legal butchery a Tribunal which, from the very severity of its functions, ought to have been most scrupulously subject to forms. It was Fouquier who, either in person or by deputy, presided over the indictments and judgments He used to say ' Things must move '

" Fouquier pretends that he only acted by order of the Committees Here are two facts which prove that, if this is so, he must have given a very great extension to his orders

" Boucher, an usher at the Tribunal, an honest and a feeling man, told me, in the bitterness of his heart, that Fouquier having given orders to the ushers to go to a prison to fetch a woman named Biron who was to be put on trial next day and to form part of a *batch*. He remarked to him that there were two women of the name of Biron, one the widow of the Duke who had been condemned to death, and the other the widow of the Marshal.[1] Fouquier said ' Bring them both. They will pass through it.' In fact, they both passed through it next day, and both were sent to the scaffold.

" The same incident was repeated and also through the agency of the same Boucher, who told it to me. Fouquier gave this usher a warrant to arrest a person named Castellane The usher remarked to him that he knew several persons of the same name. ' Arrest all who bear that name,' replied Fouquier. Only one was arrested because no others called Castellane were found.

" Finally, Fouquier said to Tavernier, a clerk in the registry of the Tribunal, when speaking of Fabricius, the chief registrar, who had been imprisoned for four months and put into solitary confinement by Robespierre, and who, since the restoration of the Tribunal, had again been appointed to his old post by the National Convention, that Fabricius was wrong to bear him ill-will, seeing that he, Fouquier, had prevented Fabricius from being placed on trial and Taver-

[1] They were Amélie de Boufflers, Biron's widow, and Françoise Pauline de Roye, Marshal Biron's wife.

nier also, and that he had prevented the witness, another friend of Fabricius, from being charged along with him, whilst there was neither accusation nor denunciation against Fabricius any more than against Tavernier or the witness; these two last have never been arrested, and, on the contrary, have always continued to perform their functions at the Tribunal, to which they were re-appointed on its restoration

"It is within my knowledge that for more than six months no registrar was ever summoned to be present when lots were drawn to select the judges and jurors; the Public Prosecutor sent to the registry the list which was afterwards furnished to the ushers in order that they might summon them; moreover, the ushers were not present at the deliberations in the Council Chamber and they were only provided with a memorandum of the proceedings so as to make out and sign the minutes; several times when persons who had been acquitted presented themselves at the registry to obtain the documents necessary in order to get the help that was granted them by the law, Fouquier forbade those documents to be given without consulting him, because he did not wish everybody to have that help, although the law made no exceptions. He would say, in order to empower himself to prevent the delivery of those documents · ' What ! these beggars are too lucky to be acquitted. It is incredible. What sort of jurors could acquit them? Give them nothing.' "[1]

Charles Nicolas Tavernier, aged 38, a clerk to the registrar of the Tribunal, residing in the Rue de la Monnaie, heard Fouquier say in the ushers' office: " I must get through with 250 to 300 accused persons in the *décade*." When any one was acquitted, Fouquier used to ask for the names of the jurors who were sitting. Several times he gave orders for certain jurors to be summoned on the pretext that one section was weaker than another. The indictments were delivered to those concerned *on the day before the trial* at seven or eight o'clock in the evening.

[1] W. 501, 2nd dossier, p 77

Gabriel Nicolas Monet, aged 38, an usher at the Tribunal, residing in the Rue du Contrat-Social in the Section of the same name, declared that Fouquier selected the jurors who were to be summoned. Those whom he chose oftenest were Renaudin, Nicolas, Desboisseaux, Lumière, Vilate, and Gravier. This choice only began after the operation of the law of the 22nd of Prairial.

Monet heard Fouquier say. " Next *décade* there must be 300 or 350 tried. Things are not moving. We must act in revolutionary fashion."

Citizeness Goureau, aged 36, of No. 18, Faubourg Saint-Martin, and her sister-in-law, née Alexandre Rosalie Pigeon, having been commissioned to bring to the Tribunal a letter to Fouquier-Tinville from Bourdon (of the Oise), saw three jurors entering the Council Chamber where Fouquier was. " Now we are free ! " said they. Fouquier asked them if the prisoners had been tried. " Yes," answered the three jurors. " We do not know of what they were accused. To know that, you have only to run after them." At this remark Fouquier burst into laughter.

Jean Baptiste Topino-Lebrun, aged 31, born at Marseilles, a juror of the Revolutionary Tribunal, residing in the Louvre, had always regarded as a problem Fouquier's activity in his duties combined with the negligence with which he followed up " the business of the great conspiracies, either to reach their real heads or to extirpate their roots." To take an instance. " In the project for rescuing the Queen from the Conciergerie, and afterwards when she was led to execution, the police administration, influenced by Hébert and Chaumette, ought to have been differently examined (*sic*)." There was the same negligence in the Ronsin affair and in that of Westermann " who was placed on trial for having violated all the forms relative to La Vendée."

" Fouquier did not seem to me to be without party spirit in the Danton affair If he did not write to the Committee of Public Safety about the alleged rebellion of the accused persons, why, when he demanded the reading of the law which took away their right to plead, did he begin by saying : ' On account of the rebellion of the accused persons ' ? Why, on the fourth day, did he and Herman go to the jurors' room to induce them to declare that they were sufficiently informed ? After that trial, did he, at the very least, act on these words of Danton, so important to our liberty · ' I demand commissioners from the Convention in order that they may receive my denunciation of the system of dictatorship ' ? It was the Convention that should have been writen to and not the Committee of Public Safety.

" It was Fouquier who caused the red shirts to be put on the 52 prisoners in the affair of Admiral and the girl Renaud. They were by no means accused of assassination.

" The writs of indictment seemed to me to strain and exaggerate the charges which could be made against prisoners. Sometimes terrible facts were in no way borne out at the trial by the documents or by the statements of the witnesses."[1]

Jean Baptiste Sambat, aged 35, a juror of the Revolutionary Tribunal, residing at No. 36 Rue Taitbout, had no acquaintance with the facts alleged against the prisoner Fouquier. However, he noticed, a little before the period of the law of Prairial, that grave accusations were often found to be void through the lack of documents and witnesses.[2]

Jean Nicolas Thierriet-Grandpré, aged 41, chief clerk of the Commission for the Administration of Civil Affairs, Police, and Tribunals, residing at No. 38, Rue de Thionville, declared that on the day following that on which Fréteau was acquitted, he went to Fouquier to consider with him what measures were to be taken for the security of the Hospice de l'Evêché. Fouquier said to him : " You do not know that yesterday they acquitted Fréteau at the Tribunal, though the man is known to me as having been a royalist and a definite counter-revolutionary under the Constituent Assembly. But I swear that before long he will be taken again and then he will not escape."

[1] W 500, 3rd dossier, p 145   [2] *Ibid.*

Another day Fouquier told him with "a mixture of pleasure and irony" how he had received in his office an individual who came to give him information about some case. For several hours Fouquier had "wheedled" him, then had suddenly handed him over to the Tribunal, "which condemned him in a quarter of an hour."

Louis Charles Hally, aged 42, janitor of the house of detention of Plessis-Egalité, only became acquainted with the famous conspiracy in the prisons through the report of Viart and Courlet-Beaulop. He immediately communicated this report to Fouquier, who said to him "I shall put them on trial to-morrow or the day after, and I shall summon you as a witness" He asked for time to inform himself about the matter. Fouquier refused it. On the following day the prisoners were placed on trial. Hally, summoned as a witness, could not make a declaration as he did not know a single fact about the case, which was adjourned Fouquier reprimanded him, and showed ill-humour towards him "because the business could not be ended as he wished."[1]

Louis Pierre Dufourny, aged 55, an architect in the House of Explosives at the Arsenal in Paris,[2] in a very long, pretentious, circumstantial, and rather obscure deposition, in which it appears that he liked pushing himself forward and distributing praise and blame to the Thermidor conquerors—Dufourny charged Fouquier with having been secretly favourable to Ronsin, "Robespierre's man, and with having contributed to suppress the clues that might have made known the causes of La Vendée, the methods employed to keep that ulcer open, and the participation in it of Robespierre and of Ronsin as well as their actual accomplices."

Summoned as a witness at Danton's trial, Dufourny said that he was systematically set aside. In vain did he write about the matter to Fouquier He was kept in the witnesses' room for the three days that the proceedings lasted. He there observed all that was taking place around him. He

---

[1] W 501, 2nd dossier, p. 61.

[2] Dufourny succeeded Lavoisier as Director of Explosives at the Arsenal.

saw several members of the Committee of General Security "sitting at the Tribunal," among others, David, Amar, Voulland and Vadier. "They were unrecognisable from anger, pallor, and fright, so much did they seem to fear that they would see the victims escape death." They kept coming in and going out, and were agitated by an activity which displayed all their passions. They communicated with Fouquier in his office as well as in the passages and even in the entrance to the witnesses' room "[1]

Jean Pierre Victor Féral, aged 39, judge of the district of Pont-Chalier,[2] residing in Paris at No. 3, Rue de la Femme-sans-Tête declared that, being present at the last session of Hébert's trial and finding himself in the Council Chamber, he heard Fouquier propose to the judges and some jurors to have Lieutenant-Colonel Quétineau's widow and a man called Armand[3] withdrawn from the proceedings "seeing that there were no proofs against them, and to send them back to the house of detention because proofs might be found in other cases." He added that he was going to make this proposal to the Tribunal when the session opened. Several judges and jurors opposed this initiative of Fouquier. The witness believed that, disarmed by this opposition, Fouquier remained silent at the session [4]

[1] W. 501, 2nd dossier, p. 41.
[2] Pont-l'Evêque, Calvados
[3] Jean Antoine Florent Armand, a medical student, implicated in Hébert's trial and condemned to death on the 4th of Germinal in the year II
[4] W. 501, 2nd dossier, p 85

CHAPTER VIII

JEAN BAPTISTE TAVERNIER, registrar's clerk of the Revolutionary Tribunal, was commissioned to pay 50 *livres* to the prisoners each *décade.* He received their claims, and presented them to Fouquier. A great number of them " overwhelmed him with claims in regard to sums deposited with the Public Prosecutor instead of being placed in the registry."

Tavernier related these facts to Judge Forestier at his examination on the 12th of Vendémiaire in the year III., and he gave details. A prisoner claimed " his *décades* out of about 1,800 *livres* in paper-money, 1,392 *livres* in gold " Another claimed them out of 2,282 *livres.* On a certain day when Tavernier " presented to Fouquier their just claims and pointed out to him that he lacked everything," the Public Prosecutor answered him sharply (" for," said the witness, " he is violent ") · " Give me the list of these beggars. I will make them pass through it to-morrow."

Tavernier knew what that meant. He pointed out to the complainants the extreme danger of their demands. They became silent. It was only after Fouquier's arrest that the deposits of certain prisoners " who had not yet been guillotined" were sent to the registry

Tavernier remembered the calculations made by Fouquier to cause a certain number of heads to fall each *décade.* One day he heard him say " Last *décade* furnished so many ; this one the number must go to 450 or even 500. Come ! Call an usher ! " The usher came. " Come, you fellows," said Fouquier, " things must move. Last *décade* things did not turn out badly. But this *décade* they must reach 450 at least."

Since Fouquier's arrest the witness had met him at the Conciergerie. Fouquier approached him and said to him :

" Are you a friend of Fabricius ? "

" Yes, you know it."

" I am told that he has a grudge against me."

" I know nothing about it."

" He could do me a great service   He knows Barras, Fréron, and other Deputies   He could serve me with them. He is wrong to have a grudge against me.   For it was I who caused the postponement of his trial.   It was even intended to join you with him, as well as Wolff."

The witness ended by saying that his astonishment was so great that he withdrew without any further explanation.

Louis François Ferrière–Sauvebœuf, aged 32, living on his private income and detained at La Force, declared that on the 28th of Prairial he was summoned at one o'clock in the morning before the Committee of General Security. Fouquier-Tinville came there, about two o'clock, to complain of having been ill-treated in a guard-room.   He heard Fouquier-Tinville say, in the presence of the assembled Committee " which contradicted him in no way " : " I have thirty-nine of them to-day who went to the Barrier du Trône Renversé for the Bicêtre plots.   To-morrow I shall send sixty of them "   And the witness heard cries of " Bravo ! "

He also heard it said to Deschamps, the registrar's secretary of Bicêtre, that Fouquier-Tinville came with gendarmes to fetch the second batch from Bicêtre, and that he refused to listen to Osselin[1] who was commenting on this transference [2]

---

[1] Charles Nicolas Osselin, a member of the Convention, had voted for Louis XVI.'s death   He was a member of the Committee of General Security and President of the Tribunal which was established on August 17.   He proposed the law against the emigrants   Informed against for having gone security for an emigrant, Charlotte de Luppé, Countesse de Charry, he was put on trial, condemned to be deported, and transferred to Bicêtre, where he was implicated in the conspiracy in the prisons   He was brought before the Tribunal, condemned to death, and executed on June 26, 1794.   He had tried to commit suicide by stabbing himself in the breast with a nail.

[2] W. 501, 2nd dossier, p. 72.

In a second deposition, three days later, Ferrière-Sauve-bœuf repeated the words of Joly, an usher at the Criminal Tribunal of the Department. On the 8th of Thermidor, this usher met Fouquier, who said to him " Your Tribunal is not keeping up. *It only makes two or three mount* (the scaffold), and I, *I shall make fifty mount it* the day after next *décade* begins "

Ferrière-Sauvebœuf observed that when he was at the Committee of General Security he heard Fouquier say · "*I have made thirty-nine of them* mount (the scaffold) to-day, and to-morrow *I will make* sixty of them mount it." Fouquier could not carry out his intention for, having been beaten in a police-station, he was ill on that day. The next day ' was that of the ' batch ' of people from Bicêtre, and the 29th of Prairial was that of the sixty which he had predicted."[1]

The following deposition is in part favourable to Fouquier : Urbain Didier Château, Fouquier's ex-secretary, afterwards an usher in the Revolutionary Tribunal, aged 34, noticed, when he was the Public Prosecutor's secretary, that almost all the letters he wrote to the Committee of General Security bore the address of Vadier only

He knew also that several citizens came, on several occasions, to ask Fouquier to bring about the trials of their children who had been prisoners for a long time, saying that if they were guilty their heads ought to fall, but if innocent they ought to be given back to the service of the country. Fouquier, reminding them of the causes of their children's imprisonment, remarked that " he did not wish to cause defenders of the country who were only guilty of foolish actions to be put to death , that if he put them on trial it would ruin them, and that he preferred to leave them longer in prison in the hope that when the great operations were ended there would come a gentler law which would set them free."

Château also knew that Fouquier several times said . " It is a tyranny and a very great annoyance that the

[1] W 501, 2nd dossier, p 79

inhabitants of Nantes should be brought before this Tribunal without any evidence against them "

Since he became an usher at the Tribunal, Château, being one day in the Council Chamber, heard Fouquier and Dumas say to five or six jurors that it was astonishing they had not convicted an accused ex-noble (whose name he had forgotten). According to them, he was a man who ought not to escape the punishment of death ; but they held him, and they would know how to take him again without it being possible for him to escape.

At the beginning of Thermidor, Château heard Fouquier say to two jurors, as he was leaving the session in the Hall of Liberty, with papers under his arm, and was at the bottom of the staircase that led to his room " It is astonishing that you have condemned that prisoner. I hope he will be set free "

At the same period there had been a number of persons tried, among whom were three who had been acquitted, and who ought to have been set at liberty twenty-four hours after the verdict Château went to find Fouquier the next day, at eleven o'clock in the evening, at the refreshment-room of the Tribunal He asked him for an order to set these three persons free. Fouquier read the three names, said that among them there was an ex-noble who had been badly tried, and that he would see about getting hold of him again For this reason it was necessary to leave them in prison until there was a fresh order.[1]

Armand Benoît Joseph Guffroy, Deputy for the Pas-de-Calais at the Convention, residing at No 35 Rue Saint-Honoré, was not well acquainted with Fouquier-Tinville. He had heard, either in the offices of the Committee of General Security, or from the members of the Convention, that at the beginning or at the end of each *décade*, when Fouquier brought long lists of prisoners to the prosecutor's office, he used to say in a gay tone, rubbing his hands " Ah! we shall unbreech (*déculotterons*) a good quantity of them this *décade.*"

[1] W 501, 2nd dossier, p 74

CHARLOTTE CORDAY

He also heard his colleague, Lecointre, say that, when Fouquier was dining with him, some one (perhaps Lecointre himself) said to Fouquier · " How is it possible that you, who were at first believed to be a just man, can lend yourself to committing or helping to commit so many cruelties ? "

Fouquier answered · " When one has one foot in crime, it is necessary to plunge right in "

The witness several times saw Fouquier coming to the Committee of General Security and asking for papers relating to various prisoners. He would then have secret conferences with Vadier, Amar, and some others of whose names he could not be certain [1]

Next came Jacques Bernard Marie Montané, the former President of the Revolutionary Tribunal, aged 43 [2] He declared that at the period of the creation of the Revolutionary Tribunal he had been appointed President, not on the nomination of a Committee, but by the Convention itself, by a majority of votes given in secret ballot. It was at the time of the installation of the Tribunal that he saw Fouquier for the first time For two months he lived on fairly good terms with him He had then no suspicion of him. It was otherwise during the following two months, when these two magistrates were at open war " either on account of the absolute despotism which Fouquier-Tinville publicly exercised over the whole Tribunal or on account of the criminal operations with which Montané publicly reproached him, or on account of the generals, the commissioners for war, the ex-nobles, the ex-captains of cavalry, the ex-marquises, whom he exempted from the sword of the law, clandestinely

---

[1] W 501, 2nd dossier, p 65

[2] Fouquier had denounced him for having erased from the sentence on Léonard Bourdon's assailants the clause confiscating their goods, and for having at Charlotte Corday's trial modified the questions propounded to the jury, giving them a sense which made her case one that could be tried by a common-law tribunal In his denunciation, Fouquier had asked that the President " should not be delivered over to the rigours of justice " When Montané was arrested, he had been humanely forgotten in prison by Fouquier, and thus saved in spite of letters in which he demanded to be placed on trial (W. 500, 3rd dossier, pp. 89, 90, 91).

and without the knowledge of the Tribunal, although they had been sent forward by the constituted authorities, by representatives of the people, and by decrees of the National Convention, and for crimes which came only within the purview of the Revolutionary Tribunal "

This latter part of Montané's deposition gives cause for astonishment. We have not been able to find out on what written proofs he based the charge of having exempted any counter-revolutionary ex-nobles from punishment.[1]

Nicolas Gastrez, aged 25, employed at the office of Public Instruction, residing at No 1342 Rue de Seine, begged Dumas, who lived in the same house, to bring him with Gobertière, one of his friends, into the Hall of the Tribunal on the day of Admiral's trial. The hearing had not begun. Dumas took him into his office " where he was brought a letter, folded in a fancy shape, coming from the Luxembourg prison, and which he told them was signed by the *ci-devant* Comte de Fleury." This letter, which he read aloud after reading it to himself, contained expressions which Gastrez did not remember, " but which did not seem to him becoming to apply to a patriot." As soon as the letter was read, Fouquier came in and Dumas told him about it, asking him " Does it not seem to you that this fine fellow is in a hurry ? " Fouquier answered · " Yes, he appears to me to be in a hurry, and I am going to send for him " This was done, the *ci-devant* Comte de Fleury was joined with the alleged accomplices in the plot against Robespierre, and underwent their fate. When he appeared at the Tribunal, the letter he had written to Dumas was not even mentioned to him.

Jean Placide Gobertière, employed in the Commission of Commerce, aged 26, appeared next, and declared that on the day of Admiral's trial he went with Gastrez to the Tribunal. He confirmed Gastrez's deposition in all details. He added that the Comte de Fleury was taken to the scaffold on the same day *in a red shirt*.

Jean Louis Joly, aged 40, usher in the Criminal Tribunal

[1] W. 501, 2nd dossier, p. 65.

of the Department of Paris, deposed that some nine months before, about eleven o'clock at night, as he was on duty at the Criminal Tribunal during the hearing of a case, there arose a tumult. He left the court in order to silence the public. "The first persons whom he perceived, exciting the trouble, were Fouquier and Coffinhal" He urged them to be silent. They answered "that he could go to ——, that the Criminal Tribunal was composed only of aristocrats, and that they would find out the secret of putting them on their best behaviour" A little later, Fouquier threatened him again, and repeated the same remarks to him.

On the 8th of Thermidor last, about seven or eight o'clock in the evening, as the witness was leaving his Tribunal, he met Fouquier on the Pont au Change. Having accosted him, the Public Prosecutor said to him "Well, your Tribunal hardly keeps pace." Joly answered that the judges could not compound with the law, and that the manner in which proceedings were conducted was different from that of the Revolutionary Tribunal; that, however, on the 16th of the same month, they were to have an affair in which there were fourteen prisoners, all charged with the printing and circulating false paper-money. Fouquier answered him. "Ah! that is something! As for me, I shall make fifty of them pass through it on the first day of the next *décade*."[1]

The witness Didier Thirion, Deputy for the Moselle, thought that at Danton's trial it was the Public Prosecutor's duty to have the prisoners judged on the facts of which they were accused by the Convention, and not himself to have become their accuser by imputing to them absolutely false and calumnious facts in order to get a decree depriving them of the right to plead, and thus shorten their trial by preventing them from being heard. The National Convention would not have passed the decree depriving them of the right to plead if it had not been deceived by the report, based, as was said, on a letter from Fouquier-Tinville, stating that the prisoners were in revolt. If then, this last

[1] W. 501, 2nd dossier, pp 65 and 67.

fact was demonstrated to be false, as it would be easy to determine from the depositions of those who were present at that session, it will be admitted that the Public Prosecutor had betrayed his trust.   Nor was it less a betrayal when, in a single trial and at a single sitting, he brought to trial at one time as many as fifty or sixty persons, taken from all corners of the Republic, the greater number of whom had never seen each other and had not the least connection or correspondence with one another.   The law could never have authorised the Public Prosecutor to make such a grouping (*amalgame*), and the Public Prosecutor should be guided, in his whole conduct, only by the Law and his own heart, which, if it had been animated by any feelings of humanity, would have indignantly repelled such measures.

" The passive instrument of tyranny," Didier Thirion concluded, " is sometimes as guilty as the tyrant himself. Tyrants could do hardly anything without the cowardly and criminal complaisance of their slaves. Fouquier-Tinville should have abandoned or abdicated his functions, or have performed them with honour and probity."[1]

Jean Lauchet, aged 34, general secretary of the Committee of General Security, residing at No. 22 Rue Nicaise, Paris, knew that Fouquier came very often to the Committee. His conferences with the members of this Committee were secret.   However, on a certain night, as Fouquier was leaving very late, the witness spoke to him, and the conversation turned on the great number of prisoners brought before the Tribunal every day.   Fouquier answered that it was the only way to empty the prisons, and that things would never go well so long as they did not guillotine a hundred a day [2]

Gilbert Liendon, aged 37, one of Fouquier-Tinville's ex-deputies, judge of the Tribunal of the Second Arrondissement, residing at No 68, Rue Beaubourg, had no knowledge of the fact that Fouquier, with whom rested the entire direction of the prosecutor's office, had been false to his trust.

[1] W. 501, 2nd dossier, p. 78   [2] W. 501, 2nd dossier, p. 64.

Bertonnier, delt.

DANTON

BORN AT ARCIS-SUR-AUBE, 1759, GUILLOTINED IN PARIS, 1796

Grébeauval, aged 41, another of Fouquier-Tinville's ex-deputies, at present without employment, gave evidence to the same effect.

Pierre Dusser, a commissioner of police, residing at No. 5, in the Rotonde du Temple, declared that he was present at the hearing on the day when the ex-Marshal de Noailles-Mouchy, his wife, and others were tried, and that Fouquier was sitting. " The woman Mouchy," said Dusser, " was at the end of the first bench, and Mouchy, her husband, at the beginning of the second The President and Fouquier, as was usual, examined each of the prisoners, and the woman Mouchy, having been overlooked, made a demand whilst her husband was being examined, saying . ' But, citizens, you have asked me nothing.' Fouquier turned towards the prisoner, and then said in a low voice to the President : ' Mouchy's wife has a right to speak now ? ' ' It is all the same,' said the President to the prisoners, ' you are together.' The proceedings went on, and I left only when the jury went out to consider their verdict. This woman was condemned to death without having been heard."

Pierre Goubaux, aged 29, secretary in the prosecutor's office of the Criminal Tribunal of the Department of Paris, residing at No. 20, Rue Hauteville, had heard from Laplace, another secretary in the prosecutor's office, the story of a rather strange scene between Fouquier and one of the secretaries in his office. It had to do with a list of witnesses that Fouquier thought far too long. Swearing at intervals, he said to the man who seemed to have made out the list : " Do you not know then what I want to come to ? I want to induce the Tribunal to do without witnesses," and other similar expressions. In fact, a few days later, Goubaux saw " with some astonishment " the decree of the 22nd of Prairial.

Personally, he had no other information to give in regard to Fouquier, except that he knew him to be a very violent man.

Citizen Claude Nicolas La Place appeared, and confirmed Citizen Goubaux's evidence [1]

[1] W 501, 2nd dossier, pp 52-54.

Jean Frédéric Martin, aged 36, a lawyer, residing at No. 2, Quai de la Mégisserie, had been imprisoned in the Luxembourg He heard it said that Fouquier had gone to the janitor's room in that house of detention in accordance with a decree of the 15th or the 16th of Messidor[1] ; and that there he had had an interview with one or several of the persons who made out the lists. Moreover, knowledge of this fact could be obtained either from Dubois, his secretary, or from Verney, the turnkey.

When transferred, with a hundred and fifty-five others, from the Luxembourg house of detention to the Conciergerie, the witness heard Fouquier give orders, through the window of the registry, that two of the hundred and fifty-five prisoners should be placed in the dark cell for having shown too much feeling in regard to the fate of fifty of their companions who were going down to the Tribunal to stand their trial ; a feeling all the more pardonable in those two prisoners as they knew that a similar fate awaited them the next day In fact, on that very day, they were guillotined. The proof of those facts could be furnished by the turnkey of the Conciergerie and others.[2]

The Richards, husband and wife, aged 48 and 49, janitors of the Conciergerie, had no knowledge of the facts imputed to Fouquier. The husband had " always known him to be a very violent man, whom he feared to approach."

Anne Ducray, aged 35, a clerk in the registry of the Revolutionary Tribunal, residing at No. 87, Rue Saint-Jacques, declared that he remembered none of the acts imputed to Fouquier. He had always recognised him to be " of a naturally violent character, which rendered him, so to speak, unapproachable." Several times he had seen him stamping his feet and showing all the signs of anger in regard to a case which he thought to be *of importance*, because an accused person had been acquitted He heard him complaining of the verdicts of certain jurors and saying that

[1] Three or four days before the great *batches* from the Luxembourg

[2] W. 501, 2nd dossier, p. 43.

they would not delay ridding themselves of them   Fouquier always took " the precaution of choosing the moment when there were capital executions in the Place de la Révolution to have exposed there to the gaze of the people those who were condemned to chains or to imprisonment so as to make them enjoy the disgusting spectacle of the executions."

Jean Robert Deschamps, aged 26½, registrar of Bicêtre, knew that Fouquier came to Bicêtre with Lanne, Herman's assistant   They sent for Valagnos and seven of his room-mates, put them in a row, and made the prisoners who were condemned to chains and the others pass before them in order that Valagnos might point out those who were guilty of conspiracy. As he pointed them out, Fouquier asked them their names.   On that day, the Public Prosecutor made out a warrant against thirty-seven individuals whom he immediately brought before the Tribunal   They were tried and condemned the next day.   On the 7th of Messidor Fouquier came again to Bicêtre.   " He made a further choice of thirty-seven individuals in the same manner " He issued a warrant against these thirty-seven, then a special warrant against Osselin, whom he caused to be taken away.   They were condemned the next day.   Bicêtre was, moreover, perfectly tranquil   Deschamps never perceived " the least germ of a conspiracy there."

Citizeness Banville, aged 41, the divorced wife of Bourdon, a gold-beater, deposed that on the day of Hébert's execution, she went out of curiosity to see him pass   In the Rue du Roule[1] she was invited to go into a house whose owner she did not know.   She there found Fouquier, whom she saw for the first time   When the condemned persons passed, Fouquier wanted to go to the window to see them.   It was pointed out to him that he ought not to show himself, that the condemned persons should not be insulted.   He immediately withdrew[2]

Louis Francis Debusne, aged 48, a lieutenant of the

[1] This street began at the Rue des Fossés-Saint-Germain-l'Auxerrois and ended at the Rue Saint-Honoré.
[2] W. 501, 2nd dossier, pp. 57 and 44

national police serving at the Tribunals, residing at 360
Cul-de-Sac de la Fosse aux Chiens, Rue des Bourdonnais,
noticed one day when he was on duty at a session of the
Tribunal and when thirty prisoners were tried, that
" Fouquier showed much ill-humour and impatience "
because they had all been condemned.

On the 18th of Messidor, when those charged with the
Luxembourg conspiracy were transferred, Debusne was
in command of the detachment. When he reached the
corner of the Rue de Harlay, Fouquier came and said to
him that he had succeeded in having only half of them
placed on trial , that their names would be taken there,
and that they were to alight at the Conciergerie, and he told
him to prevent them from communicating with one another.

Léonard Petit-Tressein, aged 36, a juror of the Tribunal,
residing at No 360 Rue Nicaise, on the morning of 18th of
Messidor, before the trial, heard Fouquier asking Coffinhal
in the Council Chamber if he wished to act as President
at the hearing next day, " *seeing that it was an important
affair.*" Coffinhal asked what affair it was Fouquier
explained that " it was half of those from the Luxembourg,
to the number of seventy or eighty."

Jean François Esprit Canaple, aged 26, residing at Paris,
in the Rue Neuve Denis, a seller of walking-sticks, on the
19th of Messidor, the day on which the trial of " the Luxembourg conspirators " began, saw and heard Fouquier, at
the window of the refreshment-room of the Palace, shouting
to the guardians immediately to place in a cell two prisoners
who had shown " feeling " towards the condemned. These
two prisoners were condemned two days later " for the same
conspiracy."[1]

Germain André Goureau, aged 36, an official defender, of
No. 7 Faubourg Poissonnière, gave details of what he
knew about the conspiracy in the prisons. He was imprisoned at the Plessis. He sought " to discover the
creatures whom Fouquier employed with the object of
multiplying the number of victims."

[1] W. 501, 2nd dossier, p. 84.

Jean Baptiste Darmaing, aged 23, secretary of the Convention, gave proofs, in his deposition, of the manner in which Fouquier allowed himself to be influenced by Vadier, who had sworn to ruin the Darmaings, his compatriots of the Ariège. When giving testimony to these facts, the witness declared that Fouquier had sought to debase the National Convention, and to perpetuate the reign of tyranny, and that he had conspired against Liberty and the Rights of Man.

The five Sansons—Pierre Charles, aged 40, a sub-lieutenant of artillery in the Parisian army; Charles Henri, aged 55; Nicolas Charles Gabriel, aged 73; his son, aged 49; and Henri Sanson, aged 27, a captain of artillery—had nothing to state in regard to Fouquier-Tinville. Sanson's assistant, Pierre François Etienne Desmorest, who, as public executioner, resided at No 11 Faubourg Saint-Denis, declared that "every morning, before judgment was pronounced, Fouquier gave him verbal orders to set up the guillotine at a certain time, and to have ready the number of conveyances he directed, and, in order to avoid irritating the public, he recommended him to keep them in different places but adjoining one another"[1]

Antoine Sézille, an official defender, aged 51, residing in the Enclos de la Raison, Section de la Cité, had known Fouquier only during the year that he had frequented the Revolutionary Tribunal. He regarded him as " a stern, violent, almost unapproachable man" Having to defend Citizen Thomassin, a priest imprisoned in the Conciergerie, Sézille went to the prosecutor's office and asked Fouquier for the documents relating to the affair. Fouquier became angry and refused to hand them over. Some days later Sézille defended Thomassin, without documents and without a memorandum, " after having only had an interview for a quarter of an hour with him in the prisoners' room" Thomassin was acquitted. In the course of the preceding month of Floréal, Sézille was charged with the defence of Fréteau, the ex-member of the Constituent Assembly who

[1] W 501, 2nd dossier, pp 63 and 58.

was acquitted, but was to be kept in prison as a suspect until the general peace For eight days the advocate begged Fouquier to deliver to him a copy of Fréteau's sentence of acquittal, without being able to obtain it. Fouquier refused to send the documents to the registry. At each ineffectual step taken by the advocate, Fouquier would answer harshly " You think you have got your Fréteau, but you shall not have him." As a matter of fact, some days after the law of the 22nd of Prairial, which suppressed the defenders, Fréteau was again placed on trial. " Thus in his case the maxim *non bis in idem* was violated by sending him again to trial for a crime of which he had been acquitted." He suffered the punishment of death.[1]

François Marie Pâris, aged 28, a lawyer, residing at 37 Rue Grenata, gave evidence as follows " A prisoner in the Luxembourg since the 29th of Brumaire of the year II., I was to have been numbered among the victims of the Terror, for, on the 10th of Thermidor, four prisoners from my Section and myself were transferred from the Luxembourg to the Conciergerie The municipality of Paris was in its entirety guillotined on that day and we were saved. During the twenty days I still remained at the Conciergerie, I met Fouquier[2] there. I spoke to him in these terms : ' You know me You know who I am. You are not ignorant that my principles have always been for the Revolution.' Fouquier answered me · ' What would you, my friend ? The order was precise Sent forward, as you were, by a popular commission to the Committees of Public Safety and of General Security, and those two Committees having sent you on to the Revolutionary Tribunal with injunctions to the Public Prosecutor to place you on trial, I had not the power to determine your freedom.'

" At that moment I regarded Fouquier rather as the kindly executant of barbarous and sanguinary orders that were given him rather than as a genuine Public Prosecutor. I ceased to speak to him. However, since I left prison,

---

[1] W 501, 2nd dossier, p 53
[2] Imprisoned, as we have seen, on the 14th of Thermidor.

I have learned that he had in no way deceived me, that in very reality I was to be one of his victims, for on the side of the papers relating to me, he had written in large letters, ' *Ready for delivery.* "[1]

Finally, on the 12th of Brumaire, at noon, an important witness appeared before Judge Forestier. This was Pierre Noel Subleyras, an ex-registrar of the Tribunal of the District of Uzès, who, during the Terror, had become President of the Popular Commission of the Museum (the Louvre). The sinister reputation of the Popular Commissions of Paris is well known, that of having been commissioned " to empty the prisons." Subleyras had formerly performed for a time the functions of judge of the Revolutionary Tribunal, functions to which he had been appointed on September 26th, 1793.[2]

Subleyras declared that ''about the middle of the preceding *décade*, Fouquier-Tinville's wife brought him a letter from her husband,[3] in which he asked him to give him collated

[1] W. 501, 2nd dossier, p 60

[2] It was he who at the trial of Hébert, Ronsin, and others, collected notes along with Naulin and Coffinhal, judges like himself, during the proceedings Every evening these three men met to collect these notes and to make them into a work which it was intended to print, a fantastic work which suppressed the proofs against Pache and Hanriot in order to place them to Danton's account, but so clumsily that it is impossible not to recognise Pache in the matter.

[3] This is Fouquier's letter ·—

" To Citizen Subleyras, President of the Popular Commission established at the former Louvre

(In Subleyras's hand—" *Ne varietur* the 13th of Brumaire of the year III of the Republic one and indivisible Subleyras ")

" I need, citizen, a copy certified by the Commission of the different letters that I have written relative to the persons who were to be placed on trial, either those who were sent forward (for that purpose) or those who were found to be implicated in conspiracies in the prisons, I particularly need the letter written by me on the night between the 18th and the 19th of Messidor these letters are indispensable to me to repel the attacks of my enemies in that direction , I hope, citizen, that you will hasten to procure this deliverance for my wife, who, for this purpose, will send you this present Trenchard groans in the same prison

" Greeting and fraternity,   A O FOUQUIER.

" This 1st of Brumaire of the year III of the Republic one and indivisible Pélagie." (W 500, 2nd dossier, p 32)

copies of the letters written by him (Fouquier) to the former Popular Commissions, and relating to the accused persons whom he had to place on trial.

When he was Public Prosecutor, Fouquier had sent to the Commission of the Museum some lists of " individuals " whom he was to place on trial for the conspiracy in the prisons. He invited the Commission to send him any documents and information it had respecting them. On this invitation, Subleyras affirmed, the Commission sent to Fouquier the documents it had and the reports that had been made out in the Paris Sections concerning some of the prisoners on the lists. Those documents remained at the Tribunal. This was all, according to Subleyras's account, that the Popular Commission knew of the conspiracy of the prisons !

He added that, on the 7th of Thermidor, two days before Robespierre's fall, Fouquier had told the Commission that some of those reports had reached him, and that he had asked it for such documents as it might have [1]

Madame Fouquier-Tinville continued to take measure after measure, step after step, in the interests of her husband's defence. Three times, during the first ten days of this month of Brumaire, she went to Subleyras. Not being able to see him, she had written the following letter —

" This 8th of Brumaire, year III. of the Republic.

No 242 Rue de la Harpe.

" I pray you, citizen, to be good enough to give me an answer relating to what I have asked you for my husband, the copy of those letters which are indispensable to him in the present circumstances, for three days in succession I have gone to your house without being able to see you. As I am a long distance off, I pray you to let me know if you have found these papers, and if you can give me a copy of them ; you will oblige your fellow-citizen.

" Fouquier's Wife." [2]

(To Citizen Subleyras, No. 108 Rue des Petits-Champs.)

[1] W 500, 3rd dossier, p 144   [2] W 500, 2nd dossier, p 31.

It is easy to understand the importance which Fouquier attached to the possession of those copies. They were indispensable to him. In his defence he had to prove that he had acted only in virtue of the orders of the Committee of Public Safety. The Committee had sent him a list of names, telling him that these prisoners had conspired in the Luxembourg house of detention. The Committee had sent him a resolution of the 17th of Messidor, ordering him to bring to trial within twenty-four hours all those charged with conspiracy in the prisons According to the expression he used in the course of his examination on the 1st of Frimaire, "when the Law speaks, the public official must act " He could not therefore avoid (it is still his own argument that we reproduce) prosecuting and bringing to trial all the individuals named on that list. He had not desired to know either how that list and others were sent to the Committee, or by whom they were made out. He had received no revelation in regard to this ; he had only " performed the imperious duty prescribed by the Law." Then he wrote to the Popular Commission of the Museum to ask it for the documents which it might have for the prosecution or for the defence. The Committee of Public Safety having decided, on the 18th of Messidor, that the 158 persons suspected of conspiracy in the Luxembourg should be tried in three sections, on the same evening, when he returned home, he immediately informed the Popular Commission. It was this letter and some others sent by him to Subleyras that he needed to clear himself. They would testify in his favour, would establish that he was only an agent of the Committees, and prove that he only carried out their orders strictly.

But this written evidence of his obedience which he claimed, and which no one would dream of refusing him, would also prove that, a servile magistrate, entirely subject, through fear or interest, to the Committees, he had been the diligent workman of a work of blood. The principal artisans in that work perished on the scaffold on the 10th of Thermidor Those who remained were denounced and

N

hunted down. It was the zealous, indefatigable official of the Terror that the Themidorian purification aimed at and pursued in his person.

As Public Prosecutor Leblois said in his speech against Fouquier "Invested for nearly eighteen months with the painful obligation of searching out and prosecuting crime, but honoured during the same period also with the holy and consoling mission of supporting innocence, of defending it, and of protecting it, it might be said that Fouquier-Tinville made it his sport to overthrow these two objects and to take them in an inverse sense."

CHAPTER IX

THE days passed. Fouquier was waiting to be examined. On the 9th of Brumaire he was transferred from Sainte-Pélagie to the Plessis-Egalité, to that house of detention which the Parisians, at the time he was Public Prosecutor, had named " Fouquier's storehouse." " The horror that he inspired was such that the prisoners nearly killed him. The janitor confined him to his room. He wanted one day to open his window to take the air ; horrible imprecations forced him to shut it immediately." [1]

He lived then apart, walled in, enclosed, alone with his thoughts, thoughts that absolved him. His heart was free from crime. It was in his opinion the heart of a good citizen. But hatred pursued him without an intermission. He was a victim of that feeling of duty which led him to perform public functions " with diligence and vigour." He did not ask himself whether the lives of all those men and women whom he had sent to execution were worth nothing. In his eyes they were the enemies of the Republic and traitors. They were conspiring against liberty and virtue. As Public Prosecutor his duty was towards the Revolution and its heads. He had fulfilled the law.

Finally, on the 1st of Frimaire in the year III. (November 21, 1794), he was taken from the Plessis house of detention to the Tribunal and examined by Judge Forestier, assisted

[1] Campardon : *Le Tribunal Révolutionnaire de Paris*, II., p. 138. Details furnished by the journal entitled *La Vedette*.

by Raymond Josse, his registrar, and Jean Jacques Granger, his deputy. Here is his examination

The Judge " Did you not, while you held your office, and especially in the last months of it, give orders every morning to the public executioner to set up the guillotine, and to prepare a more or less considerable number of conveyances ? "

A —" As regards the guillotine, there was for a time a question of leaving it up permanently. Afterwards, because the materials were kept in the Rue du Pont-aux-Choux and as it took five hours and more to erect, it has happened two or three times that the order to set it up was given, but only to execute the persons condemned on the previous day in accordance with the sentence of the court. In order to avoid the unpleasantness of seeing those materials transported from the Pont-aux-Choux, the Department was asked for premises in which to place the materials and the wood. Those premises were granted near the Place de la Révolution. At no time was an order given by me to set up the guillotine, except for the purpose of executing sentences that had been passed. As regards the other part of the question, having seen the scandal (I mean this fact had been reported to me) of allowing as many as twelve or fourteen condemned persons to be piled up on the same cart, and the Committee of Public Safety having blamed me for it, notifying to me its desire that each cart should contain only seven individuals, next day I summoned the public executioner and notified to him the order to place only seven individuals at most in the same cart, and to arrange in such a way that the executions should never be postponed until the following day. When the executioner remarked that it was often very difficult to find carts in sufficient number for the same day (for he only received the order at about half-past three), and also on account of the known scarcity of horses, I advised him to have some always ready, preferring and desiring that they should be useless rather than that condemned persons should be crowded on a single cart as had happened before

THE GUILLOTINE

" In spite of my advice in this respect, it sometimes happened that condemned persons in excess of the number seven were placed in the carts But in all this I only acted from a motive of humanity and to alleviate the sufferings of the condemned persons in so far as it lay in my power. I have never known and could not know whether any of the persons placed on trial would be condemned, nor what their number would be. The proof is that very frequently the carts were useless "

Q.—" Who raised the question of leaving the guillotine up permanently ? "

A.—" It was discussed at the Committee of Public Safety."

Q —" Have you always conformed to the exact selection of the jurors who were to sit in any given case ? Did you not intend to exclude some who might be more humane ? Have you not, on the contrary, made choice of those whose character appeared to you fitter for doing what was called *firing an uninterrupted volley* ? "

A.—" I never made any choice of jurors through preference in any given case ; if I have made a choice of them, it was not purposely or consciously , I have never known any of the jurors very intimately I point out that the ushers sometimes made mistakes in summoning the jurors ; but I never believed that those mistakes were the fruit of crime, but rather that of error. I have never made use of the expression ' firing an uninterrupted volley ' ; I have never known anything but the execution of the laws Since the terrible law of the 22nd of Prairial, the reformation of which I have perpetually but vainly solicited from the Committees of Public Safety and of General Security, every time I have sat I have never made a single opening or closing speech calculated to influence the opinion of the jurors in any way against accused persons who were already so unfortunate as to be deprived of defenders I may even add that I have never forgotten to point out to the jurors and to outline the documentary evidence for the defence provided by the accused persons as well as that for the prosecution "

Q.—" Have you not held conferences about the composition of the juries with various persons who came either to the hearings or to the prosecutor's office or to your own room ? Have not those persons influenced you ? Have you not combined with them beforehand to secure the acquittal or the conviction of certain persons ? "

A.—" I have never done anything so monstrous. Nobody has ever presumed to make proposals of such a nature to me I should have treated as they deserved any persons whatsoever who would have done so I point out that when the Committee of Public Safety proposed to me, and even pressed me to have General Kellermann and other individuals tried, I always refused, and for this reason alone, that the order was given me without the attendance of certain witnesses whom I regarded as indispensable "

Q.—' Who are the members of the Committee of Public Safety who gave you such orders ? "

A.—" Robespierre and Couthon summoned me to the Committee and in the name of the Committee for that purpose in the early days of Messidor, some time before Robespierre ceased going to the Committee. Immediately Couthon had been carried[1] to the bottom of the staircase, he caused me to be summoned to the Committee of Public Safety where he had remained for something else, and said to me ' Above all, do not fail to have Kellermann tried before Dubois de Crancé's arrival ' This injunction, joined with the quarrel that had taken place between Couthon and Dubois de Crancé, was sufficient to convince me that Couthon bore ill-will to Kellermann as well as to Dubois de Crancé. It was at two o'clock in the afternoon that I was summoned to the Committee, as Couthon never went there after dinner."

Q.—" Have you not had intimate relations or a special understanding with Robespierre, Saint-Just, Lebas, Dumas, Coffinhal, Fleuriot, and other conspirators, the enemies of the people and of liberty ? Have you not known, shared, and supported their counter-revolutionary opinions

---

[1] Couthon was paralysed —Tr

and arrangements ? Were you not associated with them ? "

A.—" I could limit myself to remarking that it was I, in my capacity of Public Prosecutor, who on the 10th of Thermidor, demanded that the law should be enforced against all those afore-mentioned conspirators, who were outlawed by a decree of the Convention, with the exception of Coffinhal, who was only captured on the 18th,[1] an enforcement of the law that I certainly would never have demanded if I had been initiated into or engaged in any way in the counter-revolutionary projects of the various conspirators But I believe I ought to give a little fuller scope to my answer.

[1] On the night between the 9th and 10th of Thermidor, Coffinhal, seeing the Commune conquered and Robespierre and his friends in the hands of the Conventionals, hurled himself on Hanriot, whose drunkenness had ruined everything, and flung him out of one of the windows of the Hôtel de Ville on to a dung-heap   Then he disappeared into the night   He was vainly sought for during several days

He had fled towards the Seine, and, disguised as a boatman, had gone down with the stream to the Ile des Cygnes, where he had hidden himself   He remained there two days and two nights, staying his hunger with the bark of trees, and drenched by the torrential rain that fell continuously

At last, being able to hold out no longer, the outlaw left the island and went to a friend to whom he had rendered some services.   He asked him for food, clothes, and money.   This man brought him into his house, and then, locking the door, went to inform against him

Coffinhal was arrested on the night between the 17th and 18th of Thermidor and taken to the Conciergerie   " Nothing can paint the tortures I have endured," he said to the turnkey   " The death that is preparing for me is a benefit and a kindness compared with what I have suffered "

As the Revolutionary Tribunal no longer existed, a decree of the Convention decided that the Criminal Tribunal should verify *the outlaw's* identity and send him to execution.   It was on the 18th of Thermidor that he appeared before Oudart   Four witnesses identified him.   Public Prosecutor Leblois demanded the application of the law   Coffinhal was then led to the Place de la Révolution, in a heavy rain, in the midst of hooting   The people crowded against the cart, and tried to stab or strike him with their umbrellas, saying, " Well, Coffinhal, guard against that thrust, if you can ! "   This was an allusion to a saying of the ex-Vice-President of the Revolutionary Tribunal to a fencing-master who had just been condemned to death. " Well, old fellow, guard against that thrust if you can "

Coffinhal died courageously

In consequence, I declare that I have never had any intimate connection with the Robespierres, Saint-Just, Couthon, and Lebas, that I have never seen them except at the Committees of Public Safety and of General Security, and then as members of those Committees; that I have never been to the houses of any of them, except once to that of the elder Robespierre, on the day of the attempt on Collot d'Herbois, just as I had been to that of Collot whom I did not find at home; the despotic tone with which Robespierre received me would have estranged me for ever, even if I had been anxious to go there; never have I been in any of the houses to which I have learned since my arrest that the conspirators repaired I have never had any private correspondence with them As for Dumas, I only knew him as President; moreover, Dumas was notoriously known to be my enemy, so much so that he tried at different times to have me replaced

"As for Fleuriot and Coffinhal, I knew them only subsequent to their becoming members of the Tribunal. I have sometimes had meals with them, as is customary among members of the same tribunal. But I never perceived that they were engaged in a conspiracy. They never made any overtures to me in this respect. Finally, I had no knowledge of this conspiracy, except on the 9th of Thermidor in common with all other citizens. The proof of my denial follows from my conduct on the evening of the 9th of Thermidor. I remained at my post up to the moment when I went to the assembled Committees of Public Safety and of General Security. It is notorious that I did not go to the rebel Commune, in spite of the repeated invitations of emissaries who were sent to me for that purpose. It also follows from the declarations made by Coffinhal, in the presence of several gendarmes, that I counted for nothing in this conspiracy; that Coffinhal, and Dumas, were the only members of the Tribunal who were initiated into it. This declaration has been drawn up in the form of a report by the officers of *gendarmerie* who despatched it to Deputy Fréron "

Q.—" Who were the emissaries and by whom were they sent ? "

A.—" I did not know them. But they announced themselves as coming from the Commune, to which all the authorities of Paris were invited to repair, according to what was said "

Q.—" Have you not shown that you were affected by the condemnation of those conspirators, and in particular that of Fleuriot ? Were you not full of reproaches at the fact that this conspirator, as it happened, was executed last of those who were condemned with him ?[1] What were the reasons for this special interest that you took in the said Fleuriot ? "

A.—" It was usual for the ushers to give me an account of the executions and to tell me if any incident took place. On the day of the execution of Robespierre, Saint-Just, Fleuriot, and others, my usher, Tavernier, came to tell me that the execution was over. I then remarked to him : ' Of course, you have taken the precaution of having the triumvirate of Couthon, Robespierre, and Saint-Just executed last ? ' On Tavernier's answer that the Mayor of Paris had been executed last, I said to him ' You are a good fellow ; but you are always doing something foolish. Did you not feel that chiefs such as those I have mentioned ought to be executed last, and not the Mayor and others who were only accessories ? ' And I added· ' Your blunder will cause me many reproaches ' In fact, the public thought it very extraordinary that those three individuals were not executed last But it was not out of any interest towards Fleuriot that I made those remarks to Tavernier."

Q.—" Did you not, in the exercise of your functions, perform many harsh and arbitrary acts ? Have you not threatened those who came to speak to you on behalf of various prisoners, various condemned persons ? Have you

---

[1] We have seen in Chapter V that, on the 10th of Thermidor, Fouquier-Tinville, who had pleaded against Robespierre, Couthon, Saint-Just, etc , rose and left the Tribunal at the moment for pleading against his friend, Lescot-Fleuriot, Mayor of Paris. It was his deputy, Liendon, who then pleaded

been exact in reading or laying due stress at the hearings upon the memorials, documents, or evidence for the defence that were sent to you in favour of those who were placed on trial ? Has it not happened that you placed several accused persons on trial before you opened the packets containing the documents for the defence ? Have not several of those persons been condemned, and do you not think that you are responsible for those condemnations ? "

A —" I have never performed any arbitrary act either out of hatred, or out of resentment, or for any other reason. I have never used harshness towards anybody whatsoever. If my quick and petulant temper has caused me to be considered a harsh man by anybody, most of the upright men who know me will not fail to do me the justice that I was as gentle as I was humane towards those who presented themselves to me for any reason whatsoever, above all towards the unfortunate. I have never used any threat of the class mentioned in the question. I have always busied myself, and I have enjoined the same upon my secretaries, in joining together all the documents relating to each accused person I carefully opened my mails every day, and even several times a day. Every time documents reached me from the Committee of General Security or from other constituted authorities, I made haste to send them to my deputies who were in Court. It is not within my knowledge that any documents for the defence relating to accused persons were not produced ; and when accused persons who were on trial claimed documents in Court, they were always searched for Moreover, as I have remarked above, I have always taken care to hand over to the jurors the documents for the defence put in either by the accused persons or by those who interested me in their fate, together with a ticket indicating the names of each of the accused persons."

Q.—" Did you not, in league with the conspirators (and in order to bring about the deaths of those whom you had designated or who had been indicated to you), resolve to

place on trial a considerable number of accused persons ?
Did you not cause them to be tried with such haste that
it became impossible for them to be heard or for there to be
even sufficient time to ask them their names and the formal
questions it is usual to put in such circumstances ? "

A.—" I have already remarked that I have had no
connection or acquaintance with any conspirator. I have
not ceased to prosecute conspirators without any regard
to person or rank, and this is one of the secret motives for
my arrest and the persecutions I am experiencing. This
question shows well enough that it is desired to make me
responsible for the rapidity with which Dumas exercised
his functions. However, nobody can be ignorant that the
President, then as well as to-day, was the master to decide
whether the accused persons should be accorded or refused
the right to speak. Further, I never made any arrangement
with him as to the prompt or slow manner of trying accused
persons As often as I sat (which was very seldom), I have
moderated, in so far as it depended on me, Dumas' frightful
celerity, and granted accused persons the right to speak.
In regard to the number of those accused persons, no law
then prescribed the maximum or minimum number that
were to be placed on trial for the different offences with
which they were charged Besides, in this respect I have
exactly followed the orders of the Committee of Public
Safety, which at that period had plenary powers It is
quite true that, in my capacity as Public Prosecutor, I have
placed on trial several persons charged with different
offences. But that is only on account of the reproach
made against the Tribunal in a report of the Committee of
Public Safety to the Convention on the 9th of Ventôse.
In a word, it has never happened, whatever may have been
the number of those placed on trial, that they have been
tried without being questioned, all of them, at the hearing
This fact is notorious. But it was not the result of a criminal
arrangement."

Q.—" How could you, at the same hearing, have included
on the same list and for the same offence, fifty, sixty, or

more individuals of all ranks and conditions, who had never either spoken to one another or known one another, and, until then, had been separated from one another by great distances ? "

A —" The placing on trial of fifty or sixty individuals or more has been very rare I believe even that this has not occurred in such great numbers except for different crimes, and that the indictments including few or more individuals characterise and specify each of the offences that were personal to them. This fact is easy to verify by an inspection of the indictments Thus it is of little importance whether they were from the same place or from distances very remote from one another and for diverse offences Moreover, I have only adopted this measure in accordance with the orders and the very pronounced wish of the Committees of Public Safety and of General Security, to whom I exactly delivered every evening the list of verdicts passed by the Tribunal, whether of condemnation or acquittal. In regard to individuals of different professions, I only determined to group the unhappy prisoners of different professions after the difficulty arose from the law of the 22nd of Prairial, which provided among other things (Article 18) that the judgments passed by the Council Chamber could not be executed without having been approved by the Committees of Public Safety and of General Security Important occupations rendered this measure impossible and void. The motive which determined the grouping was the desire more effectively to bring about the release of a crowd of individuals who would have remained in prison if this grouping had not been employed, and it took place, moreover, only in accordance with the orders of the members of the Committees of Public Safety and of General Security. Those Committees have approved of this measure, insomuch that, in a report made to the Convention on the 9th of Thermidor, they note the fact that, in spite of the measures and means employed by the Tribunal for accelerating the trials of the conspirators, the two Committees, on the previous day, resolved on new measures intended to bring to trial without delay all conspirators throughout the Republic.

" Finally, so far as concerns myself, I have never designated anybody as deserving, by preference, to be struck by the sword of the law, but I have placed individuals on trial according as the law enjoined me."

Q.—" Have you not exceeded the punishments pronounced against various accused persons ? Are you sure that, out of the great number of persons tried or condemned, there was such an identification of their persons that it is impossible that condemned persons were set free, whilst individuals who had not been placed on trial and against whom there was no indictment were none the less sent to death ? "

A.—" Far from having exceeded any of the condemnations pronounced, I have, on the contrary, given the most precise orders to execute exactly and strictly the condemnations pronounced against them In regard to the rest of the question, I very rarely sat in Court. When I did so, if I was obliged to bring a verbal indictment against the prisoners not included in the written indictment and against whom charges were brought forward in the course of the proceedings, I have always demanded, at the end of my verbal indictment, that an official report of it should be drawn up by the registrar. The same must have been done by my deputies. My functions were limited to that. The drawing up and signing concerned the President, the judges, and the registrar. I cannot be responsible for omissions or errors that may have been made in this respect, though I do not think they have been made. As regards the identity of individuals who were condemned, their names were exactly inscribed on the printed paper intended to be sent to the executioner by the registrar on duty. It is not within my knowledge that one person has ever been sent to death for another. Further, I beg the Tribunal in its justice to point out to me an instance of this. I undertake to answer it "

Q.—" Have you always faithfully secured to the accused

persons or to the nation the return of the sums of money lodged with you ? Have you taken care exactly out of these sums to provide for the needs of those for whom they were intended, and who asked for assistance ? "

A.—" I have never personally received or handled any monies These sums were received in my name by the secretaries and clerks delegated according to the court registrar for that purpose.

" Each object bore an identifying number. But those which I received in my own letters, sent for different prisoners, I always sent François to the post to cash. On my orders, François delivered them to the registrar entrusted with that duty This employee has, through his negligence, given ground for many complaints, in particular for not having distributed, each week, the sums due to the prisoners. I have never retained any sum belonging to the condemned or to the prisoners. The woman Richard, the janitor of the Conciergerie, had orders to deposit them in the registry so that the proof ought to exist in a register. Towards the end of Messidor, the treasurer of the Hospice gave me a bill of exchange for four thousand and some hundreds of *livres*, belonging to a man named Leborgne, then detained in the said hospital This Leborgne, arrested by order of the Committee of General Security, was charged with very grave counter-revolutionary offences, I believed I could see, from an inspection of this bill, that he might have considerable deposits at Paris. That is why I believed that I ought to keep this bill of exchange, which I placed in my desk, in a drawer intended for objects of this sort, and with this inscription on it · ' This bill of exchange belongs to Leborgne, detained at the Hospice. To be attached to the documents pertaining to the said Leborgne and verified ' This bill of exchange was found in that drawer (at the time of the examination of the said room made by the Deputies commissioned by the Convention to do so), by one of them whose name I do not remember, but who is five feet two inches high, with a dark face and dark hair. This commissioner declared, in the presence of Citizens

Dobsen and Petit, that he had held the said bill of exchange and had put it back among the papers."

Q.—" Have you not, in a fashion, boasted of the great number of prisoners whom you have brought to trial, and have you not addressed threats to those who begged you for the justice which you owed them and for the pity to be expected from you on account of their misfortune ? Have you not prosecuted and even punished the sensibility that some prisoners showed at the sight of the great number of those who were going away to be executed ? "

A —" These statements are as atrocious as they are new to me. My character for humanity assures me that I shall be avenged by posterity for such insults."

Q.—" At the trial of Danton and others did you not pretend that you suspected a rebellion and a lack of respect towards the Tribunal and at the hearing, in order to derive from this an opportunity to solicit a decree which took from them the right to plead and thus deprived them of the means of being heard and defending themselves ? Did you not announce beforehand that you would obtain this decree ? "

A.—" The minute of the letter written by me, on the 15th of Germinal, to the Committee of Public Safety, relative to that affair was found at the time my papers were examined It forms part of the quota taken away by the Deputies commissioned to make the search. This letter answers the question in a manner that destroys all imputations. As for the last part of the question, I declare that, on the contrary, I announced to the accused that I hoped to be able to bring about the appearance of the deputies they desired "

Q —" Have you not imagined projects of insurrection in the prisons in order to derive from this an opportunity for placing on trial a greater number of accused persons, and precisely those whose deaths had been promised ? "

A.—" Without the law of the 23rd Ventôse, which expressly provides that whoever shall attempt to open the prisons shall be declared a traitor to the country and punished as such, a law which imposed on me the rigorous duty of prosecuting and placing on trial all individuals charged with these offences, I should have had a difficulty in believing in the conspiracies on which the Committee of Public Safety lodged informations with me. But when the Law speaks, the public official must act. Now I state that the Committee of Public Safety furnished me with a list of names, declaring to me that these individuals had formed part of a conspiracy in the Luxembourg house of detention, together with a resolution of the 17th of Messidor providing that I should be bound to bring to trial within twenty-four hours, all those charged with conspiracy in the houses of detention. That is why, in virtue of the law cited above, I could not avoid prosecuting and placing on trial all the individuals named on that list.

" I did the same, afterwards, in regard to two other lists that were delivered to me in succession by the same Committee and on which were placed the names of a certain number of prisoners from the house of the Carmelites and from that of Lazare. I am entirely ignorant in what way those lists were delivered to the Committee and by whom they were made out. No member of the Committee made me the least revelation in this respect. I am equally ignorant if this measure was imagined because there were not sufficient offences to reach the persons named on those lists.

" As for me. I have performed the imperious duty which was enjoined on me by law by writing to the Popular Commission and inviting it to send me without delay all the documents for conviction or acquittal concerning the prisoners that it might have. And, for this purpose, I sent it, as fast as they reached me, the lists of prisoners who were to be placed on trial. Moreover, as a proof that I acted only in virtue of the orders and wishes of the Committee of Public Safety, I may say that the Committee having decided on my representations on the evening of the 18th of Messidor that the 158 prisoners charged with conspiracy in the Luxembourg should be tried at three sessions, namely those of the 19th, the 21st, and the 22nd, when I got back I immediately informed the Commission of this Finally, I would add that I knew so little about this conspiracy and the alleged motives for which it was imagined, that there ought to be, among the documents of the trial, a letter from Citizen Lanne, deputy-commissioner of the Administration of Civil Affairs, Police, and Tribunals, dated the 18th of Messidor, in answer to mine, giving the names of the witnesses to be heard in this affair, and that I had never seen or known the witnesses indicated in that letter, with the exception of Benoît who had appeared in the affair of Grammont and others. I have never had correspondence with this Benoît, and I have never even been willing to allow him into my room in spite of the repeated requests to do so made in his letters. They can be found among the letters I threw aside."

Q.—" Have you not caused all those makers of the lists to be heard as witnesses ? Did you not concert with them as to the nature of the depositions they were to make ? Has it not happened that you caused them to be arrested and even punished because in some circumstances they had given evidence for the defence ? Was there not an understanding with them that they would be guided in their depositions by signs that you had agreed to make to them ? "

A.—" I could not, knowingly, have caused the makers of lists to be heard, for the authors were unknown to me, and the lists, as I have already remarked, were handed to me by the Committee of Public Safety, except for one information written in my own hand, an information which was lodged with me after the Luxembourg conspiracy by a man named Verney, then a turnkey in that house of detention. This declaration is attached to the documents [1] What is gratuitously imputed to me is monstrous Moreover, those signs are clearly demonstrated to be false, for the witness's back is turned to the Public Prosecutor, and, besides, a man does not come to commit such a monstrous offence unless he has committed others before it, which cannot be proved against me It is false that I ever sought to intimidate any witness in this case, or in any other. It is true only that, on account of the ambiguities and evasions of

[1] Archives Nationales, W. 500, 2nd dossier, p 28.

ɔ

a turnkey whose name I have forgotten,[1] the Tribunal ordered this latter's arrest as a provisional measure of security "

Q —" Have you not allowed yourself to be dominated by ill-humour and violence in cases when accused persons were acquitted, where you had presumed condemnation ? Have you not claimed to retain them by your own sole authority, and threatened to seize them again and have them tried anew ? Were not some condemned in this way ? "

A —" I remember none of those cases. Further, I ask for the cases to be pointed out to me in which it is stated that I behaved in this way. Then I will answer in a manner that will leave no doubt I remember only that Fréteau, having been acquitted for a first offence, the Tribunal decided that he should be detained until the general peace. Fresh charges, not foreseen and not indicated on his first indictment, having been laid against him, he was again placed on trial and condemned on a fresh indictment."

Q.—" Have you ever acceded to proposals that may have been made to you to allow yourself to be bribed by more or less considerable sums ? "

A —" I have always been faithful to my duty Far from allowing myself to be bribed, I would not even have allowed such a proposal to be made to me To ask me such a question is to crown the persecutions that I am made to suffer. My conduct has been always frank and loyal. I ask, further, that the names of the individuals be made known to me "

Q.—" Do you intend to justify yourself, and from what do you claim that your justification will result ? "

A.—" For that purpose I make use of the answers contained in the present examination and of the printed memorial which ought to have been delivered to each of the members of the Tribunal, together with the documents found at the time of the examination of my papers and taken away by the Commission, and other papers ; finally, of means of which I reserve to myself the time and place for turning to account."

---

[1] This was Lesenne, turnkey at the Luxembourg, who was arrested on the 19th of Messidor. He gave evidence at Fouquier's trial.

Q —"Have you made choice of one or of several defenders ? "

A.—" I choose Citizen Lafleuterie."

Here Fouquier remarked that it ought not to escape the notice of the Tribunal that, as he had exercised the rigorous office of Public Prosecutor for seventeen months, individuals might come forward, moved by hatred and vengeance towards him, or on account of their own detention, or on account of the condemnation of their relatives or friends, to give evidence against him.   For this reason he asked the justice of the Tribunal " to give all the attention of which it was capable to persons of this class, leaving it also to the loyalty of the Tribunal that the present examination should not be seen by any of the witnesses who were to be heard."

The examination ended.   The accused declared that he persisted in all his answers.   He signed the official report together with Granges, the judge's deputy   Judge Forestier and Josse, the registrar, then signed [1]

On the 4th of Frimaire (November 24) Fouquier was transferred from the Plessis prison to the Hospice de l'Evêché. [2] This fact seems to indicate that he was ill, exhausted by the struggle, by the emotions which his vigorous temperament had hitherto withstood, worn out by an extremely severe winter [3] and by the prison regimen   Witnesses at his trial declared that he was recognisable though very changed and grown thinner.   He remained at the Hospice de l'Evêché

---

[1] Archives Nationales, W 501, 2nd dossier, p. 39.

[2] L'Evêché was at the same time a prison and a hospital.   As a prison it came under the Public Prosecutor's jurisdiction and had been under Fouquier's orders   " The man whom the patients must have least expected to see appearing among them was assuredly Fouquier-Tinville, who, after having taken part in organising the Hospice, after having presided over it for a long time, was now in his turn imprisoned within it and remained there until the suppression of the establishment."   We take this quotation from a very interesting monograph by M Léon Legrand which appeared in the *Revue des Questions Historiques*, July, 1890, under the title of *L'Hospice Nationale du Tribunal Révolutionnaire*

[3] A gendarme's report says, on the 10th of Nivôse, that seven persons crossing *the Seine by the ice* were engulfed   Aulard · *Paris sous le Directoire*, I., p 351

until the 26th of Frimaire (December 16), on which date he was transferred to the Conciergerie in order to appear, two days later, before the Tribunal.

Carrier and the Revolutionary Committee of Nantes came up for trial on the 7th of Frimaire. On the 24th, at half-past ten, the pleadings in the Carrier trial closed. On the 26th, at midnight, Carrier began his speech. He spoke from midnight until half-past four in the morning. He was condemned to death along with Pinard and Grandmaison [1] The other thirty accused persons were acquitted. The Carrier trial lasted sixty sittings.

On the same day, the Tribunal, presided over by Dobsen, delivered to Public Prosecutor Leblois an official certificate of the pleas for the prosecution which he had just drawn up against Fouquier-Tinville

This document comprised three propositions: 1st, Fouquier-Tinville's crimes; 2nd, Fouquier-Tinville's combinations and objects; 3rd, Fouquier-Tinville's character and moral behaviour.

" Whether we endeavour to penetrate into his connections, his views, his object, or whether we go further, and seek to know what were his manners, his habits, his moral behaviour, we see, and we could say it is already proved, that, in all these different aspects, Fouquier is criminal, mischievous, and merits punishment."

In short, Leblois laid hold of and directed against Fouquier the charges of grouping together the accused persons and of placing them on trial in a mass after the law of the 22nd of Prairial. He accused him of being the criminal author of those hasty trials, thanks to which " accused persons have been condemned in appearance and really executed without there ever being against them either a valid verdict or sentence." He affirmed that he was responsible for the substitution of one accused person for another, and of having had

---

[1] Carrier died with courage. " He offered his hand with good grace to the executioner and mounted to the theatre of death with vivacity," says the *Courier Républicain* of the 27th of Frimaire. " Pinard was dying at the foot of the scaffold; Grandmaison was weeping but did not appear to lack courage " (*Ibid.*)

the guillotine prepared and set up and the carts got ready in advance. He rebuked him for the blank sentence forms, and the eagerness, which Fouquier could have prevented, for depriving certain accused persons of the right to plead and thus leaving them without witnesses or defenders. He rebuked him for the Comte de Fleury's death. He insisted on the accusation that Fouquier had changed the jurors, and made a selection from them, that he had spoken to them and made them speak to him, that he had penetrated "furtively" into the room where they were deliberating, that he had jested in an atrocious fashion by calling them "firers of uninterrupted volleys." He influenced witnesses. He received them in his office ; he taught them what they were to say He "exercised the most pronounced despotism over all the agents of the Tribunal, and especially over the secretaries of the prosecutor's office." He kept back documents for the defence, and refused to deliver them to the defenders. He abstained from opening packets of documents for the defence. He lied by implying and trying to make it believed that some accused persons when placed on trial had rebelled against the Tribunal and shown a lack of respect towards it [1] He lied by implying and trying to make it believed that there existed conspiracies in the prisons. "He acted thus in order to snatch the terrible law of the 22nd of Prairial, which he boasted of obtaining, and of which, perhaps, he alone could have given the dangerous idea." He himself went to the prisons and the houses of detention. " He made it his task to have intercourse with those cowardly men whom one is always sure of finding inclined to injure others and to degrade themselves. He flattered them, caressed them, and influenced them to charge themselves with the very doubtful employment of common informers. . . . He established, between himself and them, a furtive, inquisitorial, sanguinary intercourse, based upon the lists of proscribed persons."

" Inexorable and pitiless, the verdict which accidentally acquitted an accused person was to Fouquier-Tinville the

[1] Danton and the Dantonists

object of a further display of rage and fury ; he almost always opposed, and that on his own authority alone, the execution of verdicts of acquittal, and if he were nevertheless forced to abstain from resisting them, he protested and threatened to recapture and sacrifice the victim ; this was especially the feeling he experienced towards, and the threat he made against, and the fate he reserved for, one of the former Parliamentarians whose ruin he had sworn."[1]

Leblois charged Fouquier with having " strangely and in all ways proved false to every part and function of his office," with having been as greedy for blood as for money, with having kept the sums sent to the prisoners through him, with having illegally taken over various deposits, chattels, and sums of money, " since there was legally no other depository than the registrar of the Tribunal," and, either from forgetfulness or from fraudulent intention, with making no note or register of those objects, some of which have been cut up or lost, and which it is impossible to trace here.

He charged him with having supported those " monsters," Robespierre, Saint-Just, Couthon, and others, " who had promised themselves to depopulate France and to cause to disappear all its genius, talents, honour, and industry." It will be demonstrated, said Leblois, " that Fouquier paid them visits in the dead of night "[2] It will be demonstrated, he said also, " that they held orgies in private houses at the period when the conspiracy was discovered "

In brief, " it is proved that Fouquier-Tinville made amusement and a sort of enjoyment out of the great numbers of those whom he placed on trial and who were condemned."

Leblois accordingly charged his predecessor with having betrayed his office, with having conspired, as author or accomplice, against the internal security of the State and of the French people , with having consequently and in

---

[1] Fréteau (Emmanuel Marie Michel Philippe), a councillor of the Parlement of Paris, at first acquitted (27th of Floréal in the year II), then placed again on trial and guillotined (26th of Prairial in the year II)

[2] These were the visits that Fouquier made to the Committee of Public Safety to which he went to give an account of his work.

this manner provoked the dissolution of the national representation, the overthrow of the Republican system, the re-establishment of royalty, and with having sought to provoke, by murder and terror, the arming of citizens one against another, and with exciting civil war.[1]

Two days later, on the 28th of Frimaire (December 18), Lecointre (of Versailles) proposed in the Convention that those who were acquitted in the Carrier trial should be sent before a criminal Tribunal on a charge of ordinary crimes. A sharp discussion took place. Some representatives of the people declared that Revolutionary justice had been too long in the same hands. Bourdon (of the Oise) proposed that the Tribunal sitting at Paris should be renewed. The Convention decreed that this should be done

The usher of the Convention delivered this decree to President Dobsen at the moment when Fouquier-Tinville was in the chair answering the questions of the judges and jurors. The President immediately prorogued the hearing And Fouquier was led back to prison. Everything had to be begun again. During more than three months that he was imprisoned, " he was frightfully bored."[2] He was still to be incarcerated for four months and a half longer before " he mounted to the theatre of death "[3]

[1] Archives Nationales, W 499, dossier 550, p 7 .
[2] Fouquier's expression in one of his letters to his wife.
[3] An expression of the time, used of Carrier.

CHAPTER X

FOUQUIER-TINVILLE'S SECOND TRIAL: THE INQUIRY BY THE TRIBUNAL ESTABLISHED ON THE 8TH OF NIVOSE IN THE YEAR III

ON the 8th of Nivôse in the year III. (December 28, 1794), the National Convention voted the reorganisation of the Revolutionary Tribunal, proposed by Merlin (of Douai). This law was put into effect a month later. The magistrates who composed the new Tribunal came from the provinces. Their duties at Paris were not to last more than three months.[1]

The first session was held in the Hall of Liberty on the 8th of Pluviôse in the year III. Aumont[2] delivered a speech of the historic type, in which he called to mind Brutus proclaiming the liberty of Rome over the ruins of the overturned throne of the Tarquins, but avoiding the shedding of innocent blood on the scaffold. He also evoked Sulla and Octavius, and of Rome placed in chains. He hailed the dawn of a happy time of justice. The new Tribunal would be revolutionary and Republican but just.

" When the sight of crime and the sad necessity of letting the sword of the law fall upon guilty heads will come to sadden our hearts, keep in sight the assurance of a not far distant future. . . . Behold France more powerful and more respected than Rome and Sparta, more intellectual than Athens, more opulent than Carthage ; above all, happier than those famous republics, because she will have

---

[1] Campardon : *Le Tribunal Révolutionnaire*, II., p. 132.

[2] Aumont, a commissioner for the Administration of Civil Affairs, Police, and Tribunals, became head of the legal and consulting office in the general police department, and afterwards until the year VII. was head of the detective department. We find no indication of him in the year IX.

more virtue, and will gaze upon the spectacle of her happiness in preparing the liberty and welfare of the world."[1]

President Agier[2] then said that he and his colleagues " ascended with fright into a tribunal of blood which recently, whilst striking as by chance at some guilty heads, had sent thousands of innocent victims to death."

" Priests of justice," he went on, " we have sacrificed ourselves to the public good ; before being the sacrificers, we become so to speak the victims , let us obey, since we must, and not being able to have the merit of refusing, let us at least possess that of resignation. If we have to pass rigorous judgments, it is not to us that they can be imputed, but solely to the Law, of which we shall be, in all the severity of the term, interpreters by compulsion ; we are really responsible only for our zeal , and conscience tells us that it could not be purer."

The prisoners to be tried by this Tribunal, established on the 8th of Nivôse in the year III , did not employ language different from that of their accusers. They also declared that they had obeyed. They also said that they could not refuse   They also entrenched themselves within the formula of the Law   They also maintained that they had only interpreted it. They also affirmed that they had behaved with exactitude, with rigorous zeal, that they had been bound to act thus, and were the victims of duty

Only, it ought to be noticed how the times had changed. The duties of the members of the Tribunal which was re-fashioned on the 8th of Nivôse could be performed without danger and without risk   They were even not without profit. The other duties, those of the members of the Tribunal established on March 10, 1793, and on the 22nd of Prairial, 1794, brought them to the scaffold   But the judges of the Terror had sent to death, between April 6, 1793, and the 22nd of Prairial, 1794, one thousand two hundred and

<hr>

[1] Archives Nationales, W 532, reg 5

[2] Agier, formerly an advocate in the Parlement of Paris and a substitute Deputy for Paris in the States-General   A judge in the Tribunal for the Second Arrondissement, he resigned after August 10 and only entered upon his functions after the 9th of Thermidor.

fifty-nine accused persons, and, between the 22nd of Prairial and the 9th of Thermidor, one thousand three hundred and sixty-six, or altogether two thousand six hundred and twenty-five victims in the space of sixteen months ; while the judges of the Tribunal established in Nivôse of the year III pronounced only seventeen death sentences—those of Fouquier-Tinville, fifteen of those charged along with him, and a woman, Marie Thérèse Marchal Jacquet, found guilty of corresponding with the enemies of the Republic.

On the 12th of Ventôse in the year III. (March 2, 1795), the preliminaries of Fouquier's trial began again on a wider basis and with new sources of information. A larger number of witnesses was heard—registrars and clerks of the Tribunal established on March 10, 1793, employees in the prosecutor's office, ushers, Fouquier's secretaries, coachmen of the Tribunal, gendarmes, lawyers, official defenders, attendants in the refreshment-room, police officials, wine-sellers, employees in the prisons, turnkeys, the executioner, the executioner's assistants, ex-prison spies, persons who had been accused but had escaped the penalties of the Tribunal, all those, in a word, who had lived the life of the Revolutionary Tribunal during sixteen months, and some persons who, in spite of the Tribunal, were still alive.

We have analysed these depositions from the originals, preserved among the Archives, made before Charles François Joseph Pissis, Judge of the Revolutionary Tribunal, a commissioner appointed by an order issued on the 12th of Ventôse in the year III., and signed by Vice-President Liger.

In these long depositions, so curious and so interesting, in these examinations signed by the investigating judge and by each of the witnesses, the living history of the trial is revealed. It is the life of the Tribunal of the Terror, Fouquier's existence during sixteen months, which lives again in those large pages covered with the close handwriting of the registrars who alternately held the pen. To reproduce *in extenso* these testimonies would be impossible ; their prolixity and repetitions would exhaust the reader's attention. We have accordingly summarised them without omitting anything essential. We hope that the reading of this summary (in which the details, collected and noted from life, are specified and particularised) will give the reader all the interest we ourselves have derived from reading the depositions in the original documents, and from transscribing and summarising them.

The first witness whom Judge Pissis examined on that 12th of Ventôse in the year III. was a young woman of twenty-two years of age who had escaped from the guillotine by a miracle—Amélie Laurence Marie Céleste Saint-Pern, the widow of Cornulier,[1] born at Rennes in the Ile-et-Vilaine, and residing in Paris, at the Rue du Sentier, Brutus Section.

She declared that on the 1st of Thermidor in the year II. she appeared before the Revolutionary Tribunal along with her husband, brother, grandfather, mother, and her two uncles. She and her husband were condemned to death There was, to her knowledge, no writ of indictment against them, and no legal documents. They had been handed a writ of indictment at the door of the audience-chamber She escaped death only by declaring herself pregnant During the hearing of the case, she was only asked her name, her age, rank, and residence. No witness was called either for the prosecution or for the defence She wanted to speak on her own behalf. The President ordered two gendarmes to separate her from her husband and to take her to the end of the bench on which the prisoners sat, so that she could not speak to him

Before the hearing, when the names of the accused were called over at the Conciergerie, neither she nor her husband had been called, for they were not on the list, and had received no writ of indictment. The bearer of the list, so Madame Cornulier deposed, immediately came back and said · " It is required that they appear at the hearing to-day, and they are not included in the list nor in the writ of indictment " He sent for one. M Cornulier refused to take his place on the benches until he was shown a writ

[1] She signs herself thus.

of indictment in which his name was included. One was brought to them immediately. Their names were included in it. It was handed to them at the entrance to the audience-chamber Her brother, Bertrand Jean Marie Saint-Pern, aged seventeen, was condemned the same day *on a writ of indictment made out against his father aged fifty-three.*

" They were named in it," says the witness, " under this form, Saint-Pern and his wife, son-in-law and daughter of Magon de la Balue," a description that only fitted her father and his wife, and could not be adapted to her young brother [1]

The public executioner's assistant, Pierre François Etienne Desmorest, who had already given evidence at the first inquiry, that held in Brumaire, repeated what he knew concerning Fouquier. He had had " no special connection with him." One day Fouquier complained to him that the executions took place too late. He told him to come to him for orders. Desmorest went every morning. As a rule, Fouquier would say to him at eleven or twelve o'clock : " The guillotine must be set up for two o'clock or half-past two. So many vehicles must be procured."

One day he told him that ten or eleven were needed. He never thought there were enough vehicles because he wished there to be only seven or eight condemned persons in each of them.[2] Still, one day it was necessary to put as many as ten in each vehicle When the sentences were passed, Desmorest would go and find the usher who was to be present at the execution, and who had the list of con-demned persons with Fouquier's order Desmorest used to go with this usher to the Conciergerie, where the janitor " would deliver over to them the condemned persons, whom it was not necessary to summon because they were usually enclosed in an apartment separated from the other prisoners and guarded by gendarmes." He would count them, with the list in his hand The condemned persons were deprived

---

[1] Archives Nationales, W. 500, 3rd dossier, p. 45 *bis*, folio 1.

[2] We have seen that he had received formal orders from the Com-mittees on this matter.

of their property before being handed over to the executioner. By a resolution of the Convention, their clothing was taken to the Hospital of the Revolutionary Tribunal. He did not know what became of it.

At the end of his evidence, Desmorest remembered that the day when Fouquier asked for ten or eleven vehicles was the 10th of Thermidor, and it was for the execution of the seventy-one members of the Commune of Paris who had been outlawed. " He received this order in Fouquier's own house."

Etienne Simonnet, usher of the Tribunal, aged 66, declared that he was too much occupied with the discharge of his duties to notice Fouquier's threats and outbursts in the registrar's office. He only knew two or three facts. One day Fouquier had changed several of the jurors on the list of those who were summoned. Several times Simonnet received " imperfect " writs of indictment from the prosecutor's office , in some of those writs the names of the accused persons did not appear, "so that the names were only given as they were asked for at the prosecutor's office." On another day, about the 22nd of Prairial, Simonnet heard him say " that he would have all those scoundrels of conspirators exterminated, that he had orders to that effect from the Committees." One morning, he saw in the courtyard of the Sainte-Chapelle, *before the trial*, a certain number of carts which seemed " intended to carry those who were to be condemned."[1]

Gabriel Jérôme Sénar, aged 35, a lawyer, residing at Tours, but at the time detained in the Hospice de l'Evêché, declared that he had " much knowledge useful for the decision of the case of Fouquier-Tinville through his connection, interviews and correspondence with him."

But it must be confessed that Sénar's evidence is highly suspicious Sénar had been an agent of the Committee of General Security. He had been president of a military revolutionary committee established at Tours ; he had been national agent of the Commune of Tours. He was at once a

[1] Archives Nationales, W 500, 3rd dossier, p. 45 *bis*, folios 2 and 3.

gendarme and an informer by profession. He knew well that his evidence could be stamped as inadmissible, since, on the first occasion when questioned, he had asked whether " a man covered with suspicion could be heard as a witness, and his depositions brought forward when his name was dishonoured in public opinion." He took advantage of this to solicit the new Tribunal to be good enough " to indict or to judge him, as, for eight months, he could obtain no decision nor even a statement of the charges against him."

Sénar said that, having come from Tours to Paris by order of the Committee, " he made the unlucky acquaintance of Héron, the principal agent of the Committee of General Security, who got hold of him." Héron took him to Fouquier-Tinville, " who appeared to be very closely associated with him." Fouquier received Héron in these terms · " Our business is going well. Heads are falling like slates." They afterwards spoke of Santerre, who had been arrested. Sénar was a commissioner in that affair. After a discussion of the official report regarding Santerre, Fouquier-Tinville answered ·—" What does it matter to me whether you are a patriot or not ? When the Committee of Public Safety tells me to have any one guillotined, I do it. .

Once more, I am only a passive being, obliged to make those persons perish whom Robespierre names. In this case I obey the Committee of Public Safety, I agree. It is displeasing to me, on your account, if, through the rivalry of the two Committees, Santerre has been kept in prison too long. I shall make him take his place on my little bench, and you will dance the Carmagnole there "

Sénar · " Ought the Revolution to assassinate, and ought we not to have justice ? "

Fouquier " It is only counter-revolutionaries and knaves who ask for justice Ask Héron how we work the heads. In Revolution you must not stop at these trifles."

Some moments afterwards Sénar heard Héron say to Fouquier : " Good, good, my friend. Cut off their heads. That is the way to enrich the Republic." After this they separated

One day, having business at Fouquier's office, to deliver to him documents by order of the Committee of General Security, he spoke to the Public Prosecutor in favour of the Revolutionary Committee of Bourgueil, and begged him not to put them on trial immediately, although they were at the Conciergerie. Fouquier answered him. "This is how it is. When one wants to carry terror into the country districts, to maintain the Revolution by fear, one finds these gentlemen of the Indulgent Faction who cry out, and our measure would fail if we listened to them. This is good business. There are rich people in it, for when they entered the Conciergerie plenty of money was taken from them"

At another time, in regard to the trial of this case, Fouquier said to him "I have so much to do that I forget what I am saying or what is suggested to me."

The members of the Bourgueil Committee were given their liberty, thanks to a reprieve.

Sénar, having notified to Fouquier a resolution passed by the Committee of General Security giving them liberty, the Public Prosecutor exclaimed : "It is always the same ! Another case of liberty given by the Committee of General Security ! But I cannot accede to it because, according to the law of the 22nd of Prairial, the Tribunal cannot set at liberty without the consent of the Committee of Public Safety" In spite of Sénar's observations, he persisted in his refusal Sénar then withdrew. As he was leaving, he met Amar, the Deputy, who told him to wait for him, so that they might go away together in the carriage belonging to the Committee of General Security

Fouquier reappeared and was stopped by a citizen, who said to him. "How many vehicles will be wanted to-day ? "

Fouquier counted on his fingers "Eight, twelve, eighteen, thirty Count on thirty."

The other, who was "attached to the public executioner," withdrew. Fouquier perceived Sénar, and said to him : "What are you waiting here for ? "

"I am waiting for Amar, the Representative of the people,

with whom I am to go away in the carriage ; I am tired, and all the more so on account of the fright your answer has just caused me. You know the number of the condemned and their case is not yet heard ! They have not and cannot be tried by this time, for it is too early in the day."

" Bah ! " answered Fouquier, " I know what to think."

He left him abruptly with the words : " You are not good revolutionaries, you formalists ! "

Another evening, at the office of the prosecutor's secretaries, where Sénar was making out an analytical inventory of the documents which he was to deliver, Fouquier came in and said · " You are very much afraid, Mr. Formalist. You are going as much into detail as if you were drawing up an inventory to be exhibited in court "

Héron [1] was there. Fouquier required Sénar to be briefer, and pressed him to end his work. He sent the secretary away. It was late. It was necessary to go to the Committee of Public Safety. Fouquier asked for two gendarmes. They went out, the gendarmes following some paces behind. Sénar walked with Héron and Fouquier. As they went, Héron and Fouquier " conversed of the victories won by the guillotine." Fouquier said . " I am pleased with its successes , but there are people who, although renowned patriots, have gone through it. Others also will go through it, and I am afraid that it may play a trick on me. I have seen the ghosts of some patriots. For some time it has seemed to me that those ghosts are following me. How will all this end ? I do not know."

Sénar answered " When a suspected person is charged, the Public Prosecutor should himself judge of the charge in his own conscience. By an exact and scrupulous summary, he ought to place the jurors in a position not to be deceived. If he is forced to do the contrary, *he ought to resign*."

Sénar affirmed that he said this. Héron silenced him.

" You are a chatterer. Fouquier ought not to take advice

---

[1] See in the first series of M. Lenôtre's *Vieilles Maisons, Vieux Papiers*, the article entitled *Two Police Officials* (Héron and Dossonville).

from a greenhorn. A few skulls like yours would be enough to ruin the revolution."

And Fouquier said : " Yes, I perceive that this fellow is not a revolutionary. We should do fine things if we took precautions."

They were then going through the door of the Louvre. Three ill-clad men seemed to be hiding there. When they heard the footsteps of the gendarmes, and saw the three others, they went away. Fouquier said to Héron : " My good friend, we shall not profit by our revolutionary labours. We shall be assassinated."

Héron replied " What matter ? Between now and then we shall make an end of some of them. Do not be uneasy. Whatever impediments I encounter at the Committee of General Security—and they sometimes unsettle my plans—I shall none the less deal with them as we have agreed, and we shall have more heads "

Fouquier rejoined · " You must be silent in the presence of Indulgents."

This was intended for Sénar.

" Good," answered Héron, " if he commit the least indiscretion, I shall soon master him."

At the entrance to the courtyard of the Tuileries, they withdrew a little from him Sénar was less able to hear what they said. He only heard Fouquier's voice and these words spoken by him : " We shall always be in agreement, and shall make them dance the Carmagnole "

Héron then rejoined Sénar. They went to the Committee of General Security. The timorous Sénar unbosomed himself to Amar, the Deputy. He told him that Héron had a grudge against him and why. Amar reassured him : " Be calm, the Committee knows you I will see that nothing is done to you. If you were arrested again, you would not be brought before the Tribunal without being heard. A resolution will be passed that will send you back home."[1]

Sénar breathed again

Charles Louis Perdry, aged 37, of No 492 Rue Neuve-des-

[1] Archives Nationales, W 500, p 45 *bis*, folios 4 to 7.

P

Petits-Champs, judge of the Tribunal of the Second Arrondissement of Paris, a compatriot of Fouquier, knew him before the Revolution. " Their families had intermarried." He had been a director with him of the jury of the Tribunal established on August 17, 1792 He had seen him less often since he was appointed deputy and then Public Prosecutor. He was present at certain sessions of the Revolutionary Tribunal. " They filled him with sorrow "

He was not able to remain for long, as he was " moved at seeing on the benches for the accused and perhaps in the midst of those who were guilty, men clothed with public confidence." He had been a prisoner in the Plessis prison. Terror ruled there. The prisoners were afraid to speak to one another. He had never been able to conceive " how any one had the effrontery to maintain that there were conspiracies in the prisons "

Anne Marguerite Devilliers, the wife of Morisan, aged 50, residing in the Palace, at the Café des Subsistances, kept the refreshment-room of the Tribunal Fouquier frequently came there to eat He often waited there in the evening until the Committees of Public Safety and of General Security were open for him to go to them. She several times heard Fouquier complain that he carried on a cruel trade, saying that he would prefer to be a labourer. He used to ask : " Were there many people present at the executions ? "

When they told him that there had been a crowd, Fouquier would answer with a shrug of his shoulders : " It is frightful ! " Sometimes he dined alone ; on other occasions with certain jurors and certain judges.

She was sometimes present at the hearings, before the 22nd of Prairial. She saw Fouquier cross-examining the accused. They could answer him freely. She heard Fouquier say to the President : " Put such and such a question to the accused, and let them answer."

After the law of the 22nd of Prairial, she heard Fouquier, who was dining in the refreshment-room, say : " The times are very cruel. It cannot last."

He complained bitterly of President Dumas. On the

9th of Thermidor he did not dine with her. He returned to the Tribunal about six o'clock in the evening. He came down to the refreshment-room about eight or nine o'clock, and said: " I do not know what is taking place or what it means."

He sent Malarme, one of the secretaries of the prosecutor's office, to get information. Citizen Botot-Dumesnil, an officer of police, sent out some men. Fouquier said: "As for me, I remain at my post, were I to perish there   I fear nothing."

He remained there, in fact, until one o'clock in the morning. He then went out, saying   " I am going to the Committee "

Madeline Nicole Sophie Morisan, aged 20, residing with her father, a restaurant keeper, at the Café des Subsistances, in the Palace, had seen Fouquier-Tinville several times at her father's, as he came to eat there at five o'clock in the evening. He often sat alone, but sometimes with judges and jurors of the Tribunal. People came to give him an account of the executions that had taken place. He would ask the usher if there had been many people there. On the usher's affirmative, he would shrug his shoulders, saying . " When will this end ?   What a wretched trade !   I would prefer to go and labour in the fields "

She sometimes went to the sessions of the Tribunal. She saw Dumas preventing the accused from defending themselves. Fouquier said to the President   " Let the accused persons speak."

On the 9th of Thermidor, Fouquier did not dine in the refreshment-room   She saw him in his own rooms, about six o'clock in the evening, with his wife   About half-past eight or nine, Fouquier came to the refreshment-room to drink a bottle of beer, " as he usually did in the evening " He asked Botot-Dumesnil what was happening   He remained until eleven o'clock at night and returned to the refreshment-room at two o'clock in the morning. He then went to bed   She heard " no conversation of Fouquier's at that time because she herself was asleep "

Of Dumas, he used to say " He is a beggar who cannot last long " She never heard Fouquier speak in her presence of the conspiracies in the prisons

Charles Gombert Bertrand, aged 41, a former janitor at the Luxembourg,[1] had had no intercourse with Fouquier-Tinville. He saw him at the Tribunal After the law of the 22nd of Prairial, he heard Fouquier, in his capacity of Public Prosecutor, cross-examining the accused. He let them answer freely.

Armand Martial Joseph Herman, aged about 36, residing at No 19, Place des Piques, the ex-President of the Revolutionary Tribunal, who had presided over the trial of Marie Antoinette and at the Danton case, declared that " all the deeds with which Fouquier was charged being subsequent to his own departure from the Tribunal, he could give no information in regard to them." While he was President of the Revolutionary Tribunal, no complaint or no information against Fouquier reached him " He would have been very pleased if there had been a little more order in his work," but he knew no fact which could be imputed to him as a crime, no betrayal of his functions.

As to the conspiracy in the prisons, he only knew it as Commissioner for the Administration of Civil Affairs, Police, and Tribunals[2] He had had to make inquiries on the subject of that conspiracy He believed that Fouquier accompanied Citizen Lanne[3] once or twice on his visits of inquiry to the prisons. He could not say in what manner those inquiries were made. " He liked to think that those two functionaries carried out their duty in this respect " He, Herman, said that he had never been in the prisons.

Joseph Verney, aged 28, residing at No 311, Rue Geoffroy-l'Angevin, Section de la Réunion, had been a basketmaker in 1790, 1791, and 1792 After August 3rd, 1793, he became a

---

[1] He had not been janitor since the 18th of Thermidor

[2] A post to which he was appointed after the condemnation of the Dantonists

[3] Herman's assistant

turnkey at the Luxembourg   Since then he had performed
the duties of janitor at Saint-Lazare until the 28th of
Thermidor.   He said that he had no intercourse with
Fouquier-Tinville [1]   When he was at the Luxembourg,
he saw only once, on the night between the 18th and 19th
of Messidor, a list brought by an usher   This list contained
the names of more than a hundred " individuals " who were
transferred to the Conciergerie   It was signed " Fouquier,"
and bore the seal of the Tribunal.   Those who were on the
list did not appear again at the Luxembourg, with the
exception of nine or ten who were acquitted

Joseph Honoré Vonschriltz,[2] aged 28, residing at Paris,
in the Place and Section des Droits de l'Homme, a police
inspector for the past year, and a carpenter before the
Revolution, saw Fouquier-Tinville only once when he came
to Bicêtre accompanied by a detachment of gendarmes on
foot, and several vehicles to take away the prisoners who
were summoned to the Conciergerie and executed the day
following, " with the exception of four or six who assisted
as witnesses," [3] and were brought back to Bicêtre.   The
others were executed as accomplices in, or authors of, a
conspiracy hatched at Bicêtre.   However, Vonschriltz
had noticed " no trace of conspiracy " in that house.   He
saw nothing but submission among the prisoners   Dupont,
the police official whose rigour made the prisoners groan,
had, along with Fouquier, caused a table to be placed in the
courtyard.   They had a list of those whom they wanted to
enter their vehicles   Fouquier took them away.[4]

Pierre Nicolas Vergne, aged 36, secretary and justice of
the peace of the Lepelletier Section, and afterwards member
of the Revolutionary Committee of that section, residing at

---

[1] This is contradicted by the facts   A document exists (Archives
Nationales, W 500, 2nd dossier, p 28) which is nothing else than the
information laid by Verney against twenty prisoners in the Luxembourg, written in Fouquier's hand, and approved of and signed by
Verney.

[2] This is how he signed himself

[3] Police spies   See Chapter III.

[4] Archives Nationales, W. 500, 3rd dossier, p 45 bis, folios 7 to 12

No. 7, Rue Favart, never had anything in particular to do with Fouquier-Tinville.

He knew him as Public Prosecutor. He had sometimes been present at the hearings of the Revolutionary Tribunal. He never saw Fouquier sitting at them He used to bring him, as member of the Revolutionary Committee, documents for the prosecution or for the defence of indicted persons. Fouquier handed them over to a clerk who counted them. Vergne made him give a receipt for them On a single occasion he dined with Fouquier, whom he did not yet know. It was about the month of June, 1793, on a Sunday when all the constituted authorities of Paris had gone to the Convention. There were seven or eight persons at that dinner, " among others Montané, then President of the Tribunal , Pâris, the registrar , and Chrétien, a juror." There was no reference made to anything in particular.

The judge asked Vergne if he had no private conversation with Fouquier at the time of the attempt on Collot d'Herbois by Admiral.

" What idea had you of that affair, and what idea had Fouquier of it ? "

" On that day, about six or seven o'clock in the morning, Admiral was examined. Accompanied by Chrétien, the juror, and another member of the Revolutionary Committee of the Section, I went to take Fouquier the declarations of those who were present at the moment of Admiral's attempt, as well as Admiral's replies. We found Fouquier in bed. We handed him the documents Fouquier asked us if we did not believe this attempt was ' the result of a more extensive plot ' We answered that we did not think so." Vergne, although summoned, was not heard as a witness in that case

Pierre Joseph Boyaval,[1] aged 26, detained in the Hospice National, a tailor, and before his arrest a lieutenant of light infantry, detained since the 20th of Brumaire in the year II , first in the Luxembourg, then in Sainte-Pélagie and the Plessis, and lastly in the Hospice, was an old *habitué* of the

---

[1] He signs thus

prisons of the Terror. But he had not suffered much from this. We have seen that he served as a prison spy.

He declared that on the 19th of Messidor, Fouquier, as Public Prosecutor, sent him to the Luxembourg to make inquiries together with Beausire, Armance, Vauchelet, Julien, Meunier, Lenain, Boispereuse, and Benoit.[1] Fouquier asked him his name, and said to him · " You are going to appear at the Revolutionary Tribunal. You must speak in the way you know."

Then he was sent back. On the 21st of the same month, Fouquier sent for the witnesses. He went to the Public Prosecutor's room, accompanied by a gendarme. He handed him the letter which a prisoner in the Luxembourg had entrusted to him. He had no conversation with him. On the same day, a little later, he asked to speak again with Fouquier. A gendarme accompanied him. Fouquier made him wait for an hour in a corridor When the Prosecutor, who had been conversing with Coffinhal, was free, Boyaval asked permission to go and dine with his relatives, under the guard of a gendarme Fouquier refused.

On the 22nd of Messidor, Fouquier sent him again to inquire, always with the same witnesses But he did not speak to him Boyaval had since written many letters to Fouquier " to denounce " to him facts relating to a conspiracy of 300 prisoners, "on the first floor of the Luxembourg." He never received a reply.[2]

Antoine Vauchelet, aged 32, a merchant in Paris, at No. 2, Rue du Gros-Chenet, Section Brutus, had never known Fouquier. But Vauchelet, like Boyaval, was an *habitué* of the prisons Like Boyaval he had rendered services. He, too, was a police spy. During his detention in the Luxembourg, which lasted from September 9th, 1793, to the 27th of Thermidor following, he " thought he noticed that Verney, turnkey in the house of detention, had intercourse with Fouquier " He boasted of going to see him Boyaval had said to him, Vauchelet, that there were still many

[1] Other police spies
[2] Archives Nationales, W 500, 3rd dossier, p 45 *bis*, folios 12 to 16.

conspirators, a list of whom Fouquier had asked of him.

On the 19th of Messidor, when summoned as a witness to the Tribunal, he had seen Boyaval going into Fouquier's room. On the same day he saw, "with astonishment," among the accused persons, a certain Morin,[1] who had reached the Conciergerie two days before and been brought before the Tribunal as the result of an error in the names. This Morin made a remark about it to Fouquier, who answered " that in truth Morin was not the man he sought, but that he held him and would keep him." At that moment " the true Morin," he whom they sought, made his appearance. Fouquier had him placed among the accused persons, "entered verbal pleading against him at the hearing, without any other writ of indictment being delivered to the accused man, who was condemned with the rest." The first Morin withdrew from the Court, but was again placed on trial the next day, and condemned like his namesake.

Vauchelet was anxious to place on Verney and Boyaval all responsibility for the " denunciations " made to Fouquier, and instigated by the Public Prosecutor. He said that Fouquier " used to keep Boyaval back " and remain in secret conversation with him. But Boyaval denied that he had private conversations with Fouquier.

Which of these two wretches are we to believe, both of them ready for anything, and seeking by accusing others to extricate themselves from a difficult position ?

Vauchelet affirmed that, being summoned a second time as a witness, on a day when Fouquier was not at the hearing of the case, all the witnesses were heard. " Six of the witnesses," he says, " of whom I was one, spoke in favour of fourteen or fifteen accused persons, and defended them with heat." Eleven were acquitted out of forty-five. A juror (whom he did not know) remarked to him that he ought to recapitulate and point out the accomplices in the Grammont Conspiracy.

Pierre Marie Bligny, Fouquier's successor as procurator at

[1] See Chapter III., p. 86.

the Châtelet, residing at No. 297 Rue Neuve-Egalité, Section
Bonne-Nouvelle, declared that he knew Citizen Fouquier
in September, 1783, " a period when he negotiated the sale
of a procurator's office and practice in the former Châtelet,
which Fouquier held, that motives of interest placed
him in a position not to see Fouquier for more than ten years ;
that the position of Public Prosecutor at the Tribunal of
the Department necessitated the witness seeing Fouquier in regard to a matter in which he was counsel "
He saw him several times in his capacity as defender when
Fouquier was Public Prosecutor of the Revolutionary
Tribunal. He spoke to him only about the cases
with which he was entrusted, and about nothing else.
He declared that he had no knowledge of the conspiracies
in the prisons, nor of " what was called firing an uninterrupted volley," as he had no cases at the Revolutionary
Tribunal for about a year.

Pierre Athanase Pépin Dégrouhette,[1] aged 43, a lawyer,
an official defender, President of the Tribunal established
on August 17th, 1792, residing in Paris at No. 25 Rue du
Sentier, Section Brutus, knew Fouquier in September, 1792,
as director of the *jury d'accusation*, of which he, Pépin, was
one of the presidents. He lost sight of him and found him
again at the Revolutionary Tribunal. Pépin-Dégrouhette
used to defend accused persons

During the first six or seven months of the existence
of the Revolutionary Tribunal, he found Fouquier " very
accessible to the complaints of unfortunate persons, very
easy in granting the delays necessary for preparing the
defence of the accused, for fetching documents and witnesses
for the defence " But towards the end of 1793 and in the
first months of the year II , " things changed cruelly "
Fouquier " became unapproachable." The days when the
accused were to appear in court were concealed from the
defenders The indictments were served on the evening
before the trial, and sometimes late at night The unhappy
prisoners often went into the dock without their defenders

---

[1] He signs thus

and without their evidence. Pépin-Dégrouhette complained vehemently of this to Fouquier The latter burst out angrily and said on different occasions · " I can do nothing about it My hand is forced."

On the 2nd of Floréal in the year II , Pépin was arrested and taken to Saint-Lazare. His wife went the next day to find Fouquier and beg him not to bring to trial the accused persons whom her husband was commissioned to defend. Fouquier received her very brutally, and said "that he would not stop the course of justice for her husband." Several citizens were, in fact, tried and condemned whilst the evidence was under seals affixed at Pépin-Dégrouhette's house.

In the case of the Saint-Lazare conspiracy, which occupied the court for three days, Fouquier only sat on the first day. He appeared to be less unmerciful than Liendon who sat on the other two days [1]

Jean Henry Voulland, aged 43, Representative of the people residing at No. 108, Rue Croix-des-Petits-Champs, had no association with Fouquier except such as he might have in his capacity as member of the Committee of General Security He could give no evidence for the prosecution or the defence. [2]

Another Deputy, André Amar, aged 38, representing the Department of the Isère, and a member of the Committee of General Security, could not say whether Fouquier held private intercourse with Robespierre. He strongly suspected that Maximilien had a good deal of influence over Fouquier, Coffinhal, and Dumas, and more particularly over the last two than over Fouquier He remembered seeing at the Committee of General Security an information in which Fouquier was accused of having dined on the 9th of Thermidor with Coffinhal and Dumas [3] This information was sent to the Tribunal with all the documents for Fouquier's prosecution. He knew nothing more.

Claude Emmanuel Dobsen, aged 53, twice President

---

[1] Archives Nationales, W 500, 3rd dossier, p 45 *bis*, folios 16 to 18.
[2] Archives Nationales, W 500, 3rd dossier, p. 45 *ter*, folio 1.
[3] This is true as regards Coffinhal, but false concerning Dumas, as he had just been arrested on that day. (See Chapter IV.)

of the Revolutionary Tribunal, residing at No 7A Rue du Cloître-Notre-Dame, Section de la Cité, had been Fouquier's colleague as director of the *jury d'accusation*. Appointed President of the Revolutionary Tribunal in place of Montané, " he had the most intimate intercourse with Fouquier." He never " noticed anything in him contrary to the principles of the strictest justice " Dobsen only left the Tribunal in virtue of the decree of the 22nd of Prairial which did not re-elect him.

When Herman, the President, was appointed Minister of the Interior, Dumas ' President in Chief," and Scellier and Coffinhal Vice-Presidents, from that moment the form of the proceedings changed It seemed to Dobsen that Dumas directed all the operations He heard him complain several times of Fouquier-Tinville and of the fact that he did not " place a greater number of people on trial at once " Since the 22nd of Prairial he sometimes frequented the Tribunal. He saw with horror almost all the accused persons tried without having any facilities for bringing forward their defence. He even saw a large number tried, in regard to whom this was confined to asking them their names and conditions The pleadings were then closed, the questions put to the jury, and condemnation pronounced Several times, when he came to the Palace, before the hearing had even begun, he saw, collected in the courtyard, vehicles intended to take the condemned to the scaffold.[1]

Denis Michel Jullien, aged 30, merchant, residing at No. 12, Quai de Chaillot, Section des Champs-Elysées, gave evidence similar to that of Vauchelet It was the story of the conspiracy in the prisons Like Vauchelet, like Amans, like Beausire, like Boyaval, etc , he was summoned from the Luxembourg, where he was detained, as a witness before the Tribunal He, too, acted the part of a police spy. Like the others, he boasted of having saved accused persons by his evidence. He gave evidence against Dumas, but said nothing about Fouquier-Tinville [2]

---

[1] Archives Nationales, W. 500, 3rd dossier, p 45 *ter*, folio 1.
[2] Archives Nationales, W. 500, 3rd dossier, p 45 *ter*, folios 1 and 2

CHAPTER XI

A S the inquiry advanced, the judge shortened the examinations of the witnesses.

From the evidence we have analysed in the preceding chapter, there result rather contradictory opinions. Many witnesses are crushing, in their answers, in regard to the moral conduct of the Public Prosecutor. Others, on the contrary, such as Château and ex-President Dobsen, are clearly favourable to him. " Never," Dobsen had said, " did I notice anything in him that could be contrary to the principles of the strictest justice."[1]

On the 19th of Ventôse there came forward a witness who owed it to his father's wonderful devotion that he was still living. This is young Loizerolles (François Simon), aged 24, in the 29th division of police. We know his story.[2] He stated, very simply, that he had never seen Fouquier-Tinville. But he knew and was sure that his father was tried and condemned by the Tribunal on the 8th of Thermidor in the year II. (a day before Robespierre's fall), on a writ of indictment issued against himself, the son. Loizerolles, the father, an ex-Lieutenant-General of the bailiwick of the Arsenal, did not protest and went to death to save his son. " By an error as extraordinary as inexplicable," said young Loizerolles, " it was my father

---

[1] Dobsen, the President of the Section de la Cité, had presided on May 30, 1793, over the insurrectional assembly of the commissioners of the majority of the sections, who met at the Hôtel de Ville and declared the people in a state of insurrection. He was a Hébertist in his opinions. Perhaps his evidence, so favourable to Fouquier, came in part from the animosity he felt against the new Tribunal because he had not been re-appointed to it.

[2] See Chapter III., p. 99, and Note p. 98.

whom the jury condemned, a mistake all the more ridiculous (*sic*) as my father was sixty years old and I was only twenty-two. The Public Prosecutor, the judges, and the jurors could easily have noticed this blunder if they had only looked at my father."[1]

François Urbain Meunier, aged 50, captain on half-pay in the 104th regiment, of No. 5, Quai d'Ecole, Section du Muséum, was imprisoned in the Luxembourg for nine months He was summoned to the Tribunal as a witness in the conspiracy case He was one of the four police spies who were heard against a large number of accused persons He affirmed that he knew nothing and said nothing. He thought that at the hearing Fouquier performed the duties of Public Prosecutor He was not sure of this.

An official defender, Bernard Jean Louis Malarme,[2] aged 44, residing at No. 531, Rue des Prouvaires, Section du Contrat-Social, spoke of the release of prisoners due to Fouquier (Sarcé, an ex-captain, and Bayard La Vingtrie, lieutenant of the bailiwick). Fouquier, on a letter from Guffroy, the Representative of the people, placed on one side the papers relating to Citizen Dupuy, an employee in the Committee of General Security, " whilst waiting for a more favourable opportunity." This saved Dupuy

When Malarme recognised that his position as official defender at the Revolutionary Tribunal had become useless, he had himself appointed secretary in the prosecutor's office, " to take charge of the correspondence there." He could thus observe Fouquier's activity and his constant obedient attention to the orders he received from the governing committees He could also observe, as did the whole staff in the office, " with what repugnance Fouquier saw artisans and labourers placed on trial "

He saw Vadier, Amar, and others in Fouquier's private room, but was never present at their conversations. He affirmed that he placed aside " in his possession " the documents relating to the ninety-four inhabitants of Nantes

---

[1] Archives Nationales, W 100, 3rd dossier, p 45 *ter*, folio 2.
[2] He signs thus

Fouquier had always given heed to the representations which he made in their favour.

He thought he noticed that Dumas was Fouquier's enemy. Twice on the night between the 9th and 10th of Thermidor, the ex-Public Prosecutor sent him to the Committee of Public Safety to tell that Committee that he was at his post at the Tribunal. When he came back, he found Fouquier having supper with the attendant in the refreshment-room, Morisan, his family, and Gillier, one of his secretaries and Morisan's son-in-law.

Next there came to give evidence, Pierre François Morisan, aged 54, wine-seller and attendant in the refreshment-room. He kept the Café des Subsistances in the hall of the Palace. He formerly kept the refreshment-room " in one of the towers, near the Revolutionary Tribunal."

Morisan repeated what his wife and daughter said. Fouquier often took his meals at their place. He believed he saw in him " much zeal and activity." He heard him complain that he performed " painful functions," and even showed " some fears on his own account."

He had not been present at sessions of the Tribunal " since the period when a great number of accused persons began to be tried there at once, because this multitude of prisoners or witnesses caused a great crowd at his place, and this obliged him to remain and serve them " On several occasions he furnished the accused with refreshments and food, by order of Fouquier, Dumas, or others.

Fouquier would say to him : " There have been so many *of them* to-day. There will be thirty more *of them* to-morrow. I understand nothing of all this "

Morisan remarked " that so great a quantity of the accused must tire him out " He asked him how he was able to hold out Fouquier answered " What would you have me do ? I have orders from the Committee of Public Safety "

On the evening of the 9th of Thermidor, Fouquier said to him " For my part, I remain at my post."

Next there came forward a sinister figure of a prisoner.

In order to get better treatment, to give himself importance, or from fear, or to obtain his liberty, he had become a police spy.

He was Joseph Manini, aged 47, he called himself a man of letters. He had been imprisoned for more than sixteen months. Just now, he was at La Bourbe or Port-Libre. He mentioned the prisons in which he had been incarcerated— the Madelonettes (four months), Saint-Lazare (five to six months), the Plessis (from the 2nd of Thermidor until about the 22nd of Frimaire), the Luxembourg, and then Port-Libre where he was at present confined He related what he knew of the conspiracies, his relations with Coquery, another police spy, the conversations he had overheard and reported. He thought that at one of the hearings to which he came as a witness, Fouquier performed the duties of Public Prosecutor. " The accused persons spoke for as long as they wished without being interrupted, except one, who defended himself with sarcasms and insults directed against the Tribunal."

François Dupaumié,[1] aged thirty-five and a half, jeweller, of No. 124, Rue de la Verrerie, imprisoned in the Plessis since the 24th of Brumaire, saw Fouquier come one day, about the end of Prairial or the beginning of Messidor, with a detachment of police and three vehicles, to Bicêtre, of which Dupaumié was governor There Fouquier had a table placed in one of the courtyards. He drew out a list, and summoned thirty-six or thirty-seven persons who had been informed against by prisoners who were sentenced to chains. This was the Bicêtre conspiracy [2]

Dupaumié took care to exonerate himself from any share in this act of Fouquier He affirmed that, so long as he was governor of Bicêtre, the house was " perfectly quiet ", that he noticed no conspiracy. Fouquier said to him: " I have been present at the hearing when thirty-six or thirty-seven individuals were condemned I knew that the witnesses were scamps The prisoners would not have been condemned if they themselves had not confessed they had

---

[1] He signs thus   [2] See Chapter III

conspired against the Convention, and had not thrown the responsibility for this fact on one another.[1]

Jean Advenier, aged forty-nine, an assistant in the depository of military provisions and forage at Orléans, had been secretary in the prosecutor's office from October in the year II (*sic*) until after the 9th of Thermidor. " In the early days," he forwarded writs of indictment. After the 22nd of Prairial, he heard Dumas and Coffinhal say to accused persons who tried to defend themselves —" You have no right to speak."

He never saw Fouquier demanding this right for them.

He saw Voulland, Vadier and Amar coming fairly often to Fouquier's room, and shutting themselves up " carefully " with him. He often saw members of the Revolutionary Committees come and ask Fouquier for warrants to arrest persons. Fouquier would answer them " Bring me the reports and documents which state the offences and I will deliver them to you. But I do not want to deliver them to you officially.' He sometimes saw Fouquier " lamenting the fate of some condemned person."

Jean Baptiste Toussaint Beausire, aged thirty-three and a half, living on his income at Choisy-sur-Seine, had been imprisoned in the Luxembourg, in Sainte-Pélagie, in the Plessis, and in the Hospice de l'Evêché.[2] He gave evidence at length on what he knew about the conspiracies, and he ended thus " On the 19th of Messidor I heard the man who performed the duties of Public Prosecutor at that hearing say, ' The Morin who is here is not the man who was to be placed on trial. But as I have been looking for him for a long time I do not want to let him escape ' This Morin was placed on trial. No witness spoke against him He was, nevertheless, condemned with the rest "[3]

Jean Baptiste Vergnhes, aged 67, living on his income in Paris, at No. 1, Quai d'Egalité, Ile de la Fraternité, gave an

[1] Archives Nationales, W 500, 3rd dossier, p. 45 *ter*, folio 3 and 46, folios 1 and 2

[2] Beausire is the husband of the woman d'Oliva (of the Diamond Necklace affair) In prison he played the part of a police spy.

[3] Archives Nationales, W 500, 3rd dossier, p 46, folios 2 to 6

account of the dinner that took place at his house on the 9th of Thermidor [1]

Jacques Marie Botot-Dumesnil, aged 36, commander of police of the Tribunal, residing at No 4, Cloître Notre-Dame, Section de la Cité, had no intercourse with Fouquier except in so far as related to the maintenance of order within the precincts of the Palace of Justice Fouquier never spoke to him except a few chance words. Every evening one or two gendarmes accompanied him to the Committee of Public Safety, waited for him until very late at night, and came back with him.

On the 9th of Thermidor, about four o'clock in the evening, Botot-Dumesnil, was arrested in the middle of his troop, by order of Hanriot. Fleuriot and Payan Set at liberty the same evening by order of the Committee of General Security, he returned about eight or nine o'clock ; he was then sent for by Fouquier, whom he found in the refreshment-room, seemingly ignorant of what was taking place. He heard him say several times —" Whatever they do, I remain at my post "

Guillaume Alexandre Tronson-Ducoudray, aged 44, a lawyer, of No. 17, Rue des Victoires Nationales, Section Guillaume-Tell, thought he remembered that in the Léonard Bourdon case,[2] Fouquier-Tinville was not so violent in his speech for the prosecution as he was in other cases later on. " He seemed to him in those cases to exceed the bounds of moderation and impartiality becoming to his office every time that the accused persons appeared to him to have been designated by the Government " Moreover, Fouquier often urged him not to press for the trial of accused persons whom he had to defend He remarked " that the moment was not favourable, and that by waiting some time they might perhaps be saved "

Mathurin Denys Lainville. aged 47, an official defender at the Tribunal, residing at No. 354, Rue de Chartres, Section

---

[1] We have given an account of it, from his evidence, in Chapter IV.
[2] In this case Tronson-Ducoudray defended some of the citizens of Orléans who were accused (July 12, 1793)

Q

des Tuileries, knew Fouquier as a fellow-student. He had observed him in his career as procurator at the Châtelet, as director of the *jury d'accusation* of the Tribunal established on August 17, 1792, and, finally, as Public Prosecutor of the Revolutionary Tribunal.

He constantly attended the sessions of the Tribunal down to Hébert's trial. During that period the official defenders had every latitude for giving effect to the means of defence of accused persons. From that moment (the date of the beginning of what was called " the Tribunal's batches ") he saw that he no longer had the same latitude in pleading his cases. He decided to tell people who claimed his services that he no longer defended cases before that Tribunal. He was desirous of pointing out that he ceased to plead because of the remarks made to him by Coffinhal and Fouquier. Those two magistrates warned him " that henceforth official defenders must be very circumspect in their defences ; the Revolutionary Tribunal was not so much a tribunal of morality and justice as a tribunal established to judge in accordance with pronounced public opinion (*sic*)."[1]

Louis Claude Adnet,[2] aged 57, captain of the police of the tribunals, residing at No 120, Rue de la Harpe, Section des Thermes, had no intercourse with Fouquier-Tinville except in so far as related to the daily service of the Tribunal. He sometimes saw Fouquier getting angry with the ushers when he did not find those whom he had asked them for. He was often present at hearings. From the 22nd of Prairial to the 9th of Thermidor " persons were no longer tried, they were condemned." Accused persons were barely asked their names, their ages, and conditions. Several times he complained to Fouquier " of the rigours and horrors of the assistant executioner towards the condemned women." Fouquier answered him : " What would you have me do ? "

However, Fouquier caused one of the executioner's assistants to be imprisoned for twenty-four hours.

Fouquier said to him, on the evening of the 9th of Ther-

---

[1] Archives Nationales, W 500, 3rd dossier, p 46, folios 7 to 13.
[2] He signs thus.

midor, after having acquainted himself with the events of the day : " I remain at my post "

He refused to go to the Commune in spite of the solicitations of certain persons. He asked several times if " those scamps, Dumas and Coffinhal, had been arrested." That same day Adnet remarked to the Public Prosecutor that to secure the execution of the condemned persons would endanger the police. Fouquier answered him " I cannot stop the course of justice."

Jean Baptiste Christophe Jullienne, aged 27, a lawyer, of the Quai Conti, near the Mint, frequented the Tribunal a great deal in his capacity as official defender He was sure that, in a great number of cases, particularly those of the Farmers-General and the Members of the Parlements, the haste was such that well-intentioned jurors were scarcely able to fit the name of the accused to the person they had before them. Several times he saw the jurors declare themselves sufficiently informed when the proceedings had hardly begun.

" It was what was called ' strangling the proceedings.' "

Fouquier often prevented cases from coming to trial. He would say that the moment was not favourable. Several persons thus owed him their existence.

Louis Charles Hally, aged 42, janitor of the Plessis house of detention, Rue Saint-Jacques, knew that Fouquier went there sometimes to make visits Hally went to the prosecutor's office to give Fouquier an account of the state of affairs in the house of detention. The Public Prosecutor did not give him a good reception. Manini and Coquery, summoned to the Tribunal to give evidence concerning the alleged conspiracy in the prisons, came back enchanted with the welcome that Fouquier had given them, so they said.

Gabriel Nicolas Monet, aged 38, an usher of the Tribunal, frequently saw Fouquier giving orders in his office " with great violence " He very often erased names from the lists of the accused who were to be placed on trial next day, and added others He used to say he had received orders from the Committee The ushers, owing to those charges, were compelled to spend nights copying out indictments. They were often compelled to take in "extra writers to work night and day."

Sometimes when the indictments were very long "and many copies were required for which they had only from the evening until the next day," there came to them from the prosecutor's office the first folio of the memorandum, then the second, then in succession all the others until the indictment was completed.

Jean Louis Marie Villain d'Aubigny, aged 42, ex-assistant to the Minister of War and General Agent for Military Transports at Paris, of No 60, Rue Montpensier, at the time detained at La Bourbe, had the following story from Sénar, who told it to him in the presence of several persons at the Luxembourg.

Sénar was one day with Fouquier   They had a discussion, and Fouquier said to him   "Do you know that I will place you in the dock ? "

"How could you do that ?   You know that I am a patriot, and that I have served my country as well as I could."

"Bah ! " answered Fouquier, "what does that matter ? Do you not know that when the Committee of Public Safety has decided on the death of any one—patriot or aristocrat—he has to go through it ? "[1]

Philippe Marie Tampon, aged 30, judge of the Tribunal of the Third Arrondissement, at present in the service of the Criminal Tribunal of the Department of Paris, heard Fouquier say, at the dinner on the 9th of Thermidor, in the house of Vergnhes, when he learnt of Robespierre's arrest · " My post is in the prosecutor's office, where I may receive orders at any moment, and I am going there."[2]

Next, a man who owed his life to an error in the writ of indictment came forward to give evidence of this. His father had been guillotined in his place.[3]

Guy Marie Sallier, aged 31, a former Councillor in the

[1] Archives Nationales, W. 500, 3rd dossier, p 46, folios 13 to 14.
[2] Archives Nationales, W. 500, 3rd dossier, p 64.
[3] See Chapter II, p. 60

Parlement of Paris, a lawyer, residing at No. 7, Rue du Grand-Chantier,[1] Section de l'Homme-Armé, declared that Henry Guy Sallier, ex-President of the Cour des Aides, his father, was included by mistake in the arrest, made by the Committee of General Security on the 9th of Germinal in the year II , of the ex-Presidents and Councillors of the Parlement of Paris, who were charged with having signed or adhered to the protests made by the Vacation Chamber of that Parlement. On the 29th of the same month his father was examined before a judge of the Revolutionary Tribunal. Fouquier was present.

His father declared that his name was Henry Guy Sallier, *a former President of the Cour des Aides*, and said that there was an error regarding his person, as he did not belong to the former Parlement of Paris.

This made no difference. A letter was produced against him, signed " Sallier," and couched in general terms, from which an alleged adhesion to the protests of the members of the Parlement was inferred He answered that he did not admit that letter to be his, but his son's (the witness's).

Nothing more was said to him about it. He was conducted to the Conciergerie Fouquier, without taking any other information, hastened to make out a writ of indictment, in which he stated that, by resolution of the Committee of General Security, Henry Guy Sallier, ex-President *of the Cour des Aides*, would be charged before the Revolutionary Tribunal with having taken part in the protests of the Vacation Chamber of the Parlement of Paris. This was false, for the resolution of the Committee of General Security had mentioned Sallier, ex-President or Councillor *of the Parlement*.

" Forgetting his first statement," Fouquier attributed the son's letter to the father He had the father brought to trial. The father was condemned to death on the day following (the twenty-fifth prisoner) in spite of the evidence and notwithstanding his protests.[2]

[1] Rue des Vieilles-Haudriettes et des Quatre-Fils
[2] Archives Nationales, W. 500, 3rd dossier, p 64.

Louis Severin Guyard, aged 29, a farmer from Mandres, near Brunoy, had been imprisoned at the Plessis. He saw Fouquier-Tinville there for the first time. " He had just loaded the vehicles with victims for his Tribunal " Guyard tried to speak to him to beg him to have him tried. Fouquier answered roughly " You will come in your turn. You are all scoundrels."

Fouquier seemed to be very familiar with Hally, the janitor.

" They consulted together on the surest and quickest method of being able to take a greater number of victims from the houses of detention, in order that the lists might always be provided complete."

In order " to satisfy Fouquier's impatience, Hally—according to the witness's account—answered him one day that he had to satisfy himself with sending him the surnames without the Christian names, that this method would be quicker "[1]

After the 25th of Ventôse, Judge Pissis gave place in the inquiry to Judge Jean François Godart. It was before him that the younger Sallier and Guyard, the farmer, appeared. It was also before him that, on the 27th of Ventôse, there appeared Pierre Urbain Deguaigné, aged 48, an ex-usher of the Tribunal, now living on his income in Paris, at No. 4, Quai de la République.

He was acquainted with Fouquier " His principal characteristic was irascibility. He frequently gave way to violent outbursts. He often drank wine in the evening, and came and made a horrible racket in the offices, breaking and damaging the portfolios, and using the hardest language to the employees."

But " at bottom, he never saw him cruel or ferocious."

He frequently saw him with jurors—Chrétien, Auvray, Topino-Lebrun, Prieur, Trinchard and others—eating in the refreshment-room, " together or separately."

The witness was particularly charged " to attend to the death sentences." The only question that Fouquier used to

---

[1] Archives Nationales, W 500, 3rd dossier, p 64

ask when he came back from the executions was —" Were there many people there ? "[1]

Marie Pierre Joseph Fonteines-Biré,[2] aged 27, living on his income at No 113 Quai Malaquai, Section de l'Unité, had been imprisoned for a long time in various houses of detention during the Terror. At the Plessis, he noticed that Fouquier often came there, and consulted with the janitor. It was said that he had dined several times with him. But that was merely " a report "

André Contat, aged 50, formerly a clerk in the ushers' office of the Tribunal, residing in Paris at No. 1, Rue des Rats, Section du Panthéon, declared that he only knew Fouquier-Tinville when he was employed in the ushers' office. He often saw the Public Prosecutor come, swearing and shouting " either at the ushers or at the clerks." He used to complain that the work was not done fast enough. He broke the portfolios by the way he struck them with his hand. He made everybody tremble He went so far as to say · " If you do not hurry, I will lock you up. I will have you locked up "

It was more particularly after dinner that he gave way to those " violent and frightful " outbursts

The amount of work was such that the " trembling " clerks would tell him that they would never have time between the evening and the following morning to copy and serve all the writs of indictment which he ordered them to prepare. He would answer them . " Do as you like ! There will always be enough of them. Hurry ! Things must move ! "

They were often brought indictments to copy which were signed by him but not by the judges. They pointed this out to him. He answered : " Go on with your work. They will be signed "

It was Contat who, meeting Fouquier on the 9th of Thermidor " in the archway adjoining the ushers' office," remarked to him that " something was taking place in Paris,"

[1] Archives Nationales, W. 500, 3rd dossier, p 64
[2] He signs thus

and that perhaps it would be prudent to put off the execution of the condemned persons until the morning, so as not to " expose " the police. To which Fouquier answered, speaking to the executioner's assistant : " The course of justice must not be stopped "

Fouquier afterwards went out to dinner. Contat had since learnt that that dinner took place in the Ile Saint-Louis.

Twice the witness noticed that writs of indictment were signed by Fouquier although the names of the accused were not written in them. For this purpose he left a long space of blank paper on which to write them

Next came a deposition that was terrible for Fouquier. It was that of Nicolas Joseph Pâris, called Fabricius, chief registrar of the Revolutionary Tribunal, residing in Paris in the Rue des Fossés-Saint-Germain-des-Près. He was appointed registrar of the Tribunal by Danton. He did not hide his indignation after Danton's trial. Four days after Danton's death, he was imprisoned in the Luxembourg and placed in solitary confinement. Set at liberty after Robespierre's fall, he had been re-appointed registrar by a decree of the 22nd of Thermidor in the year II. He hated Fouquier with an implacable hatred. He said " Towards the end of September in the year II., the Tribunal was almost entirely reorganised. This reorganisation was the work of the Committees of Public Safety and of General Security, along with Fouquier and Fleuriot,[1] who presented various members as candidates. Those members were appointed. The cause of this reorganisation was that it was desired to get rid of honest jurors

" It was at this period that the Committees of government took possession of the Tribunal, which became an instrument in their hands. There is no case of any unhappy wretch being acquitted, who was sent by those Committees to the Tribunal ; if that happened he was again arrested and guillotined.

[1] Lescot-Fleuriot, one of the Public Prosecutor's deputies, then Mayor of Paris, was guillotined with Robespierre and the members of the Commune on the 10th of Thermidor.

"The Tribunal being composed of four sections, there ought to have been a selection by lot of judges and jurors ; instead of such a selection it was *a choice* that was made of them ; this was done above all when there were important cases to be tried ; it was done, to my knowledge, in the case of Hébert and Vincent, and in that of Philippeaux, Camille, Danton, and others   This choice was made by Fleuriot and Fouquier in the Council Chamber, in the presence of several judges.   The jurors chosen were those whom Fouquier called ' solid ' persons on whom one could count—Trinchard, Renaudin, Brochet, Leroi, called ' Tenth of August,' Prieur, Aubry, Châtelet, Didier, Vilate, Laporte, Gautier, Duplay, Lumière, Desboisseaux and Bernard (these last three were guillotined as members of the rebel Commune), as well as several others known at the Tribunal as *firers of uninterrupted volleys*   Those jurors, when they were serving, went in the morning to Fouquier's room where the judges on duty often were.   There they discussed the case for the day. Instructions what to do were given them

"From there they went up to the refreshment-room, through the windows of which they saw with pleasure the victims passing by whom they were about to sacrifice, and against whom they allowed themselves to make insulting remarks.   One day I was in Fouquier's room   Some one came to announce that the hearing in the hall, formerly called the Hall of Saint-Louis, had ended, and that several of the persons placed on trial had been acquitted.   Fouquier burst out against the jurors, stamping with his foot, and saying ' Give me the names of those beggars   One can count on nothing with those people   Here are safe cases breaking in our hands ! '

"Fouquier repeated similar statements on several occasions when accused persons were acquitted

"In the course of Ventôse in the year II., the case of Hébert, Vincent, Ronsin and others came on.   Lengthy informations were lodged.   More than two hundred witnesses were heard.   A large number designated Pache and Hanriot as heads of a faction, the one as the chief judge and the other as chief soldier of that faction. One evening, before the trial, the Tribunal assembled in the Council Chamber and deliberated on the charges which were brought against Pache and Hanriot in the various declarations it had received. Dumas, *who was drunk*, proposed that a warrant for arrest should be issued against Hanriot. Fleuriot opposed this on the pretext that they ought not to arrest the head of the Parisian army without referring the matter to the Committee of Public Safety. His opinion prevailed, and on the same evening Fouquier, Dumas and Herman went to the Committee of Public Safety to inform it of the debate that had just taken place. I knew the next day that they were reprimanded by the Committee, and particularly by Robespierre, for having deliberated about arresting Hanriot. They received orders to get rid of any proofs that might exist against Pache as well as against Hanriot. Ronsin, Hébert and others were placed on trial ; the proceedings began, and when certain witnesses wanted to speak of Pache and Hanriot, President Dumas interrupted them, saying it had nothing to do with those persons, that they were not on trial. He uttered a eulogy of them, speaking of the virtue of Pache, who had the confidence of the people, of Hanriot's good citizenship and his courage. The witnesses were reduced to silence. Fouquier was present and performed the duties of Public Prosecutor. He took care not to contradict the President.

" Afterwards came the proceedings entered into against Camille Desmoulins, Philippeaux, Danton and others. It was in this affair that I saw the Committees of Public Safety and of General Security employing the most refined Machiavelism, and Fouquier, like Dumas, lending himself basely and willingly to the perfidious projects of those two Committees, who wished to sacrifice the most enlightened citizens and the firmest defenders of our liberty, in order that they might more surely succeed in establishing their own tyranny and the barbarous system which they have since employed.

" At eleven o'clock the accused were brought into the room where the court sat. After the reading of the indict-

ment, Westermann and Souher were sent for and joined
with Danton, Camille and Philippeaux, just as these last
had been joined with d'Eglantine, Chabot and d'Espagnac.
In this way there were brought into the case three groups
of persons who had never seen or known one another—a
refinement of perfidy often made use of by the Committees
and still oftener by Fouquier, confounding men of the
highest probity, the most intrepid defenders of our liberty,
with low scoundrels and the declared enemies of the
Revolution.

" At this session Camille Desmoulins challenged the juror
Renaudin, and gave reasons for his challenge. Those
reasons seemed to me to be well founded   Fouquier ought
to have requested the Tribunal to pronounce upon these.
But a juror such as Renaudin was too much needed , and
care was taken not to allow the challenge, which was not
even considered. The accused, seeing a marked partiality
on the part of the Tribunal, which was surrounded by members of the Committee of General Security, who were placed
behind the judges and the jurors, asked that several Deputies
(to the number of sixteen) should be summoned and heard
as witnesses. Danton also asked the Tribunal to write to
the Convention in order that a commission of its members
should be appointed to receive the protest that he, Camille,
and Philippeaux desired to make against the dictatorship
exercised by the Committee of Public Safety. These requests were in no way acceded to , they were refused by the
President, by Fouquier, and by his worthy friend, Fleuriot,
who, with Fouquier, filled jointly the post of Public Prosecutor   As the Tribunal had no valid reason to offer the
accused for not granting a request that could not be refused
without injustice, the President closed the session

" The next day the hearing began very late. Some
questions were put to some of the accused. Danton asked
leave to speak in order to answer the charges brought against
him. This was at first refused under the pretext that he
should speak in his turn. As he insisted, it was impossible
to persist in the refusal. He took the indictment, and as

One day Dupré saw and read an indictment made out against a certain Dietrich,[1] Mayor of Strasburg ; and not having found offences deserving condemnation, he pointed this out to Château, a clerk in the prosecutor's office, who answered him · " You are right. You think that is nothing. But the 300,000 *livres* of income that are not put down there are something."

By this observation, and by the tone in which it was uttered, Château seemed to the witness to reflect the state of mind of the prosecutor's office

Dupré was present at several sessions of the Tribunal. He noticed " great vehemence against the accused on the part of Fouquier." He scarcely left them " time to collect themselves," especially in the case of Magon la Balue, in which the grand-daughter of the last-mentioned and her husband were condemned on the sole ground that they belonged to the family. There was no document, no witness, against them. Dupré could not, however, assert positively that it was Fouquier who performed the duties of Public Prosecutor in that case [2]

For a month the two investigating judges, Pissis and Godart, endeavoured to establish the Public Prosecutor's responsibility for the criminal haste with which indictments were made out, his attitude at the sessions of the Tribunal when he sat, the part he played in Danton's case, in that of Léonard Bourdon, and in the Prison Conspiracy, and his relations with the jurors.

We have made a lengthy examination of the indictments preserved among the Archives. We have demonstrated that they were made out with precipitation and negligence, and we have heard many depositions relative to Fouquier's attitude in the course of the proceedings.

We know the terrible evidence of the registrar Pâris in regard to Danton's case. When Pâris was confronted with Fouquier at the trial, Fouquier exclaimed against this

---

[1] Frédéric Dietrich, Mayor of Strasburg, was guillotined on the 8th of Nivôse in the year II

[2] Archives Nationales, W 500, 3rd dossier, p 63, folio 7.

deposition, saying : " It is Danton's death that they would revenge here."

But he was unable to deny the facts of this clear, precise, and circumstantial statement.

Another witness, Villain d'Aubigny, a prisoner at Sainte-Pélagie, met Fouquier in that house of detention, in Fructidor. He said that he reproached the ex-Public Prosecutor vehemently for his conduct in Danton's case. Fouquier answered that he had no cause for self-reproach as he had gone to the Committee of Public Safety and transmitted the request of the accused, who desired to have sixteen Deputies heard as witnesses. He believed that the Committee would offer no opposition to this The Committee refused.

" I insisted," said Fouquier to Villain d'Aubigny.

" It was therefore," answered the witness, " a crime for you to have deceived the accused and made them lose precious time which they might have spent in taking other measures for their defence. I tell you that your letter of the 15th, written to the Committee, is a crime, for from what had been told you on the previous evening, you should have known beforehand what would be the answer of the Committee to your letter."

" I wrote it," Fouquier affirmed, " because the people who were present at that case demanded, together with the accused, that the witnesses they claimed should be heard. But I did not foresee the atrocious use that the official reporter of that Committee would make of that letter, by bluffing the Convention and wringing from it a decree depriving the accused of the right to plead. That decree was gained by not allowing the Convention time for reflection A rebellion against Law and Justice on the part of the accused was spoken of. That rebellion never existed "

" It is very strange," rejoined Villain d'Aubigny, " that at the moment when this decree reached the Tribunal, at the moment when the Tribunal was informed by its contents of the horrible manner in which the good faith of the Convention had been imposed upon, you did not ask all

the members of the Tribunal, all the judges and all the
jurors, to go with you, that very moment, to the Convention,
and enlighten it concerning the frightful perfidy by means
of which it had been surprised into passing a decree that
sent the accused to the scaffold without hearing them."

" Restrained myself by the threats that were made to me
each day, I was unable, in this case as well as in many others,
to obey the inclinations of my heart," answered Fouquier.[1]

In regard to the Léonard Bourdon case, François Basseville, a tiler from Orléans, declared that he found Léonard
Bourdon, his witnesses, and Fouquier-Tinville assembled
in the same room.[2] Those witnesses, belonging to " the
clique that devastated the Orléans district," threw themselves on Léonard Bourdon's neck, and he gave them
unequivocal evidence of his friendship for them.

In the course of the preliminary investigations and of the
trial, Basseville saw Fouquier several times lunching in the
refreshment-room with those witnesses.   When the municipal officers of the Orléans district, who had been summoned
to give evidence, presented themselves in court, Fouquier-
Tinville silenced them, and said to the President : " Take
notice, President, that it is a municipal officer who is
speaking, and that he will never tell you the truth."

Another witness, Charles Cornu, aged 37, a farmer of
Orléans, declared that Fouquier and those of the judges
who had examined the Orléans witnesses in the Léonard

---

[1] Archives Nationales, W. 500, 3rd dossier, p 64, folio 1.

[2] Léonard Bourdon, a teacher and the founder of the Society of
Young Frenchmen, a boarding-school at which lectures in morals
were to be given by Robespierre, Collot d'Herbois, Billaud-Varenne,
etc , had been elected to the Convention by the Department of the
Loiret   Sent on a mission to Orléans, as he was passing the City Hall
on March 15, 1793, he had been surrounded by a crowd, dragged
into the ante-room of the Hall, struck by a bayonet and slightly
wounded in the left arm and in the head   Was it a premeditated
assault, or was it a brawl ?   The incident happened after a fraternal
dinner   Had the sentinel of the City Hall been attacked and provoked by one of the citizens who accompanied the Representative
of the people ?   The Convention, indignant at the attempt against
one of its members, ordered that the instigators of the attack should
be tried by the Revolutionary Tribunal

Bourdon case " appeared to be astonished at the importance which the Representative sought to give to that case, and did not seem to find in it any serious offence." Léonard Bourdon held frequent conferences, morning and evening, with Fouquier, down to the moment when the indictment was made out and signed.   It was at this time that Léonard Bourdon had printed what he called *Details Concerning the Attempt against a Representative of the People, Committed at Orléans.*   This statement was, in part, copied out in the indictment.   Fouquier, meeting the witness in the registry of the Tribunal when he had just left there some documents for the defence, told him that he was sorry he had consented to his provisional release, that he was guilty, and that he had been deceived regarding him.

" You cannot have been deceived," Cornu answered him, " since you have in your possession all the charges relative to this case."

The witnesses who had been summoned were daily at Bourdon's with Fouquier-Tinville.   Young girls from Orléans, who were summoned to give evidence, had, on the evening before the hearing, related that Bourdon had feasted them, had paid for bouquets for them, and promised them dresses. The witnesses had lunched several times in the refreshment-room of the Tribunal with Fouquier and some jurors. Cornu caused this to be told at the trial, by Julienne, one of the defenders.   Fouquier showed a good deal of ill-humour at this, and said to Julienne " that he would not be the happier for it "   He asked the Tribunal for the arrest of several witnesses for the defence.[1]

As regards Fouquier's complicity in that famous phantom conspiracy which has been called the Conspiracy in the Prisons, here follows a certain number of depositions which seem to establish it.

On the 15th of Ventôse in the year III , a police officer, Charles Mercereau, who had been imprisoned in the Luxembourg for two months, gave evidence before Judge Pissis that he saw " lists of proscribed persons " being made.   Some police

---

[1] Archives Nationales, W 500, 3rd dossier p 64, folios 6 and 7.

administrators proposed to him that he should share in the work. They told him that Fouquier-Tinville and the Committees had people in the Luxembourg " to discover the conspiracies " On the night between the 8th and 9th of Thermidor people came *from Fouquier* to fetch twenty-five of those alleged conspirators, among whom was an old man of about 70 years of age, so infirm that he could only move with great difficulty, blind, and in his second childhood. He was condemned like the others " for having conspired in the prisons "[1]

It is noticeable that the greater number of the witnesses declared that the conspiracies were imaginary. One " had heard them spoken of " but that was all. Another said : " A conspiracy which they said was being hatched." Many affirmed that " far from having noticed a conspiracy they, on the contrary, had noticed the greatest tranquillity and the greatest submission on the part of the prisoners who had been terrorised." Another, confined in Saint-Lazare, could attest that there was no conspiracy there. " He shuddered at seeing ninety persons carried off in three days on informations lodged by Manini." Brunet, a wine-seller of the Rue de Buci, formerly employed as a wine-seller at the Carmelites, " was acquainted with no trace of a conspiracy." The sole care of the prisoners was to amuse themselves and to soften the rigour of imprisonment. Several times, when some new-comer or other allowed a rather bitter expression, provoked by despair, to escape his lips, he even saw them " recalling him to gentleness and hope." Dufau, a colonial, imprisoned at the Carmelites, said " that in his opinion the alleged conspiracy in the Carmelites was a myth invented by men greedy for blood It had for its object only a plan of escape contrived by five or six prisoners who planned to escape during the night with the help of a bell-rope "

Chavard declared that this conspiracy was " absolutely imaginary." The plan of escape of five or six prisoners who had found a rope in the bell-tower alone gave birth to the

[1] This was M. Durand Puy de Vérine. See Chapter IV., p. 105.

idea   " The basis of the indictment which Fouquier drew
up was as atrocious as it was slanderous, for it related to a
conspiracy that had no existence except in the brains of the
Public Prosecutor and his accomplices " Millet, a commissioner from San Domingo, a Deputy in the Convention,
had been imprisoned in the Carmelites. He noticed no
conspiracy, what he was witness of was the " heroic patience"
of the prisoners, " the harshness and rascality " of the janitor,
Roblâtre, the turnkeys, and the police officials   Joly,
an artist of the Théâtre des Arts, " imprisoned for a long time
by his Revolutionary Committee," never " noticed any
suggestion of a conspiracy or even of a plan of escape."
Nevertheless, " in order that that house might be emptied
more quickly there existed makers of lists of proscribed
persons." Guyard, the janitor of the Luxembourg, " heard
a conspiracy spoken of." Nevertheless, within the building,
he observed no proceedings and heard no remarks that
pointed to a conspiracy, or it was a very secret one. He had
no reproach to make against the prisoners [1]

There are similar declarations regarding the other houses
of detention   Those who imagined the conspiracies, those
who used that monstrous imagination to escape the galleys
and to enjoy a relative liberty since they used to leave the
prison and go to the Tribunal to give evidence against the
unfortunate beings about whom they lodged informations,
they alone knew what the conspiracies were. They gave
details about them. But their evidence was suspect and
tainted beforehand, for they were branded with an igno-
minious name. They were police spies—Benoît, Boyaval,
Beausire, Manini, Coquery, and Jobert (the Belgian)

Now follows what the inquiry says about the jurors of the
former Tribunal, with whom, in a few days, Fouquier was
to stand his trial   They were his " solid persons," ready to
condemn *for eighteen livres a day.*

Citizen Didier, the juror, had been a locksmith at Choisy-
sur-Seine. " He could hardly live by his work. He had
even been obliged to toil at carrying loads in the port. Since

[1] Archives Nationales, W 509, 3rd dossier, p. 64 and p. 58.

the Revolution, and especially under Robespierre's reign, he had been in very easy circumstances and very familiar with Maximilien. As a juror of the Tribunal he acquired great prestige at Choisy, where he was the leader of the Popular Society, and where he made the citizens of the district tremble."[1]

Causeret, a building contractor from Choisy, declared that Didier, " a journeyman locksmith, really became one of the destroying scourges of the district," that he was " an inseparable companion of Hanriot, and an accomplice in all the arbitrary acts and arrests that took place in the Choisy district " On one occasion " he pushed his temerity so far as to have burned, in his presence, in the middle of the Popular Society, a letter from the receiver of taxes who asked him to advise its members to pay their taxes." Didier said that it " was only aristocrats who paid ; that he was the friend of Robespierre and Duplay "[2]

It was Didier who, at a hearing of the Tribunal, asked for permission to speak, and said to one of the accused " Is it not enough to prove you an aristocrat that you waited on a noble ? Bah ! that is enough of it."

On which they passed to the next accused person.[3]

The juror Brochet, another " solid man," twice caused the arrest of his tenant, Mury, a soap-manufacturer of Paris. Brochet was an intimate friend of Momoro. Together they had created a Popular Society " in which they only received people of their own party or those who wished to belong to it." He held at the same time the positions of Captain in the National Guard, President of the Revolutionary Committee, and juror of the Tribunal. "This man, by the arrests and condemnations with which he stained himself in the exercise of the offices which he accumulated, had made himself the opprobrium and execration of his whole Section." One day the witness went to Brochet's to pay his rent (two or three days before the trial of the woman du

---

[1] Archives Nationales, W 500, 3rd dossier, p 64, folio 3.
[2] Archives Nationales, W 500, 3rd dossier, p 64, folio 5
[3] Archives Nationales, W 500, 3rd dossier, p 58, folio 1.

Barry). The juror put him off to another day, saying: "They are waiting for me at the Tribunal I have forty rascals to try."

The witness spent nearly ten months in prison " owing to Brochet's attentions."[1]

The juror Chrétien, a member of the Revolutionary Committee of the Lepelletier Section, " was the scourge of his Section." He kept a café in the Rue Favart off the Place de la Comédie Italienne. " It was from the infernal divan that he kept at his house that there issued forth all the sabred and moustached gentry who wandered either into the theatres to make disturbances, or on the boulevards to drive away the respectable women who were taking the air." He always had " the word guillotine in his mouth, and threatened with Fouquier-Tinville those whom he desired to frighten " He boasted of the influence he had with the Public Prosecutor. He had been several times on missions in his own Department, with powers and warrants which he said he held from Fouquier-Tinville. He spread forth Terror on these missions

When he came back from the Tribunal and was asked by the *habitués* of his " divan " about the judgments passed during the day, he used to smile, and " with an insulting and barbarous joy " he would answer . " There will be twenty or twenty-three to-day."

" He would then picture, with barbarous gestures, the attitude which the condemned persons were to adopt at the moment of their execution "[2]

Another witness said that Chrétien often associated with Collot d'Herbois, and that he was the terror of all the respectable people in his Section. He described how he guided the Committee of his Section with cunning and ferocity.[3]

Another gave a picture of his " divan," which was frequented by " a society of bullies and cut-throats." People

---

[1] Archives Nationales, W 500, 3rd dossier, p 58, folio 4
[2] Archives Nationales, W 500, 3rd dossier, p 64
[3] Archives Nationales, W. 500, 3rd dossier, p 58, folio 1.

were only admitted to this den if they could prove that they had taken part in the September massacres "Every time that Chrétien mounted the tribune, it was to display his thirst for human blood."[1]

Another declared that Chrétien never showed himself in his Section " except armed with a sabre, pistols or a cudgel " ; that he often threatened people with those weapons , that he never exercised power except to oppress his fellow-citizens , that he regarded as *aristocrats* every rich or noble person and even those who held just and virtuous principles. " He made this clear on one occasion when he was complimented on a moral speech which he had delivered in the Temple of Reason of his Section, by replying that he had only delivered that speech in order that by their applause he might recognise the aristocrats and moderates, two classes of men whom he persecuted " His conduct on the 9th of Thermidor was very suspicious. He did not go to his Section. He remained at his " divan," where he held a council His sole aim was " to join the winning side." He had Fouquier-Tinville's name continually in his mouth, and called him his friend It seemed that Fouquier had given him blank warrants to arrest people, and that he had employed them at Luzarches in the case of an officer whose horses he wanted to take. Dubois-Crancé was the possessor of a document which proved this.

Chrétien had a great deal of influence with his friend, Fouquier-Tinville, and lodged informations with him against all those of whom he wished to rid himself. He used to speak of Fouquier as the best patriot in the Republic, and, when the Revolutionary Tribunal was re-organised after the 9th of Thermidor, he said " that there was a heap of intriguers such as Tallien and others who wanted to oppose Fouquier's nomination, but that the latter could not fail to win "[2]

Citizen Beudon, keeper of the furnished " sailors' house " in the Rue Gaillon, Lepelletier Section, " knew the man called

---

[1] Archives Nationales, W 500, 3rd dossier, p 58, folio 9
[2] Archives Nationales, W 500, 3rd dossier, p. 58.

Chrétien, the ex-juror of the Tribunal, as one of the greatest drinkers of blood it was possible to see." As an agent on mission he used to go into the Departments with " blank credentials which it was said he held from Fouquier."[1]

Similar evidence about Chrétien was given by Renault, a mason and building-contractor of Paris, residing at No. 810 in " the unfinished street " in the Lepelletier Section. He had been his comrade in arms in the artillery company of the Section. At first he appeared to him to be " rather quiet and gentle, not doing much duty, and employing his waiters as deputies for him " On the day when the question of Marat and Robespierre was discussed and when Louvet denounced them in the Convention, Chrétien, who was on duty that day, displayed his dissatisfaction with the Convention in a far from respectful manner, saying —

" Let these beggars go away ! They waste our time."

Since then " he had taken a more imperious tone, and began to make himself more feared than liked by his comrades." He brought into the company men like Maillard, September massacrers, so-called conquerors of the Bastille, who belonged with him to a so-called Popular Society.

In proportion as the Republican Government became established, he gained greater " preponderance," and he tyrannised over his Section. He had always been a friend of Fouquier, Ronsin, Vincent and Hanriot.[2]

Another witness, Lanchon, a wine-seller of the Rue Neuve-Saint-Marc in the Lepelletier Section, one day when he went into Chrétien's house to drink " a small glass of brandy," and expressed astonishment that so many sentences of condemnation had been pronounced at the Tribunal in such a short time, was answered by Chrétien with the words

" Bah ! are you surprised at that ? You are not up to date. We are almost useless for our part ; but with Fouquier-Tinville, who is a patriot, things are done at once. The gaol-registers are read and the thing is ended."[3]

---

[1] Archives Nationales, W. 500, p 58, folio 10.
[2] Archives Nationales, W 500, 3rd dossier, p 58, folio 11.
[3] Archives Nationales, W 500, 3rd dossier, p 63, folio 4.

Pierre Armand Le Petit, formerly a distiller, of the Rue Marivaux, saw Chrétien "dominating over his Section for three years" He gave details which confirmed the preceding depositions [1]

The ex-juror Aubry, a tailor, of the Section de l'Unité, " could neither read nor write." He was an " evil man of sanguinary instincts." A witness at Fouquier's trial heard him say, at the time of the reorganisation of the Tribunal, after the 9th of Thermidor, that " the choice of Fouquier-Tinville as Public Prosecutor was the best that could be made, that only aristocrats could oppose his appointment, and that another like him would never be found." It appeared that Aubry, in his capacity as a juror, never voted except for death. " Two classes were to him *food for the guillotine*—priests and nobles." It was useless to examine the documents relating to them. [2]

Another witness, Langlois, a haberdasher of Paris, of the same Section as the ex-juror Aubry, knew him " to be an ignorant tailor, unable to read or write, and an evil man whom he had often heard proposing revolting and sanguinary motions. He saw him take some citizens by the collar, and threaten others."

" He congratulated himself on the victims whom he had helped to send to the scaffold He publicly boasted that he had never voted except for death at the trials of priests and nobles, who, to him, were all food for the guillotine." [3]

Citizen Porcher, a cabinet-maker, of the Rue Mazarine in the Section de l'Unité, knew Fouquier-Tinville only by repute and from sometimes seeing him at the Tribunal. But he knew Aubry, the ex-juror, who threatened to denounce him to the Jacobin Club, because one day, when on guard with him, he had expressed indignation at the condemnation of four or five prisoners who had not been allowed to speak and whose accusations had not even received the final sanction of the Public Minister. Out of this there

---

[1] Archives Nationales, W. 500, 3rd dossier, p. 63, folio 5.
[2] Archives Nationales, W. 500, 3rd dossier, p 58, folio 1.
[3] Archives Nationales, W 500, 3rd dossier, p. 58, folio 2.

arose a quarrel, and the officer of the guard intervened " He had always known Aubry to be a man of blood " He had seen him at several trials. He was either asleep, or scarcely listening.

In the affair of Ferrand and Laruelle[1] who were charged with complicity in an alleged conspiracy at Montauban, on May 10, 1790, the witness pointed out to Fouquier that the accused were in no way accomplices, seeing that one of them had been at Brest and the other at Gondrecourt in the Meuse. His evidence might have been of value. Fouquier did not think it fitting to have it heard.

Nevertheless he had followed the course of this trial, which took place in one of the halls and was presided over by Dumas He had been revolted by the partiality of the judges and jurors Aubry slept. The accused were cut short in their speeches. The witnesses for the prosecution were listened to " complacently " ; the witnesses for the defence " in a body." They made a hubbub. Aubry woke up. When the jurors returned after a short deliberation, Aubry, like the rest, was convinced of the facts and of the culpability of the accused.[2]

" Aubry could neither read nor write," declared Robert Wolff, the registrar's clerk. " He belonged to my Section. He could only write five letters in print, and these were enough to bring him in, every month, five hundred and forty livres as the price of his assassinations." He used to boast, besides, in the café at the corner of the Rue de Buci and in that of Rue de la Chaumière, where he went daily, that he had always earned his money well, and that he had no cause to reproach himself, for he had never acquitted anybody.[3]

André Barraly, aged 39, hairdresser, of No. 34 Rue Neuve-des-Petits-Champs, facing the Rue Neuve-des-Bons-Enfants, Section Guillaume-Tell, had never known Fouquier-Tinville except by reputation. He never had

[1] Captain Ferrand and Captain Laruelle were guillotined on 9th of Ventôse in the year II
[2] Archives Nationales, W 500, 3rd dossier, p 58, folio 10.
[3] Archives Nationales, W 500, 3rd dossier, p 63, folio 7.

any relation, direct or indirect, with him. " In his capacity
as hairdresser, either he himself or his assistant, Lingault,
had dressed Robespierre's hair for twelve or thirteen
months at the house of Duplay, an ex-juror of the
Tribunal, in the Rue Saint-Honoré, opposite the Rue Floren-
tin. He had dressed Duplay's hair two or three times by
chance when he went to Robespierre, because Duplay happened to be in a hurry. The said Duplay, who was very
reserved and haughty, would not lower himself to speak to
a hairdresser." [1]

There was further evidence of what the other jurors were
like—Renaudin, the maker of musical instruments and
the keeper of the ball-room at the Lumière Barrier ; Lohier,
the grocer ; and Trinchard, the carpenter.[2] Trinchard said :
" It does not take me much time to try an accused person.
The mere inspection of his appearance discloses to me the
morality or immorality of a prisoner. It is enough for me
to see people in order to settle on my verdict."

It was also Trinchard, after the 22nd of Prairial and when
he was no longer a juror of the Tribunal but had been
appointed a member of the Popular Commission of the
Museum district, who, as he was lunching one day with
several of his former colleagues, said to them : " The Commission is going to begin its operations by sending to you
at the Tribunal all the priests and nobles in the prisons.
I hope they will be sent to the guillotine."

The others applauded.[3]

But the examinations of the witnesses tell us nothing
more concerning the relations between those jurors and
Fouquier-Tinville We are, therefore, compelled to stop
here.

On the 4th of Germinal, Judicis, the Public Prosecutor
of the new Tribunal appointed on the 8th of Nivôse preceding, had drawn up his indictment against Fouquier and

---

[1] Archives Nationales, W 500, p 58, folio 12.

[2] For Trinchard, " Nature's man," see A Dunoyer . *Deux Jurés du
Tribunal Révolutionnaire*, Paris, Perrin, 1909

[3] Archives Nationales, W 500, 3rd dossier, p 63, folio 6

his accomplices. The accused numbered thirty. At their head was Antoine Quentin Fouquier-Tinville, ex-Public Prosecutor of the Revolutionary Tribunal Then came Delaporte, ex-judge ; Foucault, ex-judge , Maire, ex-judge , Scellier, ex-Vice-President , Harny, ex-judge , Deliège, ex-judge , Garnier-Launay, ex-judge , Naulin, ex-Vice-President ; Félix, ex-judge , Bravet, ex-judge ; Barbier, ex-judge ; and Liendon, ex-deputy to the Public Prosecutor. Finally came seventeen former jurors—Lohier, Trinchard, Leroy, called "Tenth of August," Renaudin, Chrétien, Gauthier, Didier, Ganney, Vilate, Duplay, Prieur, Châtelet, Brochet, Girard, Trey, Pigeot, and Aubry.

Judicis declared that he had made a fresh examination of the documents delivered either to his predecessor or to himself.

From this it followed that Fouquier " abetted the projects of a liberticidal faction known under the name of that of Robespierre, Saint-Just, Couthon, and others who fell under the sword of the law after the 9th of Thermidor " The writs of indictment which he presented were full of erasures, commitments, and interlineal insertions that were without authority. He signed these. He presented others that were not filled in, others in which the names of the accused were inserted after the indictments had been made out, or at the moment when the case was being heard, by a different hand and in different ink from that in the body of the documents, others in which several names written in small characters were sometimes intercalated, sometimes written on the margin without authority, and from which the names of other accused persons had been erased and effaced He presented other indictments in which the statements relative to the names of the accused give those of certain persons of whom no mention is made in the remainder of the indictment. He inscribed in one indictment the name of a person already condemned to death and executed He pleaded in court that the corpse of a prisoner who had stabbed himself should be taken to the scaffold He pleaded in court for the execution of women who had declared themselves pregnant,

s

and that before the medical officers had pronounced on their condition.

He knew that Fouquier had protested his humanity, the rectitude of his conduct as a magistrate, and his absolute probity. For his own part, as Public Prosecutor, so far from admitting that Fouquier has given proof of his innocence, he considered that he was guilty, and that he had been abetted by the ex-judges, his ex-deputies, and the ex-jurors of the Tribunal, men whose bad moral character was known and who were closely allied with the conspirators, those despots and tyrants who murdered instead of judging.

If Judicis had been unable to make out a detailed list of the documents incriminating Fouquier by their faults of form and the omissions with which they swarmed, the reason was that their number was too great, and he would have risked " causing confusion."

" Whilst recognising that among those who were condemned there were guilty persons who deserved to be punished, one cannot, however, distinguish those from the innocent, and *the forms even severer than those of martial law* that were employed to secure condemnations are enough to prevent us from making the distinction, so that we can legally regard all those acts of condemnation as pure murders." [1]

[1] Archives Nationales, W. 499, dossier 550, p. 9.

CHAPTER XIII

THE FINAL EXAMINATION OF FOUQUIER-TINVILLE. THE PROCEEDINGS IN COURT. VERDICT AND DEATH

THE preliminary inquiry had come to an end. An order of the 4th of Germinal in the year III., signed by Judges Agier, Liger, Debregeas, Favart, Mazerat, Grand, Godeau, Gaillart-Lecart, Godard, Pissis, Devillas, and Bertrand d'Aubagne, granted the demand of Judicis the Public Prosecutor, and gave him a writ of indictment against Fouquier.

The hour was approaching when Fouquier was to appear before his judges ; but, previous to this, he had to undergo a fresh cross-examination

On the 6th of Germinal, commissioners went to the Plessis prison whither the prisoner had been taken. These commissioners were Jean Debregeas, Vice-President of the new Tribunal, and Cambon, Judicis' deputy.[1]

From its beginning the examination was directed to the capital point—the indictments. The commissioners had in their hands those terrible documents, fatal to those whom they had sent to the scaffold, fatal also, by a reaction, to him who had signed, initialled, annotated, or compiled them. They existed. He was responsible for them. They were filled with erasures, commitments, and unauthorised insertions. The names of the accused were written after the indictments had been made out, and in a different hand and with different ink from that in the body of the documents. There were family names presented in a sum-

---

[1] At his first examination, on the 1st of Frimaire in the year III., he had been questioned by Forestier in the presence of the latter's deputy, Jean Jacques Granger. On that occasion he had been taken from the Plessis prison to the Tribunal (See Chapter IX., p. 195.)

mary form without the Christian names, descriptions, ages, or designation of the place of origin. It had not been possible to identify them, from lack of time, between the evening and the following morning.

Fouquier claimed that all the indictments which he presented were regular ; that these indictments had been written by his secretaries   This was his system—to throw all responsibility on others. *But these indictments were signed by him.* The judge did not point this out to him. He allowed him to go on speaking.   Fouquier declared that if these indictments were shown him, he would explain what " people affected not to know."

Never, he said, had he presented blank indictments to the judges to sign.   But as, after the law of the 22nd of Prairial, private preliminary examinations had been suppressed, the Christian names, ages, descriptions, and places of birth could only be filled in after the prisoners had been asked to state them.   Family names had always been inserted in the indictment as well as in the text.

Never, to his knowledge, had he made any additional insertion between the lines of the indictments.

He did not remember that he had ever made out an indictment against a person who had already been condemned.

The judge asked him whether he had not pleaded in court to have carried to the scaffold the corpse of a prisoner who had stabbed himself at the moment he heard his death-sentence (Valaze, the Girondin Deputy).

" Having regard to the public clamour," answered Fouquier, " and in order to avoid the greater disorders that were threatened at the moment when Valaze stabbed himself, I believed it prudent to ask that he should be taken to the place intended for the execution.   I may have been mistaken.   But a mistake cannot be imputed as a crime. I had to execute the judgment of the Tribunal "

Q.—" Have you demanded the execution of women who were pregnant, instead of waiting for the opinion of the doctors ? "

A.—" I have respected declarations of pregnancy "

Q.—" Have you ever gone into the jurors' room at the moment when they were deliberating? "

A.—" I have never gone alone into the room. I have never interrupted the deliberations. I have never taken part in the jurors' deliberations."

Q.—" Have you presented an indictment against 155 persons charged with conspiracy in the prisons ? Was not the word, *twice*, placed alongside three names to indicate two persons under a single name, so that the total number of persons was 158 instead of 155 ? "

A.—" I have in fact made out an indictment against 155 persons charged with conspiracy in the Luxembourg, on the 18th of Messidor According to President Dumas, the intention of the Committee of Public Safety was that they should all be tried at the same time But I had been to the Committee that evening, and it was decided that there should be three trials I do not know what is meant by the word, *twice*, which cannot have been written by my hand or by orders from me. Moreover, the indictments were handed into the registry, after the trial

" Now, I have all sorts of reasons for suspecting that omissions and additions were made at the registry. I can be in no way responsible for those that may have been made either in the indictments or in other documents. Moreover, when I am shown the documents, I shall be in a position to give the most precise explanations. But I am persuaded that the number in question never exceeded 155.

" Besides, I have never meddled with the writing out of the sentences "

" In the first sentence on a section of the Luxembourg prisoners," asked the judge, " was not a man named Morin included, although he was not mentioned in the indictment ? "

This was an embarrassing question, for here, certainly, there had been a judicial error, and a Morin or Maurin had on that day been guillotined instead of another man

Fouquier answered imperturbably : " I am always faced

with indictments that I have nothing to do with. This Morin, so far as I remember, was not tried on the 19th but on the 22nd. Before him, a man named Morin, Madame du Barry's steward, was tried and condemned. Moreover, a Morin, the ex-Maréchale de Biron's steward, had been tried and condemned at a period which I do not precisely remember. The Morin of the Luxembourg Conspiracy had been quartermaster in Capet's guards. When the documents are shown me, I will give the most precise explanations."

Were the documents shown to Fouquier in the course of the proceedings? What were his explanations? In regard to this we know nothing.

Denys Morin, Madame du Barry's servant, had been guillotined on the 3rd of Nivôse in the year II., more than twelve months previously A Nicolas Morin, a farmer, had been acquitted on the 26th of Germinal in the year II. A Jacques Morin, a farmer and carter, had been set free on the 6th of Fructidor in the year II. A Jean Morin, a trooper in the Revolutionary army, had also been set free on the 11th of the same month. A Charles Sosthène Morin, grocer, auctioneer and tax-collector, had been guillotined on the 13th of Messidor in the year II But the error in regard to the persons with which Fouquier was charged, concerned Louis Clerc Morin, quartermaster in the King's Guard, guillotined on the 22nd of Messidor in the year II., and Jean Dominique Maurin, the Maréchale de Biron's bookkeeper and estate-agent, guillotined, instead of the last mentioned, on the 19th of Messidor in the year II. Fouquier's answer, on this matter, was decidedly evasive The cross- examination continued.

" Did not Fouquier demand the punishment of a witness who said that no conspiracy existed in the Luxembourg? "

" This witness[1] was arrested for the evasions, tergiversations, ambiguities, and vacillations in his statement, which appeared to disclose a dishonest person."

For his own part, he, Fouquier, took care not to base his speech for the prosecution on the conspiracy. He even

---

[1] The turnkey, Lesenne

had on that day, " a very sharp altercation with Dumas "
regarding the latter's refusal to allow some of the accused
to defend themselves.

Before allowing the cross-examination to close, Fouquier
was desirous of taking his own precautions, and he made the
following declaration regarding Pâris, the registrar, and
Robert Wolff, the registrar's clerk. He pointed out that
" Pâris, the present registrar of the Tribunal, had declared
himself to be his mortal enemy, both in public and in
private." He spoke of the dinners that were held by the
registrar's clerks (particularly that of the 27th of Frimaire,
the eve of the day on which he was sent for trial). At those
dinners, " they occupied themselves with Fouquier's trial
and the means they would take to ruin him."

" Pâris," he said, " has even boasted that if he were
wanted to hang me, he would pull the cord "

Fouquier said he employed every means for releasing
from prison this very man who was to appear against him
in the capacity of accuser and lover of justice.

" About three weeks ago," Fouquier went on, " Pâris
went to the Café de Chartres, in the Palais Egalité, with
several persons. There he published and indicated the day
on which I should be placed on trial He aggravated the
alleged crimes that are imputed to me He went back there
again and spoke in a perfidious manner and one likely to
rouse public opinion against me."

Then came a capital charge.

" In order more certainly to reach his end, Pâris had
carried off by force, on the 19th of Nivôse last, all the
extracts from the sentences and the receipts of the Commission of National Revenues which were in the prosecutor's
office, and which were my guarantee in regard to the trial
we are dealing with to-day, because I had taken the precaution of having handed to me each day the extracts from the
sentences bearing the names of the condemned persons,
both in order to have those sentences proceeded with, and
to transmit them to the National Estates and to the Commission of National Revenues The number of these docu-

ments has neither been ascertained nor verified. Thus it has been within the power of Pâris to take away those he judged fit. These facts are known to the brothers Toutain,[1] who have done all they could to stop them. They are known to Citizen Leblois,[2] who had then no position there, and to François, one of the attendants in the prosecutor's office.

" Moreover, Pâris had previously taken away a hundred notes of papers relating to cases that had been tried, without giving any receipt for them, though I would have given these to the constituted authorities as fast as they had been transmitted to me.

" I have learnt that, at the time of the departure of Citizen Granger, the Public Prosecutor's deputy who was entrusted with the documents relating to the present trial, that magistrate had handed them over to Pâris and to Wolff ; that they had been deposited with them up to the period when the trial had been committed to Citizen Cambon. One cannot doubt for a moment that they did not neglect to read those documents. It was Pâris who presented the first indictment for signature in court. On the 28th of Frimaire, the day when I appeared before the Tribunal, it was also Pâris who acted officially, for he publicly brought into court a bundle of documents which he placed on the Public Prosecutor's table. Lastly, he also acted officially in this same trial by signing the judgment passed by the Tribunal on the 30th of Ventôse last, and by writing a letter to the Public Prosecutor dated the 2nd or 3rd of the current month "

In accordance with those facts, and others which he intended to develop later, Fouquier-Tinville declared that he knew no law permitting a witness to act officially, in any manner whatsoever, in a trial at which he was a witness. Here, in this trial, not only had Pâris, Wolff, and others acted officially, but they had even displayed, in several

---

[1] Employees in the prosecutor's office.
[2] The Public Prosecutor of the Tribunal established on the 23rd of Thermidor, who drew up the first indictment against Fouquier.

public and private places, their excess of hatred against the accused, a fact that ought to cause the Tribunal henceforth to look on them with suspicion.[1]

The judge asked Fouquier if he had chosen a defender. The ex-Public Prosecutor answered that Citizen Lafleuterie, whom he had chosen as his counsel, having informed him that he had been summoned as a witness for the defence by Citizen Naulin and other fellow-prisoners, and that he was too scrupulous to accept the position of defender in the case, he knew of nobody else whom he could entrust with his defence. An official advocate, Citizen Gaillard,[2] was assigned to him.

The list of jurors was then communicated to Fouquier— Lapeyre, Bressand, Husson, Tournier, Taillerat, Lebrun, Mesange, Bouygues, Duprat, Vignalet, and Laporte

He was acquainted with none of those jurors, except Duprat. He said that his brothers, the Duprats of Avignon, had been tried and condemned, and that he, Fouquier, had appeared against them , that Duprat was an intimate friend of Jourdan, who had been condemned and against whom he had appeared, etc. For all these reasons he challenged Duprat. As regards the others he invited the Tribunal to ask them to remember whether they had any relatives or friends or clients condemned between March 10th, 1793, and the 9th of Thermidor, 1794 In case there should be a fresh selection

---

[1] In the course of his trial, on the 22nd of Germinal, Fouquier sent a note to the Tribunal, " hoping to convince it that, since his imprisonment, documents had been taken away from his room and from the registry by Pâris, a witness whose hate and partiality had been displayed yesterday." Fouquier requested that it might please the Tribunal that in his presence and in the presence of the Public Prosecutor a search should be made in the judges' rooms for papers that might have been hidden in there by Pâris

The Tribunal immediately acceded to this request   (W 499, dossier 550, p 3)

Pâris was heard as a witness at the trial in spite of Fouquier's protests   The President read to the jurors the law relating to the grounds on which a witness could be challenged, and declared that the Tribunal would receive the evidence of Pâris   (Archives Nationales, W. 499, dossier 550, p 6)

[2] Gaillard de la Ferrière.

of jurors, Fouquier challenged in advance Citizen Delorme, with whom he had " a very sharp scene in 1790 at the house of Commissioner Dubois in the Rue de Chabanais," and for further reasons which he enumerated.[1]

On the 8th of Germinal the public proceedings in the trial opened in the old Grand Chamber of the Parlement of Paris, in that vast hall where Fouquier, Dumas, and Coffinhal had sat, with plumed hats on their heads, and their small black cloaks over their shoulders. An enormous crowd had invaded the court, a curious, attentive, and rather quiet crowd.

Twenty-four prisoners[2] took their places on the benches. Seated in the front rank, Fouquier had before him a table on which the documents which he was to employ in his defence were arranged. Two large portfolios served him as a desk. He took notes, writing rapidly.[3] Whilst he wrote, not a single word, either from the President or from a witness, escaped him.[4]

Fouquier was very thin, very much worn by his imprisonment. But he was neither exhausted nor depressed. He had all his faculties about him, that extraordinary gift of memory which never failed him when he needed it. He was there, thrown back on himself, tense, ready for the supreme struggle, for thrust and parry in this judicial duel in which he felt that, in spite of everything, the chances were all against him.

The Public Prosecutor's seat, his own former seat, was occupied alternately by Judicis and his two deputies, Ardenne and Cambon.

[1] Archives Nationales, W. 501, 2nd dossier, p. 38, folio 15.
[2] They were Fouquier, Deliege, Delaporte, Foucault, Maire, Scellier, Harny, Gernier-Launay, and Naulin, ex-judges of the Tribunal of the Terror ; Lohier, Trinchard, Leroy, Renaudin, Pigeot, Aubry, Vilate, Duplay, Prieur, Châtelet, Brochet, Chrétien, Girard, Trey, and Ganney, ex-jurors. Félix, Bravet, Barbier, Liendon, Didier, and Gauthier had fled the country.
[3] We know from Mercier that he wrote with extreme rapidity. (Vatel : *Madame du Barry*, III., p. 257.) And see Archives Nationales, W. 180, liasse 26.
[4] Mercier : *Paris pendant la Révolution*, II., pp. 127, 128.

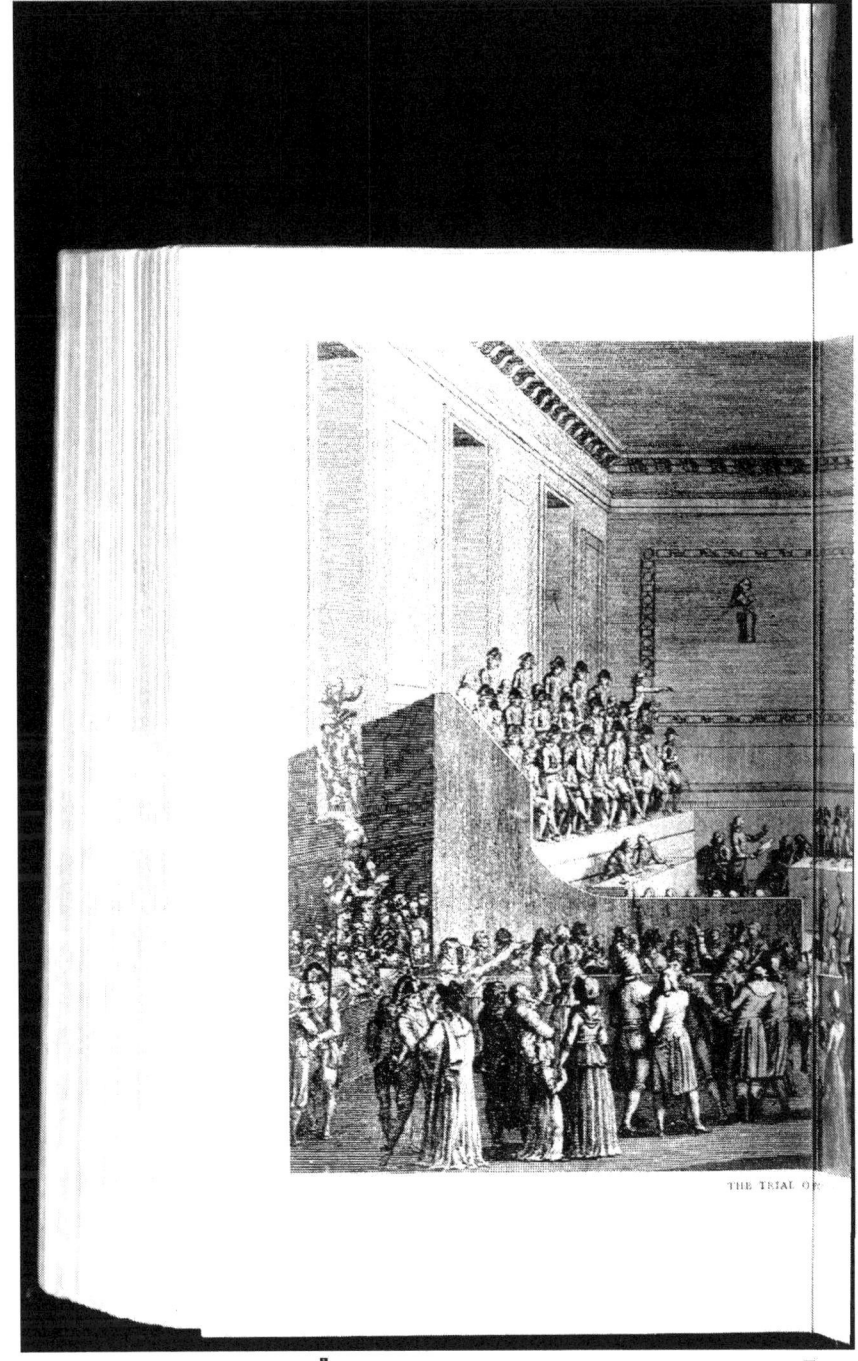

THE TRIAL OF

FOUQUIER-TINVILLE

Liger,[1] the Vice-President, presided over the proceedings, with Godart, Grand, Gaillard-Lécart, and Bertrand d'Aubagne as assessors. Fifteen jurors[2] were seated facing the accused. Very different from the former jurors of the Terror, from Chrétien the lemonade-seller, Renaudin the maker of musical instruments, Vilate the dandy, Duplay the carpenter, Prieur the painter, Trey the tailor, etc, whom they had before them, these Thermidorian jurors were provincials who had come from a distance, strangers to the fevers that had shaken Paris during the sixteen months of the Terror They were people who clung to order and did not love blood The violent acts they had witnessed in their Departments during the Terror, the denunciations, depopulation by the guillotine—these they reprobated. They had seen danger and death at close quarters They were determined to cause those who were responsible for the system that had been overthrown, to expiate the evil they had done. But they would know how to follow the proceedings patiently. They did not declare that they were convinced by the indictments They would listen attentively to the evidence. And at the moment when they gave their verdict, they would show themselves moved by feelings of moderation, for they would admit extenuating circumstances, and would not condemn in the mass. The advocates were, Cressend, Villain, Boutroue, Gobert, Gueneau, and Domanget. Gaillard de la Ferrière assisted Fouquier Lafleuterie had had to abandon his defence for reasons which Fouquier explained at the end of his cross-examination on the 6th of Germinal

[1] He had been President of the Criminal Tribunal of the Loiret In the year VIII., following upon the decrees of the 13th, 14th, 15th, 16th, 17th and 18th of Germinal (April 3 to 8, 1800), Liger-Verdigny was appointed a member of the Court of Cassation He was re-elected by the nomination of February 15, 1815, and remained a member of the Court of Cassation until 1830 He then appears in the Royal Almanac under the name of Liger de Verdigny. From 1830 to 1832 he was an honorary counsel, and he does not appear in the Royal Almanac after this date He had been a chevalier of the Legion of Honour since 1816

[2] Routtborel Abadie-Verduisant, Cadet, and Gabriel Saint-Horrent had been elected as supplementary jurors.

Four hundred and nineteen witnesses were to give evidence in the trial. The case promised to be a long one. What a contrast with those rushed through in a few hours before the 9th of Thermidor !

The proceedings in the trial of Fouquier and his "accomplices" lasted a month and nine days, from the 8th of Germinal until the 17th of Floréal   How are we to relate these proceedings ? So far as we know there remains no written account of them [1] We have to-day only two documents bearing upon them—the printed account of the trial, and that in Buchez and Roux's *Histoire Parlementaire*. Both are open to the suspicion of partiality. They are often curtailed, especially towards the end of the proceedings. They are inexact on many points, and full of printer's errors   Proper names are wrongly spelled. They do not give us the answers of the principal prisoner, Fouquier, except in unsatisfactory and colourless condensations. Fouquier, in spite of his fatigue, must have defended himself fiercely, and with talent

We believe, then, that his real defence consisted of : (1) the memorials he had drawn up and which we have reproduced in full, as they exist among the National Archives, written in his own hand , (2) his answers at the two cross-examinations which he underwent and which we have also reproduced impartially.

At the opening of the proceedings, at the hearing on the 8th of Germinal, a statement was made of the charges brought against Fouquier and his accomplices.

" Citizens and jurors," said Cambon, the Public Prosecutor's deputy, " I come in the name of the Public Prosecutor to unmask great crimes and to denounce great offenders.

" These crimes are those of the liberticidal faction which, by its infamous plots, was able for eighteen months to beat down the courage of all, to repress even the energy of the national representation, to spread terror and consternation on the soil of liberty.

[1] Except the official report of the hearing, which is preserved among the Archives (W 499, dossier 550, p 7).

" Yes, citizens, whilst on the frontier valiant defenders of our country were cementing young liberty with their blood, whilst the noise of their victories was resounding on all sides, the most shameful defeats of morality as well as of justice were in this building dishonouring the magistracy and degrading the French name "[1]

At the hearing on the 9th, Fouquier, questioned by the President on the arrest of Lesenne, the turnkey of the Luxembourg,[2] who had declared that he had no acquaintance with the conspiracy in the prisons, answered · " The witness shuffled in his evidence He contradicted himself I never asked for more than his provisional arrest But Dumas, whose ferocity everybody knows (laughter and murmurs), Dumas had the judgment made out in a different sense. Then that is not my fault "[3]

Later, he said " I received the orders of the two Committees "

On the subject of the carts which he ordered in the morning without knowing whether any persons would be condemned during the day, he answered " It was because of the scarcity of carts "

Then he pointed out that the witness who was accusing him (Sénar), " had let slip the words, *the Thermidorian faction*," an insult to the Government actually in power.

As regards the sentence on the Comte de Fleury, who was sent to death in a red shirt, Fouquier denied all responsibility Gastrez, an employee in the Commission of Public Instruction, charged him with this, and formally identified him as having said to Dumas " This gentleman seems to me to be in a hurry I am going to send for him "

" You are Fouquier," said Gastrez " You were a little stouter then, but I recognise you "

Fouquier " I do not remember that trial "

(And he searched for it in his portfolios.)

---

[1] Buchez and Roux, XXXIV, p 292, and W 499, dossier 550, p 7
[2] He was the first witness to give evidence
[3] *Ibid*, p. 304

In general, to the evidence concerning the conspiracies in the prisons, the lists, and the *amalgamations*, he answered that the facts did not concern him, that he had had his orders. He denied the remarks attributed to him, or said he did not remember them. Or he quoted, with precision, the resolutions of the Committee of Public Safety, that of the 17th of Messidor, for example, relating to the 155, in order to shelter himself. Or he said " I was not sitting on that occasion."

" What answer have you in regard to Morin ? " Cambon asked him.

Fouquier " The witness did not say that it was I who was sitting. Besides, I was the prosecutor. I was neither judge nor juror. Moreover, I deny the remarks. Morin, the quartermaster, is on the list."

This was not answering the question. For an examination of the indictments proves to-day that there had been a mistake in the persons, and that that mistake was to be attributed to the negligence or precipitation of Fouquier and his subordinates.

Moreover, he replied to Baraguay d'Hilliers, ex-General of the Army of the Rhine, who gave evidence against him in regard to the Luxembourg conspiracy·

" The witness gave his evidence with resentment. He had been placed on trial. And yet he had been acquitted."

To which Baraguay d'Hilliers rejoined. " Fouquier had relations with Boyaval at the Luxembourg in order to obtain lists of proscribed persons. It was Boyaval himself who told me so "[1]

Later, Leroy, called "Tenth of August," having exclaimed: " You are vilifying the institution of the jury ! " Fouquier added " It will be ended all the sooner. You must condemn us. Condemn us."

He laid stress on the immoral character of the spy, Benoît, the maker of lists. " I never wished to listen to him "

Benoît, who was in court as a witness, declared " I have never made a list."

[1] Buchez and Roux, XXXIV, p. 332.

Fouquier then, in order " to roast " Benoît, got Cambon to read some compromising and instructive letters written by that witness.

Other witnesses, one of whom was Vonschriltz, a carpenter and police inspector, affirmed that they had seen Fouquier come to Bicêtre, and that he had a list ; that Fouquier caused four or five informers to be sent down to him and had their irons removed.[1]

Fouquier answered " I have carried out the orders of the superior authorities."

In the course of the long discussion that took place on the affair of the Luxembourg Conspiracy, the President asked Fouquier . " Why did you not arrange for the court to hear all the witnesses who were summoned to give evidence at the time of the first ' batch' ? "

Fouquier " I always asked for this to be done I asked on that occasion for all the witnesses to be heard. I do not know why they were not heard It sometimes happened that the President closed the case."

The President · " You ought then to have asked for and demanded the continuation of the hearing of the witnesses."

Fouquier · " I did so."

Cambon : " I have in my hand the official report of the hearing ; there is no mention in it of that demand."

Fouquier : " That is an omission. I was not commissioned to make out the official report. I did not sign it. Besides, the matter must have reference to the circumstances and the persons who assisted me "[2]

In regard to the condemnation of Loménie de Brienne, a witness declared " I remember the trial of Elisabeth, Louis Capet's sister. The ex-Comte de Loménie de Brienne was tried with her. Dumas reproached the ex-Comte de Brienne with having been a Minister in 1788, with having caused himself to be invited to be Mayor by forty neighbouring Communes, and he was guillotined "

Fouquier " On that day I returned from the Committee

---

[1] Buchez and Roux, XXXIV , pp 349-355
[2] Buchez and Roux, XXXIV , p 365

of Public Safety at five o'clock in the morning   I was unable to appear in court.   I recommended that the greatest precaution should be taken regarding several of the accused   I wished to save Brienne.   The invitations of the forty Communes were produced   They were handed over by a resolution of the Government   I may add that Brienne was charged with being the accomplice of the woman Canisy, his niece "[1]

At the same day's hearing, a witness, Thierret-Grandpré, said that on the 26th of Prairial Fouquier had gone to Bicêtre along with Lanne to draw up a list of thirty-three alleged conspirators, and he read the following letter, written and signed in Fouquier's hand ·

" The Public Prosecutor of the Revolutionary Tribunal to Citizen Lanne, assistant in the Commission of Civil Administration Police and Tribunals

· Paris, 26th of Prairial of the year II.

· Citizen, enclosed is a statement of the suspected persons who were found in our inquiry, made to-day at Bicêtre. I invite you to send me, to-morrow at latest, all the documents concerning this case, especially the resolutions

" Greeting and fraternity,

" A. Q. FOUQUIER."[2]

On the next day Lanne filled in the blank space in the resolution which the Commission had passed the day before, inserted in it the thirty-three names, and sent to Fouquier the resolution of the Committee of Public Safety of the 25th of Prairial, and that which the Commission had just passed. Those thirty-three persons were tried, as we have seen. Fouquier answered " that he had no initiative "

At the opening of the hearing of the 18th of Germinal, Fouquier explained that he found himself in an awkward

---

[1] Anne Marie Charlotte de Loménie, the wife of Canisy, was guillotined on the 21st of Floréal in the year II   Buchez and Roux, XXXIV, p 421

[2] Buchez and Roux, XXXIV, p 432

position owing to the arrest of Collot d'Herbois, Billaud Varenne, and others.[1] He had not foreseen this when he wrote his memorials for his defence.

Thiernet-Grandpré spoke of Loménie de Brienne, and said that he enjoyed an honourable reputation, that he was regarded as the father of the unfortunate.

Fouquier answered that this was true that 'imbued with respect and veneration for ex-Minister Loménie, he had made arrangements to sit at his trial and to lay stress on all that was memorable and advantageous to that worthy ex-Minister, but that having been prevented in his laudable intentions, Liendon, his deputy, had anticipated him in court and had succeeded in having the case tried before his arrival at the Tribunal so that he had not been able to carry out his good intentions towards him.''

Then Cambon said ' I have in my hand the indictment presented and signed by you against Loménie You have just uttered a pompous and merited eulogy of ex-Minister Loménie, and yet, in your indictment, you make it out to be only a crime for him that he captured votes in order to become Mayor of his Commune, and that he asked for invitations from neighbouring Communes Why then, do you shelter yourself to-day under his merit in order to excuse a conviction that your eulogies now destroy ? Did your heart formerly deny what your mouth utters to-day ? ''[2]

We have not Fouquier's answer

On the subject of ' the red shirts, he answered that the sentence which condemned them had provided that they should be clad in that garment which was reserved for assassins

Cambon Here is the minute of the sentence which states that, in accordance with the jury's verdict, the sixty-nine (sic)[3] were not convicted of an individual assassination but of having conspired to assassinate the people by

---

· Condemned to be deported
[1] Buchez and Roux, XXXIV, p 441
[3] In reality there were 54

T

famine. The sentence does not contain this provision for red shirts."

Fouquier· "I claim that this is a mistake of the registrar, because the sentence so provided."

Harny, one of the accused, who had been one of the judges in that case, said : " The Tribunal did not so provide. I expressed my astonishment at it, but I was told that it did not concern me."[1]

Regarding the charge of having influenced the jurors in the case of Danton and the Dantonists, Fouquier explained his attitude thus· "The jurors were getting impatient in their room because the hearing did not begin   We went up there, I think, on the 16th, to inform them of the reply of the Committee of Public Safety "

It was pointed out to Fouquier and to Herman that they ought to have had the reply of the Committee read publicly in court   They answered that that reply was only verbal, and stated that the Deputies demanded by the accused should not be heard as witnesses.[2]   Fouquier added : " It was Voulland and Amar who brought the decree.   .   .   I do not remember that Danton was deprived of the right to speak. I made no summary in that case."

The registrars of the Tribunal, Tavernier, Pâris, Wolff, and Neirot, gave evidence that went severely against him. He cried out· " I have learned that Fabricius (Pâris) bears me ill-will.   I am surprised at it.   I did all I could to get him out of prison.   A warrant was issued by the Committee for the arrest of you, Tavernier, and for Wolff's arrest.   I had that decision revoked "

Then he exclaimed   " It is Danton's trial that has brought us here   This is our reward for saving these fellows."   (Murmurs) [3]

Long and tiring hearings succeeded one another.   Sometimes a juror would fall ill and be replaced by one of the four supplementary jurors. ' The jury pointed out to the Tribunal

---

[1] Buchez and Roux, XXXIV , p. 463.
[2] Buchez and Roux, XXXIV., p. 477.
[3] Buchez and Roux, XXXIV., p. 6.

" that a matter of this importance demands attention and, consequently, rest." Some sessions were adjourned to the next day or the day after.

The Convention having passed a decree that the Revolutionary Tribunal should remain in permanence until the end of the trial, Ardenne, the Public Prosecutor's deputy, addressed the court on the 1st of Floréal to say that " the painful position of the accused during the hearings necessarily demands a rest , justice, moreover, should give them time to think over their defence. It will, therefore, be perfectly in the spirit of the law if we devote to this trial all the time that our moral and physical strength allows us."

Fouquier, on the 19th of Germinal, after a long and bitter discussion with the witness, Robert Wolff, became indisposed, and the proceedings were brought to an end for that day. However, on the morrow, he recovered all his energy to argue with the witness, Pâris.[1]

Mercier, in his *Paris pendant la Révolution*, has given us some details concerning Fouquier's attitude during the hearing. " He was like Argus in the fable, all eyes and ears. His attention did not appear to relax for a moment during this long case. It is true that he pretended to sleep during the Public Prosecutor's summing up, but this pretended sleep was only to mislead spectators. He wanted to have an appearance of calm when hell was already in his heart. His fixed look made one lower one's eyes in spite of oneself. When he prepared to speak, he frowned with his eyebrows and wrinkled his forehead. His voice was loud, rough, and threatening ; it suddenly passed from shrill tones to deep, and from these to the lowest whisper. He listened to himself speaking when he asked a question. No one could put more assurance into his denials, or more skill in the distorting of facts, isolating them, and, above all, marshalling them so as to prove an *alibi*. When a judge showed him a blank sentence signed in his hand, *he denied his signature in a firm voice*, and did not tremble before that accusing witness.

[1] Archives Nationales, W. 499, dossier 550, p 6.

When the proof was irresistible he filled the whole court with his terrible roars."[1]

The ushers give evidence against him just as the registrars did.

Boucher (an ex-usher, then a registrar's clerk in the Tribunal) said "Fouquier complained that we did not work fast enough. 'You do not keep up,' he used to say. 'I want two hundred to two hundred and fifty each *décade*'"[2]

Tavernier, also an ex-usher and then a registrar's clerk, said that the jurors chosen by Fouquier were called *the solid men*.

Fouquier answered that when jurors were wanted, they were taken from those in the following column; that he knew neither strong jurors nor weak jurors.[3]

In regard to the trial and sentence of the Marquise de Feuquières, guillotined without witnesses appearing against her, before the documents arrived, without having signed the official report of the preliminary examination, and while Château, the usher, was by the Public Prosecutor's orders at Chaton to look for a document and to summon witnesses, Fouquier answered Ardenne · "If from the proceedings that took place, and if from the confession of this woman, the jurors came to a decision, there is no crime."

Ardenne. "Did you mention to the jurors, during the proceedings, that you were waiting for documents and witnesses concerning the woman Feuquières?"

Fouquier: "If you are attacking the trials, I can no longer reply."

Ardenne. "We are not revising the trials here. But I point out that you ought to have procured and presented the documents for the prosecution and the defence, and produced the appointed witnesses I tell you, therefore, that you have carried out your duties in a dishonest manner by

---

[1] Mercier *Paris pendant la Révolution*, II , pp 127, 128. Quoted by Campardon *Le Tribunal Révolutionnaire*, II., p. 209
[2] Buchez and Roux, XXXIV, p 12.
[3] Buchez and Roux, XXXIV, p 15.

not presenting this letter. If crime ought to be punished, we ought to endeavour to discover innocence by every possible means. I tell you that your precipitation is a crime."

Fouquier · "This woman was arraigned before the Tribunal. The proceedings opened. She confessed. There were no further proceedings. You are here trying the Tribunal as if a Revolutionary Tribunal were an ordinary tribunal ! You ought to refer to the Revolutionary laws."

Ardenne · "No matter how imperious circumstances then were, and no matter how severe these laws, you ought not to had added cruelty to them You ought rather to have carried your head to the scaffold." (Loud applause)

Fouquier "You are holding me responsible for the sentences "

Ardenne "No. But I charge you with having transformed ordinary deeds into counter-revolutionary offences, and with having been at least one of the principal agents of the former Committees of Government Besides, you were not ignorant of the decree of amnesty passed after these events "[1]

At the hearing of the 25th of Germinal, nine other prisoners were brought in and associated as accomplices with those who were being tried, viz.. Boyaval, Beausire, Benoît, Valagnos, Guyard, and Verney, former police spies and notorious informers , then Lanne, Herman's assistant on the Commission for Civil Affairs, Police, and Tribunals ; lastly, Herman himself, and Dupaumier, a former police official. They passed from the position of witnesses to that of prisoners on trial, and this owing to their answers and the very compromising documents that had been brought together against them The part they played in the business of the conspiracies in the prisons seems to have been monstrous. As for Herman, it was evident that he was " paying " for his attitude during the proceedings at Danton's trial During the sessions that were to follow, these new

[1] Buchez and Roux, XXXV., p 18, and Archives Nationales, W. 499, dossier 550, p 6, folio 19

prisoners were on trial, and fresh light was thrown on
this dark affair. Once more Danton's trial was referred
to, and Herman affirmed that " Danton had an opportunity to speak several times "

Didier-Thirion, a representative of the people, objected
that Danton had not answered the third charge in the
indictment against him, and that he had not spoken of the
Belgian affair before he was deprived of the right to speak.

Herman " I knew nothing of Belgium. The accused
were not deprived of the right to speak. At the end of the
period appointed by law, on the fourth day, I asked the jurors
if they were sufficiently informed to give their verdict.
They answered in the affirmative."

Pâris. " Danton was deprived of the right to speak.
Herman and Fouquier went into the jurors' room and told
the jurors to say that they were sufficiently informed."

Fouquier : " Pâris was Danton's friend ; it is Danton's
death they want to avenge." [1]

There was a certain number of other cases about which
the witnesses gave evidence, and this evidence was over-
whelmingly against Fouquier. These were the Sallier case
(1st of Floréal year II), the Fréteau case (26th of Prairial
year II.), the Pérès case (18th of Messidor year II.), the Saint-
Pern case (1st of Thermidor year II), the Maillé case (6th
of Thermidor year II), and the Puy de Vérine case (9th of
Thermidor year II).

We have seen in an earlier part of this work how Henry
Guy Sallier, an ex-noble and President of the Cour des Aides
of Paris, had been guillotined in a " batch " of members of
the Paris Parlement condemned for having protested against
the decrees of the National Assembly in 1790. It was his
son, Guy Marie, who was aimed at. There had been a
mistake as to identity

Guy Marie Sallier gave evidence at the trial in a letter
in which he charged Fouquier with having committed a wrong
act in arraigning the President of the Cour des Aides instead
of a member of the Parlement.

. [1] Buchez and Roux, XXXV , p. 130

To this Fouquier answered that they were making him responsible for the proceedings; that they would finish trying him all the sooner; that he had no more to say—he was ready [1]

Concerning the case of Fréteau, the ex-councillor of the Parlement of Paris who was acquitted on the 27th of Floréal in the year II, but whom Fouquier had nevertheless kept in prison and again brought to trial, and who had been condemned to death on the 22nd of Prairial in the year II., the Tribunal heard the evidence of Sezille, an official defender, which has already been quoted [2] Fouquier answered: "The Fréteau case does not concern me, on the second occasion he was arraigned for another offence, I do not remember having refused to send the warrant for Fréteau's release."

But a witness, Didier Jourdeuil, chief registrar of the Tribunal of the Third Arrondissement, formerly a juror of the Revolutionary Tribunal until the 23rd of Prairial, revealed that the juror Girard, then on the benches of the accused, said to him. "Do you not know that Fréteau has an income of sixty thousand *livres* ?"

Thierriet-Grandpré said that one morning Fouquier said to him in a heated tone · "Do you know what they did yesterday? They acquitted Fréteau, that ex-councillor of the Parlement, that Deputy of the Constituent Assembly, that known counter-revolutionary. But I swear on the word of a Public Prosecutor that that scoundrel will be taken again in a few days, and that once in my grip he shall not escape again ! "

Fouquier denied this remark, and said that Fréteau had been tried for another offence [3]

Regarding the case of Pérès, a former councillor of the Toulouse Parlement, who was guillotined without having been included either in the questions propounded to the jury or in the indictment, and on the authority of a blank sentence, Ardenne remarked to Fouquier that in this matter he had

---

[1] Buchez and Roux, XXXV, p 101   [2] Chapter VIII, p 189
[3] Buchez and Roux, XXXV, pp 75 and 97.

deceived the Convention by giving it false information, and he ordered the proofs of Pérès' good citizenship to be read.

Fouquier threw all responsibility on Liendon, who sat on that day.

Ardenne thereupon replied to him, pointing out that, in the papers concerning the members of the Toulouse Parlement, there was no document for the prosecution, whilst there was a crowd of documents for the defence which he had not presented [1]

In the matter of Saint-Pern, the son, who had been guillotined instead of his father on the 1st of Thermidor, Madame de Saint-Pern, Cornulier's widow, appeared in person at the session of the 1st of Floréal.

" On the 1st of Thermidor I appeared here on trial along with my grandfather, my father, mother, brother, husband, and several other prisoners. My brother, aged seventeen, against whom there was no indictment, was condemned to death instead of my father, aged fifty-five, who regained his freedom after the 9th of Thermidor. Neither my husband nor I received indictments. My husband refused to go into court without one. We were brought one in which it was said that we had assassinated the people on August 10 "

Ardenne read the documents relating to this trial. In the indictment, only Saint-Pern and his wife were mentioned. The son was not included in the indictment nor in the list of charges. The jury's verdict contained, " J. B Saint-Pern, aged seventeen, unemployed, born at Rennes." " The Tribunal condemned the son instead of the father." (Murmurs of horror.)

Madame de Saint-Pern then addressed Fouquier

" Why did you not also place on trial those who were named in the indictment, Boucher, Custine, and Thomas, for instance ? "

And she named the jurors who sat in that case, Renaudin, Châtelet, and Prieur " I remember their names because when my husband was going to execution he handed me

[1] Buchez and Roux, XXXV, p 141.

BERTRAND BARÈRE

some of his hair in a paper which turned out to be the list of the jurors for that day "

Ardenne · " The judges who sat on the 1st of Thermidor are Harny, Lohier, and Dumas "

Fouquier   " I did not sit "

Lohier : " I have nothing to do with the indictment."

Harny : " After the 22nd of Prairial the judges here were merely figure-heads." [1]

In the matter of young de Maillé, who was condemned to death as a conspirator for having thrown a rotten herring at the head of a turnkey in Saint-Lazare, his mother, Madame de Maillé appeared, and was asked by Ardenne : " Can you prove that your son was only sixteen years old ? "

The witness produced a copy of his birth certificate certifying that he was born on August 25, 1777. And he had been condemned to death on the 6th of Thermidor in the year II

Fouquier answered · " If young Maillé is included in the indictment, the reason is that he was impeached by a resolution of the Committee of Public Safety."

Ardenne   " I submit to Fouquier that no resolution of the Committee of Public Safety is to be found among the documents relating to the case, and that there is no date on this indictment "

Fouquier · " There ought to be a list on which is written, ' To be sent to the Public Prosecutor.' It is signed by three members of the Committee "

Ardenne · " It is not in existence "

Fouquier   " Documents have been taken away. That being so, I have nothing more to say " [2]

Ardenne read the article in the indictment which concerned the case of Loizerolles, the father, who, on the eve of Robespierre's fall, was guillotined instead of his son. We have already discussed this case [3] Ardenne added that the warrant bore the words " the girl Loizerolles."

---

[1] Buchez and Roux, XXXV , p 92.
[2] Buchez and Roux, XXXV , p. 57 and following
[3] See Chapter III , p 99 and note p 98

" There was no girl Loizerolles brought to trial," answered
Fouquier. " It was the son. After the law of the 22nd of
Prairial, no preliminary examinations were held. Ushers
or other persons were sent to the prisons, whose duty it
was to take the prisoners' names and bring them to the
Tribunal The person who went to Lazare took the father
for the son. My deputy, I think it was Liendon, ought
to have stopped the proceedings against the father." [1]

When, at the evening hearing, on the 2nd of Floréal,
a witness[2] charged Fouquier with having said concerning a
paralysed woman, " It is not the tongue, it is the head we
want," Fouquier denied the fact. But Cambon immediately said " Fouquier has just told you that he had never
placed paralysed persons on trial. I am going to show that
he placed on trial not only paralysed persons, but also a
man who was deaf, blind, and in his second childhood."

He then spoke of M Durand Puy de Vérine and read the
certificates relating to his case.

Fouquier answered : " Those certificates ought to have
been presented. I cannot be responsible for everything.
I do not know, besides, whether I was sitting on that day.
They were not charged with conspiracy. They were impeached by the Committee."

And (what seems to contradict his statement a moment
before that he did not know whether he was sitting on that
day) he added . " Besides, that blind man did not seem to
be in his second childhood Moreover, he confessed in court."

But Cambon had the official report of the case, and he
read the names of the members who composed the court on
that day, " Dumas, Maire, Félix, judges. *Fouquier, Public
Prosecutor* " [3]

Among his witnesses for the defence, Fouquier had
summoned Carnot, one of the members of the Committee of
Public Safety whose orders he has executed , but on the 12th

[1] Buchez and Roux, XXXIV., p. 439.
[2] Retz, a merchant, formerly steward of the Hospice de l'Evêché.
[3] Buchez and Roux, XXXV., p 137, and see the official report in
W. 433, No: 973.

of Floréal (May 1), at the morning hearing, the President read a letter from Carnot, apologising for not being able to come, and enclosing a certificate of illness.

Fouquier then declared that "he abandoned his witnesses." The hearing of evidence came to an end on that day.[1]

At five o'clock in the evening, Cambon, the Public Prosecutor's deputy, summed up for the prosecution. Fouquier slept. He was heard in his general defence from eight o'clock until ten o'clock. On the 13th, at nine o'clock in the morning, he continued his defence until half-past eleven. Naulin, Herman, Leroy, Lanne, Chrétien, Scellier, and Vilate spoke afterwards On the 14th, at half-past nine in the morning, the other prisoners were heard. In the evening Garnier-Launay, Delaporte, Trinchard, and Dupaumier defended themselves Guyard and Verney entrusted their defence to their advocates

Fouquier-Tinville addressed the court. He said that part of his defence was lacking. This was the evidence of Billaud-Varenne, Collot d'Herbois, and Barère, who had been deported, and that of the members of the former Committees of Government who were then in prison.

"It is not I who ought to be arraigned here, but the chiefs whose orders I have executed I have acted only in virtue of the laws of the 14th of Frimaire and of the 23rd of Ventôse, laws passed by a Convention invested with full power Through the absence of those members, I find myself the head of a conspiracy that I have never known. Here I am, a target for the calumny of a people always eager to find persons guilty. (Vehement murmurs) Only men of ill-will can find what I say to be wrong"

Afterwards he replied to several facts that had been alleged against him.

On the morning of the 15th, Gaillard de la Ferrière, his advocate, spoke on his behalf The other defenders addressed the court on behalf of their clients. In the evening, Cressend, Gueneau, and Domanget spoke.

---

[1] Archives Nationales, W. 499, No. 550, pièce 7, p. 47.

On the 16th, at nine o'clock in the morning, Domanget continued his speech until eleven o'clock Leroy, Fouquier, Ganney, and Valagnos made some observations, and Fouquier again addressed the court, and presented to the jury some facts in his defence

The pleadings closed at eleven o'clock. The Tribunal declared that the jury should not disperse until the verdict were given. The President summed up at the evening session The questions were propounded The jurors retired to their room to consider their verdict at nine o'clock in the evening, and at noon on the 17th they came back to declare their verdict. This declaration lasted until three o'clock. The Tribunal retired to the Council Chamber to consider it It came back at five o'clock. The accused were brought into court. Judgment was pronounced.[1]

Fouquier-Tinville was convicted of machinations and plots tending to favour the liberticidal plots of the enemies of the people and the Republic, with provoking the dissolution of the national representation and the overthrow of Republican government, with exciting citizens to arm against one another, particularly by causing the deaths, through the disguised form of a trial, of an innumerable crowd of French people of all ages and both sexes ; of inventing, for this purpose, conspiracies in various houses of detention in Paris , of making out and causing to be made out, in those various houses of detention, lists of proscribed persons, etc ; of having acted with evil intentions. He was unanimously condemned to death by the votes of all the eleven jurors [2]

Foucault, Scellier, Garnier-Launay, Leroy, called " Tenth of August," Renaudin, Vilate, Prieur, Châtelet, Girard, Boyaval, Benoît, Lanne, Vernier, Dupaumier, and Herman were convicted of having been accomplices in Fouquier's machinations and plots, and of having acted with evil intentions. They were condemned to death.

Maire, Harny, Delsège, Naulin, Delaporte, Lohier, Trin-

---

[1] Archives Nationales, W. 499, dossier 550, pièce 7, p 57.
[2] Archives Nationales, W. 499, dossier 550, p. 13.

chard, Brochet, Chrétien, Ganney, Trey, Guyard, and Valagnos were not convicted of being principals, but of being accomplices in those machinations and plots They had not acted with evil intentions. They were acquitted. Duplay and Beausire were also acquitted.[1]

It was six o'clock in the evening. The *Courrier Républicain* tells us that when the verdict was announced Fouquier appeared to be " furious." Scellier hurled a pamphlet which he held in his hand at the President's head. Herman took off his hat " in a moment of rage " and flung it out of the window. Most of the condemned persons called the judges and jurors scoundrels, and predicted for them a death similar to that which they were going to experience. " Yet forty days," they exclaimed, " and Nineveh shall be destroyed ! "[2]

As for the crowd that filled the court, it seemed to have been moved by various feelings Some police inspectors wrote in their report of the day · " Yesterday (16th of Floréal in the year III., May 5, 1795), Fouquier-Tinville's case was talked about in several cafés. Opinions on this matter were very much divided. Some citizens held that this scoundrel and his accomplices were to be sentenced to death. Others maintained that the Convention had provided otherwise, that it had given orders that they should only be condemned to deportation, that this measure was of importance in order not to expose Fouquier to the public gaze, for he would not fail to disclose many horrors that it was the Government's interest to keep secret "[3]

The condemned persons asked to be executed that same evening. But it was late. Twilight was coming on, and the executioner was not to be found. The execution had to be postponed until the following morning

Fouquier-Tinville then wrote these few words which have been preserved for us :

---

[1] Archives Nationales, W. 499, dossier 550, p. 15.
[2] *Courrier Républicain* for the 9th of Floréal, quoted by Aulard : *Paris sous la Réaction Thermidorienne*, I , p 707.
[3] *Ibid.*, p. 701.

" I have nothing to reproach myself with : I have always conformed to the laws , I have never been the creature of Robespierre or Saint-Just ; on the contrary, I have been four times on the point of being arrested. I die for my country and without reproach . I am satisfied ; my innocence will be recognised later.

" A Q. FOUQUIER."[1]

On the 18th of Floréal (May 7, 1795), early in the morning, the quays and streets adjoining the House of Justice and the Place de Grève were black with people. The immense crowd was waiting for the arrival of the carts. Before the Hôtel de Ville, the scaffold reared itself up in the dazzling light of day. "The spirit which seemed to animate this multitude was not that ferocious joy which joy (*sic*) inspired in the cannibals who were the daily spectators of the Revolutionary butcheries ; the curiosity which leads us to go and see extraordinary monsters seemed to be the only feeling that reigned in this crowd of individuals of every position, and age, and of both sexes."[2]

Among the groups only one voice was heard : " He has deserved it. He was given plenty of time and every means of defending himself." And many people told how " the monster " had deprived them of a friend, a father, or a relative Some congratulated themselves on having escaped his carts by a miracle He was called " a man-eater."

The windows were filled with curious persons of both sexes, " on whose faces one read that satisfaction which the destruction of crime procures to virtue "[3]

Suddenly, in the midst of the crowd, above their heads, the three carts were seen advancing. Fouquier-Tinville was in the last. A torrent of invectives and insults poured upon him. Desperate voices cried out to him : " Give me back my father, give me back my family, give me back my brother, give me back my friend, my wife, my sister, my

---

[1] Archives Nationales, W 499, dossier 550, p. 41.
[2] *Messager du Soir* for the 19th of Floréal, quoted by Aulard : *Paris sous la Réaction Thermidorienne*, p. 707.
[3] *Messager du Soir* for the 19th of Floréal.

husband, my mother, my children !" Others jeered · " They
are going to deprive you of the right to speak !" " In
two minutes the pleadings come to an end !" " Is your
conscience sufficiently enlightened ? " " The people are
going *to fire an uninterrupted volley* in its turn !" " Go,
scoundrel, and join your victims ! "[1]

Shrill cries and cheers of triumph were raised. The
multitude rocked in continuous movement. Fouquier was
pale and livid, all the muscles of his face contracted, his eyes
" bloodshot." Doubtless he had wept as he thought of his
wife, of his sons, of his children, of the beings whom he was
leaving in the most frightful destitution. Some thought
they saw him smile and sneer. A journalist heard him
answer the groans with these words " Vile riff-raff, go
and look for bread !" The people cried out, " Long live
justice ! "

The three carts stopped before the scaffold. The condemned men alighted from them. One after another, they
were balanced beneath the bloody triangle of the guillotine.
Fouquier-Tinville was executed last. The people howled
and asked his head to be shown to them. " The executioner
seized it and displayed it to the eager gaze of the public."[2]

It was eleven o'clock in the morning. The crowd withdrew slowly. It flowed over the Place, along the quays,
through the streets, over the bridges, commenting on the
events, quiet or noisy, satisfied with the execution, and
pleased with the fine day beneath the Floréal sun.

But, not far off, in a modest lodging in the Rue de la Harpe,
a widow was weeping A life of opprobrium, of terrible
poverty, of absolute, irremediable isolation, was beginning
for her She was Madame Fouquier-Tinville.

[1] *Messager du Soir* for the 19th of Floréal
[2] *Courrier Républicain* for the 19th of Floréal.

CHAPTER XIV

CONCLUSION

" I WAS the agent of the Committees of Government. What would you have done in my place ? " Fouquier-Tinville said and repeated in his defence before the judges. And that, upon the whole, is his only defence

It is a hundred and eighteen years since the ex-Public Prosecutor of the Terror asked that question. Can we answer it to-day in a clear, straightforward, and precise manner ?

In order to judge Fouquier-Tinville let us go back to the time when he held his terrible magistracy, to that epoch when, in Revolutionary France, public order was so profoundly troubled, when the judicial body was a body of servile officials, ready to obey in any way the ephemeral chiefs of an unstable Government pledged to the changing humours of the multitude and the infuriated struggles of parties.

Fouquier-Tinville was amazed that he was sacrificed by the Thermidorians, after the fall of Robespierre, Couthon, and Saint-Just, after the exile of Billaud-Varenne, Collot d'Herbois, and Barère He advocated in court the sending to the scaffold of the victims of the 9th of Thermidor. And on the 14th of Thermidor he was preparing to be Public Prosecutor " under the Thermidorian faction." If he had lived and kept his place, he would have been a diligent Public Prosecutor under the Directory and he would willingly have made an Imperial Procurator under Napoleon.

For his defence, he claimed that he only executed the orders of the Committees of Government. It is true that he executed their orders. But he did more than execute them.

He outstripped them. In Wolff's words at the trial, Fouquier transformed into a slaughter-house a Tribunal which, from the very severity of its functions, ought to have been the more scrupulously subject to forms. He alone did not transform that Tribunal into a slaughter-house. But, aided by President Dumas, Vice-President Coffinhal, and others, he contributed to that transformation.

He defended himself against the charge of having instigated the deprivation of Danton and the Dantonists of the right to plead. He said that he had nothing to do with the idea of a conspiracy intended to empty the prisons and depopulate France. He affirmed that he had never known the police spies, the compilers of lists of proscribed persons. He said that he had always been faithful to his duties. He had shown himself humane, " especially towards the unfortunate." The conspiracies in the prisons ? He would not have even thought of such a thing but for the law of the 23rd of Ventôse and the Committee of Public Safety " which imposed on him the rigorous duty of prosecuting and bringing to trial all individuals suspected of such offences." The mistakes in drawing up the indictments ? They were due to the negligence of his deputies or to errors committed by secretaries in the prosecutor's office. He had no knowledge that, by his act, one person was ever sent to death instead of another. He only carried out orders, for, he said loudly, " when the law speaks, the public official must act." And he laid informations against Robespierre, Couthon, and President Dumas.

He himself, on the other hand, had resisted, in certain cases, the wishes of members of the Committee of Public Safety and of the Committee of General Security (this was not the case, however, when Vadier made him bring the Darmaings and de Pamiers to trial), and he had perpetually, courageously, but vainly " demanded the revision of the terrible law of the 22nd of Prairial " He appealed to a posterity which would avenge " the insults he was made to experience " in the course of the proceedings at his trial.

Certainly these denials are very clear No prisoner had

u

more assurance, defended himself more skilfully, knew better
how to deny the evidence of facts, to distort them, to present
them in a special and favourable light, to isolate and destroy
them, to say that he did not sit on a given day, to throw all
responsibility on others   None was more stubborn, more
imperturbable, less disconcerted.   His defence was specious.
But the documents remain among the papers relating to the
Revolutionary Tribunal, and they bear his signature.   There
are indictments with erasures, filled with commitments,
unauthorised insertions between the lines, blank spaces.
There are pleadings for the prosecution against accused
persons, with no evidence to support them.   There are witnesses for the prosecution summoned by him who were
nothing more than police spies from the prisons or compilers
of lists.

He said that he had never brought to trial any persons
except conspirators, and that he had had orders.   But what
of the paralysed Durand Puy de Vérine and his wife ?   What
of Toupin, the Breton, who could not speak French ?   What
of Madame de Lavergne ?   Were they conspirators ?   He
did not know that any person had ever been sent to death for
another.   What of M. de Saint Pern ?   What of Madame de
Maillé ?   What of Pérès ?   What of Maurin ?

He exonerated himself from the charges that weighed on
him by throwing all responsibility on the members of the
Committee of Public Safety, on his colleagues, on his
subordinates.   But Robespierre, Couthon, and Saint-Just
perished on the scaffold.   He made himself out to be innocent
by accusing President Dumas   But Dumas perished on
the scaffold.   It is easy to incriminate dead men.   They
cannot reply.   And there were convenient witnesses whom
he should not have feared to face.   Why did he not think of
incriminating Billaud-Varenne and Collot d'Herbois until
they had gone into exile and been deported to Sinnamarie.

And all the negligence, all the errors, all the omissions that
were pointed out in the indictments, how easy it was for him
to attribute them to Liendon, his deputy, who had fled the
country, and who, consequently, could not contradict him !

He invoked the laws. But above the Revolutionary laws, are there not superior and imperishable laws which enjoin pity, humanity and courage? If, on the 22nd of Prairial, when he recognised that the task imposed on the Revolutionary Tribunal became henceforth abominable, he had firmly given in his resignation, he would undoubtedly have been immediately brought to trial and sacrificed. But posterity would not have to dishonour his memory, as it has hitherto done, and that without any party distinction.

It is a rare thing in studying the men of the Revolution for us not to find ourselves faced by most interesting moral cases, and it often becomes almost impossible to explain them in the final analysis.

Fouquier-Tinville, thorough instrument of the Terror though he was, was accessible to feelings of humanity and pity.

He caused the acquittal of Garcé, a captain in the Guyenne regiment; Bayard de la Vingtrie, lieutenant of the bailiwick of Bellesme, Depuis, an employee in the military transports; and Mouchet, the King's architect. He wished to save Angram d'Alleray, a former civil lieutenant of the Châtelet, who had rendered him services as Procurator at the Châtelet. He told him to deny everything [1]

He signed a letter in which he declared that, in spite of the decree of the Convention, General Harville was not guilty, " and that it was impossible for him to find grounds for an indictment." Montané, the ex-President of the Revolutionary Tribunal, owed him his life And yet they did not care for one another, and had had violent arguments. Many prisoners who were languishing in prison wrote to him asking for a prompt trial, he systematically ignored them in their prisons Systematically—and humanely—he laid on one side the papers concerning them, thus taking into consideration the remark of his friend Lavaud, the advocate, *Volenti mori non creditur*. (For he loved Latin quotations, having been an excellent student, and he sometimes allowed

---

[1] But Angram d'Alleray did not pay attention to these overtures, and allowed himself to be condemned to death by the Tribunal

himself to be disarmed by them.) Lastly, he saved the ninety-four men of Nantes.

How then are we to explain him ? What was there behind that high, firm forehead on which the raised arch of the eyebrows marked a note of interrogation ? What was the real thought that lived in those restless, attentive eyes, in that dark and oblique glance, so fixed that others could not hold out against it ?

We have freely sought, without prejudice or hatred, to understand him and to make him understood. And this, in the final analysis, is what we think of him

There was a conflict in his nature. There was a rupture between what pertained to his middle-class, human character and what pertained to the official, to the magistrate, to the agent of the Committees of Public Safety and of General Security, to the priest of Revolutionary justice. Between the magistrate and the private man, there had been, in his inmost being, terrible conflicts. We have proof of this in his letters to his wife He was good to his wife and children. He loved them tenderly.

But let us endeavour to see into him more clearly still, to peer clearly into his very depths. Fouquier was an arbitrary, violent man, ill at ease within the narrow limits of a tribunal. He was impatient of his colleagues and his official equals, especially Dumas. He had a despotic character. And he had the education, all the education and habits of a lawyer, of a procurator, of a man brought up and trained in legal chicanery and procedure

He wanted to win his cases at whatever cost. He confused his part as Public Prosecutor with his old quibbling habits. He wanted to win his cases, and he won them all with a high hand during the Terror and until the 9th of Thermidor. But he lost one case, his own, and that in spite of a vehement defence, full of talent, in which he confronted an entire Government. Public vengeance was waiting for him. He was hooted at. Too much blood had been shed. Paris had had enough of seeing so much blood flowing every day.

And now must we accept the objection made by Fouquier

during his trial that Pâris, the registrar, and Wolff, his mortal enemies, had had the documents for that trial in their hands, and could and did remove some of those that told for his defence ? Must we conclude from this that perhaps Fouquier was not guilty, that the evidence for the prosecution alone remains against him, and that, in this position of the question, all definite judgment ought to be suspended ?

But, as we have said above, the most terrible of the proofs that exist against the ex-Public Prosecutor are his own indictments. They are to be found among the National Archives. Anyone can consult them and verify the frightful precipitation with which " batches " of unhappy persons were sent to the Revolutionary Tribunal, and thence we know to what end—women dragged from their husbands, girls from their mothers, old men sent to death. Nothing is so moving and so cruel as the reading of those innumerable indictments, even for the student whose profession has accustomed him to impassiveness

As regards the charges brought against Fouquier of having been bribed in his duties by more or less considerable sums, we think they cannot be maintained. No proof of such corruption exists against him, and he died very poor, leaving his wife and children in the most appalling want.

To conclude, it seems to us just and opportune to borrow a quotation from Ardenne, the Public Prosecutor's deputy, one of the judges belonging to the Thermidorian party it is true, but a man who used language as honest as it is resolute.

" No matter how imperious the Revolutionary laws were, you ought not to have added to their cruelty. You ought rather to have carried your head to the scaffold. I do not hold you responsible for the sentences, but I charge you with having transformed ordinary deeds into counter-revolutionary offences."

This seems to us to be the only answer to Fouquier's question which we placed at the beginning of this conclusion.

INDEX

OLD FAMILY RECORDS

I N the muniment chests of many County Families there exist, without doubt, papers and records of very great historical and biographical value. From time to time a book will appear based upon such material. A preface will explain how the papers that appear in the volume were brought to light through the industry and enterprise of some antiquarian or man of letters, and how he had persuaded their owner to allow to be published what he had thought possessed interest only for himself and members of his family.

NOT only documents and correspondence relating to literary, political, or historical matters are likely to prove of interest; but also family papers that tell of the social or domestic life of a past century or a bygone generation. Messrs. Herbert Jenkins Ltd. will be pleased at any time to advise the possessors of Old Diaries, Manuscripts, Letters, or any other description of Family Papers, as to their suitability for publication in book form. When deemed desirable the papers themselves, duly insured against loss or damage during transit, will, with the consent of the owner, be submitted to experts.

ON all such matters advice will be given without involving the possessor of the original documents in any expense or liability. In the first instance a list of the papers upon which advice may be required should be enclosed, giving some particulars of their nature (if letters, by whom and to whom written), dates and approximate extent.

DIRECTORS: ADDRESS:

SIR GEORGE H. CHUBB, BT. HERBERT JENKINS LTD.
ALEX W. HILL, M.A.   12 ARUNDEL PLACE,
HERBERT JENKINS.   HAYMARKET, LONDON

UNIVERSITY OF CALIFORNIA LIBRARY
Los Angeles
This book is DUE on the last date stamped below.

Form L9–

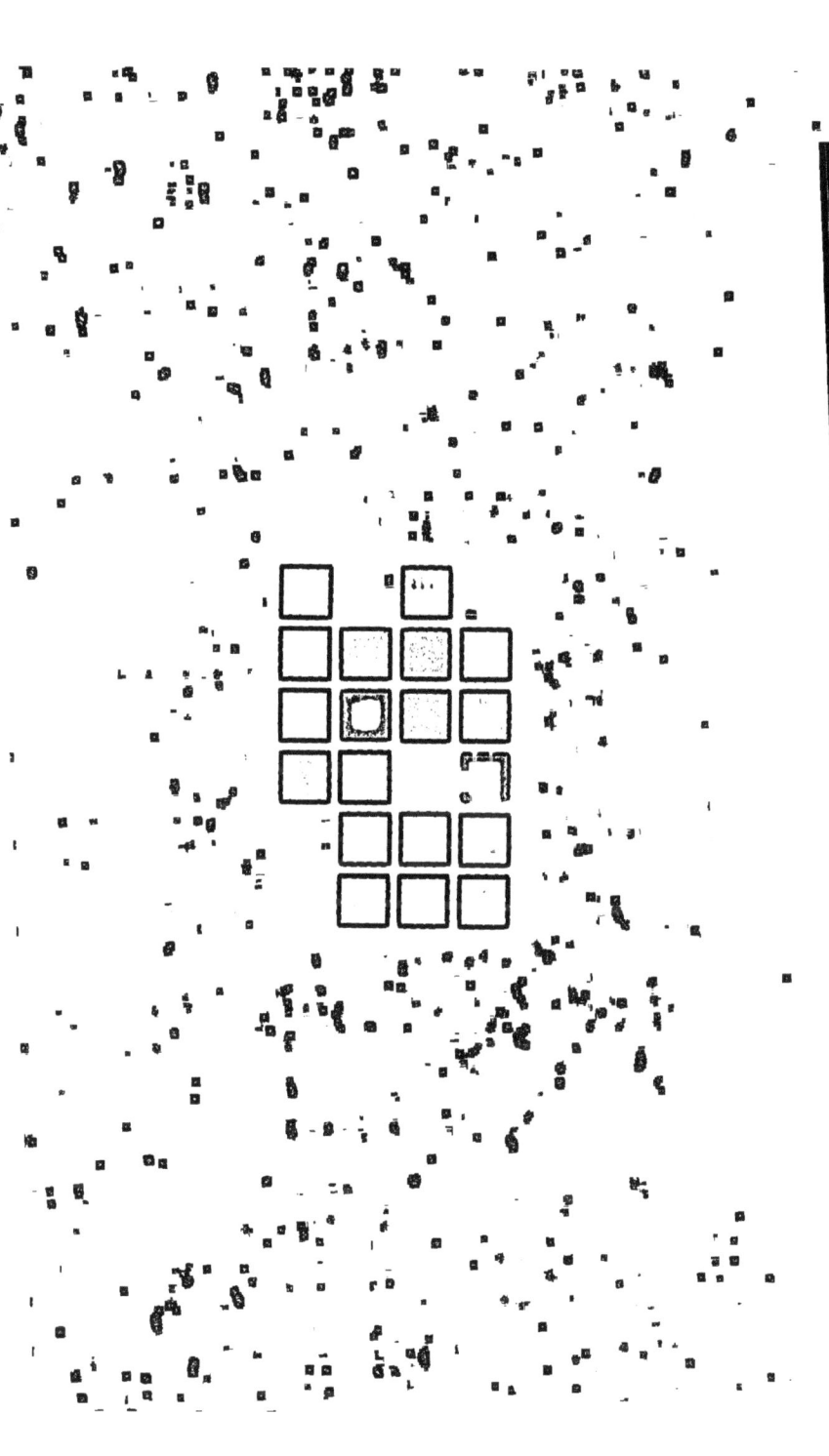